THE OCCASIONAL SAILOR

THE
Occasional Sailor

ANGUS GLENNIE

For more information contact gusglennie@sympatico.ca.

ISBN 978-0-9920825-0-5

Design and layout by Vancouver Desktop Publishing Centre Ltd.
Printed in Canada by Ray Hignell Services Inc.

To Sylvie and Jocko

Foreword

In reading the book the reader will quickly note that there is a shortage of names. Individuals have been replaced with, the boss, crewman, he or she or, in some instances, simply no mention at all. There are three reasons for this. First whilst digging deep into my faded memory, and beyond the extent of my records, there is simply no recollection. Secondly in more than one instance I wanted to protect the identity of those who had come under the scrutiny of my 'pen'. This was my story and there was absolutely no reason that these poor souls should be dragged into the lime-light due to my vanity. Thirdly, and perhaps most importantly, enormous gratitude. The men I worked for were ambitious and extremely successful. These men had also given me an opportunity to work in a career that I loved and for that I could never thank them enough and therefore, have made every effort to respect their privacy.

Notwithstanding the above I have kept to the facts and hope the reader will enjoy a lighthearted account of a life that followed a less than usual career path.

ONE

Nelson Trembles

The buttons of his waistcoat strained to contain its portly contents. The waistcoat was impeccable, as indeed was the rest of the suit. It matched its owner well as he flicked each leg in turn, tugging at his trouser leg, making himself more comfortable as he perched on the edge of the armchair. I studied him for a moment. He had no hint of color among his thinning grey hair, which sat neatly atop a rather elderly face. The last vestiges of intelligent humor still twinkled in his eyes. His thickening neck swelled over the tight, crisp collar of his white shirt, which seemed sealed shut by a well-centered tie that along with the shirt, disappeared into the confines of his three-piece suit. As a retired captain from Her Majesty's Royal Navy, he looked every inch the part, right down to his neatly polished shoes. I was sitting with him in the headmaster's study at Strathallan Public School in Scotland in the early summer of 1982. I had not the faintest idea what to do with my future, but it appeared that this fellow did. He reached inside his jacket and pulled out a pen, which with a twist, was then poised above the paper, ready for action. There followed a barrage of questions that forced me to concentrate and think, two attributes of which I was in very short supply. I began to stare out the window at the green fields beyond, losing myself to another world, but he was not to be deterred and continued his cross-examination, dragging me back from my daydreaming until he pronounced himself satisfied. The papers were gathered up and disappeared inside his briefcase. The pen slipped back inside his jacket. He declared that he thought I would be excellent material for a short service commission as a young officer in the Royal Navy. I had my doubts! However, seeing as I couldn't think of anything better to do, my fate was sealed. It was the Admiralty Interview Board for me.

We were not at war. There was no conscription and no national emergency, so quite what possessed the Royal Navy to let me through the hallowed doors of Britannia Royal Naval College Dartmouth (BRNC) as a young midshipman was beyond me. However, thanks to this obvious clerical error I found myself surrounded by the highly motivated, closely cropped naval future of Britain. All around were people who were smart, fit, motivated and determined. These four attributes seemed highly necessary for success at Dartmouth. It appeared that liking girls, television, the pub and sleeping ten hours a day were not quite so important.

Located in the small town of Dartmouth in Devon, England, BRNC sat atop a steep rocky outcrop on a bend of the river Dart. It was guarded by the usual military security. Having passed through that security, the driveway snaked up the hill surrounded by neat, short-cut grass. Arriving at the top of the hill, the college, designed to impress, was revealed. It was fronted by a large parade ground encompassed by two driveways curling round each end, with a slight incline up to the front door. The building itself was red brick, with white sills and cornerstones. Along the front were placed numerous brass cannons, glistening in evidence of endless cleaning. Surrounding the main building were the usual assortment of buildings one would expect to find in a military establishment.

With little introduction, the recruits were launched into training. The days were long and busy and began well before the sun showed the slightest inclination of rising above the horizon and ended long after it had shoved off to keep others awake on the far side of the globe. The normal daily routine began with one of two delicacies. The first, a long undulating run around the college grounds, was undertaken on the naval plimsoles. These had the barest amount of rubber between foot and ground, ensuring a powerful, jarring connection with Mother

Earth. The second was marching under the watchful eye of either a chief petty officer or, if very unlucky, a large barrel-chested color sergeant of the Royal Marines. This fellow marched around bolt upright with a stick tucked under his armpit and metal studs on his boots, which made a fearful racket. The color sergeant seemed hell-bent on waking all lifeforms within a five-mile radius with his barked orders. He had a nasty habit of approaching very close and spraying the remnants of his breakfast all over our faces while being very rude about the origins of our birth. He would always finish off his little talking to with a very polite "sir"! I was lucky because marching and running I could handle; however, staying awake in weapons engineering, navigation and naval history was more of a challenge. Following our early morning activities and a quick shower, it was time to exercise another of my talents—eating. Breakfast was a magnificent affair with an eating hall lined down one side with eggs, bacon, sausage, beans, toast and porridge, as much as you could eat, but Dartmouth had the taxpayer's interests at heart and ensured we had no time to eat it. We were obliged to operate as vacuum cleaners and hoover up as many calories as quickly as possible, which was never enough, before dashing to class. The rest of the morning required studying everything from intricate rope work, presumably just in case the Navy felt the need to put HMS Victory to sea, to weapons engineering, which even today I couldn't even begin to explain. We also covered the science of gas turbine propulsion systems and all aspects of navigation, from tidal calculations to the corrections to be applied to a sextant. Rather like weapons engineering, the use of long sight reduction forms for star sight calculation work remains to this day a mysterious science to which I was not privy.

The mathematical intricacies of sextant navigation were introduced to us by a dapper Lt. Commander, who liked to tell us that after a hard night's drinking in the pub, he would stare at the heavens to find his way home. Personally, I found it easier to remember the road network, but perhaps this was why Dartmouth failed to dig out the Vasco de Gama in me. There was only one thing I could remember from the Naval history class, which for some reason was partly taught to us by an attached Army officer. He told us, "Remember, lads, WRACS (Women's Royal Army Corp) are designed to be screwed up against the wall!" That I should remember this above the heroic exploits and tactical supremacy of Collingwood, Hawke and Nelson was not a good sign.

Morse code was another proficiency that we cadets were supposed to master, and most did with alarming speed and accuracy. Class normally took place outside with us students working in pairs. Half the cadets had their backs to the instructor, who was armed with the signaling lamp. The other half wrote down the letters being spoken by those facing the lamp. The lad I often worked with had rowed for England before coming to Dartmouth and eventually left to join the Royal Marines. He was smart as a whippet and drummed out the message without pausing. When my turn came, he was poised with pen in hand to take down my every syllable, only to stare incredulously at me as not a word came out of my mouth. However, later in the term, we did manage to hook up together and win the rowing regatta on behalf of our division in the coxless pairs, which put me in a somewhat better light as far as he was concerned.

Following the morning of intellectual stimulation, came lunch. Once again, it was a magnificent display of variation and bulk in the finest traditions of British cuisine, and once again, a superb opportunity not to enjoy. We could only inhale and dash.

The afternoon brought forth much of the same as the morning, with time split between the classroom and Sandquay, the waterside headquarters of all riverside operations for the college. Being the Royal Navy, it was decided, very sensibly, that the cadets should spend a considerable amount of time on the river in a variety of motor and sail vessels to ensure the required levels of seamanship were well-instilled. The college was separated from Sandquay by a seemingly endless supply of steps, and nothing gave the staff greater pleasure than seeing us turn up in one set of clothes only to be told, "No, no, no, go back up and change!" If they were feeling particularly malicious, they would repeat the process upon our return.

With the completion of either naval maneuvers at Sandquay or more classroom work, there generally followed a furious round of cleaning. Now, there were a great many rules at Dartmouth, but there were two that covered the essentials. First, if it moves, salute it. Second, if it doesn't move, clean it. I didn't mind the saluting; I found it could be dealt with quite quickly. However, this cleaning business really got in the way of life.

All midshipmen in their first term were arranged in dormitories or cabins, with up to a dozen cadets in each room. There could be bunk beds or single beds, and just as in Hollywood movies, you had a small locker next to each bed. Within each locker, your clothes or kit had to be arranged to perfection. Each item had to be washed and ironed into neat squares. The bed had to be made in a certain fashion, and absolutely without creases. Boots and shoes were polished or "bulled" to a mirror finish. The rest of the cabin was cleaned in a team effort, and then, the communal bathroom had to be washed and polished on hands and knees. The first inspection was normally conducted by the senior divisional officer, or housemaster in plain English. He would go round each bed and locker individually. In a methodical and infuriating fashion, he would lift each neat and beautifully arranged item and send it flying across the room. This was followed by taking the bed and tipping it upside down. Now, as a thoroughly normal young man, I had to suppress my natural urge to grab him by the throat and tear it out while issuing a torrent of foul language. Instead, I was required to stare straight ahead, ignoring him as he moved around tearing my life apart. When he had quite finished, the mess was impressive. Being a naval officer, or at least one in training, the basics of mathematics were never far from my mind, and as each item of clothing arced gracefully through the air, I would quietly compute just how long it would take to get my belongings washed, cleaned, ironed, polished and precisely arranged before tackling the required homework from the day. In other words, when the hell was I going to get some sleep? Following all this excitement, never before midnight or one a.m., I would collapse exhausted into bed.

This frenetic daily activity continued for one full term, roughly equal to a school term. At the end of this time, the Navy decided they should send their young officers to find out what life was like at sea. The ship we were sent to was the HMS *Fearless*. She was a high-sided vessel with the usual accommodation decks at the bow, but from amidships aft, she had a flight deck. She also had the capability to sink the back end before lowering a huge transom door to unleash landing craft laden with Royal Marines. As long as there was no crisis in the world, *Fearless* was free to carry several hundred of us young recruits, instead of snarling, war-hungry Marines. So my comrades and I were dispatched to Portsmouth to join the ship. Upon passing through the dockyard gates, we drove past endless nondescript buildings, some with a sense of history, all with a sense of activity and purpose, and all the while, we could catch a glimpse of the funnels and masts of the larger warships ahead. At last, *Fearless* hove into view, and with some excitement, we descended the bus. The smell of paint and diesel oil assailed my nostrils as we gazed upon our new home. We were lined up in our squads and received instructions from a Chief Petty Officer, to which none of us paid the slightest attention. The excitement of staring at this mighty warship shut down our auditory senses. We clambered aboard, and several hundred midshipmen wandered aimlessly around the ship completely lost, asking eye-rolling crewman where our bunks were.

My initial excitement soon wore off when it became quite clear this was to be no cruise with pina coladas on the flight deck. The general idea of life at sea was to introduce us to every aspect of running a warship. This covered everything from bridge watch keeping and cooking to engineering and painting. It was with great relish that the full-time crewmen of *Fearless* could watch their future officers on hands and knees, cleaning out the heads, which we seemed to have to do a considerable amount.

Armed only with a few hundred excitable cadets and a training-weary crew, *Fearless* departed for the Baltic. At the crack of dawn, the shrill tones of the bosun's call were piped over the ship's broadcast system to announce the arrival of a new day. This was accompanied by a verbal announcement of "Call hands, Call hands, Call hands—it's 0600, rise and shine." Rising was obligatory; shining, I was beginning to realize, was near impossible in the Navy. There followed the usual dash to breakfast and the requisite cleaning and tidying of everything in and around our bunks. At this point, the midshipmen would find themselves split among the operations of the ship. Some would report to the bridge to observe the piloting of a warship for real, others to the porter cabins attached on deck to attend classes. In addition, there was scrubbing pots in the galley and checking out the oil-fired steam boilers in the engine room. One of my first visits to the bridge scared me more than the report of an incoming missile. The bridge on a naval warship appeared to require an armada of humanity, most of it covered in large quantities of gold stripes and of considerable seniority to myself. They felt the need to pester midshipmen mercilessly with endless questions regarding speed, distance and time equations, as well as rule of the road issues. Utterly intimidated, I found a quiet corner with a view through the bridge windows overlooking the bow. The view took my breath away. Before my eyes was the majestic view, far below, of rust-streaked naval grey rising and falling to the rhythm of the oncoming seas. As the bow fell into the North Sea troughs, she shuddered before sending skyward a cloud of spray, which paused for the briefest of moments in midair and was then torn away to leeward. I remember being mesmerized and deeply resented being called to other pressing tasks of naval operations.

As the days rolled by, many of them in tedious repetition of onboard tasks, I eventually found myself assigned to the galley for the day. I relished the prospect of a chance to cook, an opportunity to understand some culinary magic and feel the satisfaction of feeding a hungry crew. Ah, to understand the complexities of a white sauce and the subtlety of baking bread! As I strode in and reported to the head chef, all around were scrubbed stainless steel countertops laden with activity and vast acres of stove tops and boiling liquids. Which was to be my station? I reported in with appropriate naval flare. The response was not quite what I had hoped for. The head chef pointed to the farthest dimly lit recess of the galley. There was no mistaking the sink he pointed at and, more ominously, the dangerously high pile of assorted pots and baking trays caked deep with the remnants of the last meal, waiting for my attention. I glanced once more at the head chef just in case he was now pointing at the saucier station, but no luck. No matter, I was due to be in the galley for twelve hours. A brief half hour of scrubbing to show what I was made of was fine with me. Following twelve hours of pan scrubbing, I was seriously considering reporting to sickbay with leprosy of the hands. The cratered, raw slabs of meat at the ends of my arms no longer functioned. Nor did my arms, neck or back, and I was left to hobble back to my berth as a shattered remnant of my former self. However, after good night's sleep, all seemed well. It was time for our first port visit.

Most of the places and ports we visited passed by in a haze, but one stuck in my mind—not by name but by activity. On this particular occasion, I was assigned to a small band of midshipmen chosen to attend the cocktail party for dignitaries and extras. This was a standard practice by visiting naval warships of almost all nations when visiting other countries. You send out invitations to local mayors, ambassadors, businessman, and all others considered worthy of the host naval warship. Now, being sailors, it is never considered in poor taste to invite a large contingent of unattached ladies. *Fearless* was particularly suited to the task of hosting a party. The cocktail party was to be held at the forward end of the landing craft deck, and to access it, you had to descend down a long ramp from the flight deck. At the top of this ramp, on each side, mounted high up, was a pair of powerful spotlights to ensure adequate visibility all the way down to the cocktail party. We were fully briefed on our tasks for the evening, which were to ensure no person be left alone or without a drink. The party area looked fantastic, with a bar set up down one side, the entire place enclosed with material draped from ceiling to floor, and plenty of flags to brighten up the place. With a few people inside, it was a cozy and relaxing place to enjoy the evening.

Just before the evening started, we were reminded once again of our duties. Then, the guests began to arrive, at which point the lights at the top of the ramp were switched on. All was going fine until the first consignment of single ladies arrived in their sheer summer dresses. All our polite ambassadorial chit chat stopped, and we gazed dumbstruck up the ramp. With the brightness of the arc lights shining down on the sheer dress material, these ladies might as well have been walking through an x-ray machine. The view was spectacular, but rather more than our youthful testosterone could handle. We all forgot about mayors, ambassadors and businessmen and began to elbow our way past our shipmates to be first in the queue to greet the ladies as they arrived at the bottom of the ramp. It very nearly descended into a shambles, and following a severe reprimand the next day, neither us nor the arc lights were invited to future cocktail parties.

It was not long after this that the OTO, or "Officer's Training Officer", summoned me. He was the naval officer in charge of all midshipmen, and he told me I would be joining a small naval vessel of one of the local navies while a combined naval exercise took place. I was excited at the change in routine, and the opportunity to get off the ship for a short while was an unaccustomed break. To which navy this vessel belonged, I really can't remember, but I can certainly remember the lecture I was given about being an ambassador for the Royal Navy and being polite, courteous and hardworking. With all this in mind and feeling a thousand years of British maritime history resting on my shoulders, I was dispatched ashore to report aboard my new ship. I duly arrived at the gangplank, saluted and requested to come aboard. I was shown to the bridge, and there, perched atop the captain's chair, was the captain, with his feet up on the dashboard, wearing a Hawaiian shirt. Once again, I leapt to attention and saluted with all the dignity a midshipman could muster. The captain informed me I could relax. RELAX? I had no idea what he was talking about. In the British Navy, relaxing for midshipmen seemed to be against the law. At which point, the captain told a nearby sailor to get the steam bath ready. A steam bath!? My mind couldn't compute this. A towel was thrust into my hands. I was told to change and report back to the steam room. Change into what? I thought this must be joke time for visiting British Naval Cadets and that I had better smile and go along with it. What changing meant, I didn't have the faintest idea, so from my cabin, I cast nervous glances down the corridor. Sure enough, others appeared with boxers and towels draped over their arms before disappearing through a door from which clouds of steam appeared each time it was opened. Nervously, I opened the door, and in fine Scandinavian-accented English, I was welcomed. A glass of some liquid was thrust into my hand.

So here was the captain and all the officers, who appeared most interested in chatting with me. I really didn't know quite why, but this was of no importance, because a never-ending supply of assorted alcohols was thrust upon me. I quickly lost track of time and, shortly thereafter, lost track of consciousness. I awoke to find the entire exercise had been completed and that it was time for me to return to my ship. Of course, I was expected to report in with a full verbal account of all areas of the exercise I had observed and duly did so with a long diatribe about how difficult it was to follow all its many aspects due to the foreign language being spoken. This, of course, was indeed true. Most of the talking within the warship had been conducted in their own tongue. Quite how they managed to leave port, conduct a full naval exercise and return without me noticing a thing is beyond me. Having reported back to *Fearless*, I do think it was in the operations room and not the steam bath that it was assumed I was struggling to understand what was going on, but I was not asked to make this distinction. Without lying, I was quite relieved to be told I seemed to have done a fine job and dismissed.

Life back aboard continued on at the same frenetic pace until one day we found ourselves on the landing craft deck conducting "leadership" drills. This particular exercise required one cadet to take charge of a small group of other cadets to build an arial runway to, as usual, escape the Russians over an imaginary chasm. We were given quite a bit of equipment, including six poles and one very thick rope to run between the poles, which could be anchored to the deck at either end. There was also some small length of rope for lashings and a huge aluminum block from which we could hang an individual before pulling him across. Eventually, it was my turn to take charge, and I set about using three poles at each end and lashing the tops before pushing them upright into a tripod position. Once done, we ran the thick rope across between the two tripods and placed the aluminum block on the rope, ready for action. At about this time OTO, the officer in charge of our training, appeared, took one look at me and one look at what I had set up and declared himself disgusted with both.

"I'll show you how it should be done. Stand over there!" he said.

I did as I was told and watched as he barked orders to the hassled cadets until the new rig was set up.

"Now, Glennie, hang from that block and we'll pull you across."

Once again, I did as I was told and hung suspended in mid-air as the rest of the cadets began heaving on the line and pulling me over the "empty void" below. About halfway across, the entire rig collapsed, and I hit the deck, followed by a sickly thud as the massive aluminum block smashed down on my head, splitting it open. Now, if you want blood, then a head wound is a great place to get it. In the blink of an eye, I looked like a survivor from a war zone, with blood gushing all over my face and clothes. The mess was impressive. I got up and somewhat groggily started off towards sickbay for stitches, but as I went past OTO, I asked, "Was that a little better sir?!"

I don't think he was very impressed.

The rest of my time aboard *Fearless* passed by with little more excitement, but we were now approaching the time to return to Dartmouth and face final exams. These did not go well, particularly navigation and weapons engineering, and despite the best efforts of some fine assistant divisional officers, I was marched before the captain of Dartmouth and told I was rather a waste of taxpayers' money. There was no arguing against it, and the captain felt compelled to agree. With that, my naval career came to a shuddering halt.

TWO

Onwards

The Royal Navy had done me a huge service, but I was not able to see this straight away. I was adrift again. I returned to my parent's home in Lymington, Hampshire to try and decide what was next.

So what of me? As my parents love to remind me, I was conceived in a hotel in Chicago, and not wishing to dwell on the subject of my parents' "in flagrante", I shall leave it at that. I was born 6th June 1964 in Lyndhurst Hampshire, quite normally, I am told, following a quick stop and a stiff drink at the local pub on the way to the hospital. This could account for quite a lot, but I digress. My father was a dashing naval officer, and my mother a good-looking naval wife. Together, they made quite the couple. Their first son, Andrew, my brother, was a model child, and I assume he made parenting seem so easy that my folks thought they should do it all again. They did not stop at me, and there followed my younger brother James. Andrew was indeed a model child, and for a while, they thought I was too, but they mistook my quiet demeanor in the crib and failed to realize my apathetic attitude and generally idle disposition.

Still, the busy naval life sent my father on regular tours of duty abroad interspersed with postings at home. During this time, due to a generous government, my father was able to put us in private school, starting with Walhampton Preparatory School in Hampshire. A thoroughly enjoyable affair, where I seemed to slip under the radar, play lots of sports and barely be noticed. At the age of twelve, I failed common entrance, or in plain English, my exams to get to my next school. It was beginning to dawn upon my parents that they had their work cut out for them to find an establishment willing to take me on. However, there was one school in the United Kingdom that agreed to undertake the task, with the proviso that I was dispatched to crammer school to improve my common entrance mark. The private crammer selected was in Seaford, Sussex. The school consisted of a number of houses arranged around a medium-sized grass common, all of which were located about a hundred yards from the waterfront. Our time was spent running between different houses for different classes, with the dormitories on the top floors. Two teachers stand out, one who taught French and was rumored, although none of us was brave enough to ask, to have survived a Nazi interrogation that involved having his fingernails pulled out. The other, the headmaster, was a chain smoker and took great pride in using a dirty handkerchief to polish his yellow-stained fingers as he waited for your answer to a particularly taxing math question. As you can imagine, if this was the highlight of my time here, then it was intended as such to focus young men on working hard, passing common entrance and getting the hell out. This was achieved, but God only knows how. Barely a teenager, I found myself dumped at Strathallan public school in Scotland. I am not going to dwell on Strathallan for long, except to point out that to understand how I felt, you must imagine the following: a young Englishman arriving a term late, after everyone else has settled down into a school of Scotsmen, with a father in the Navy, which had just released a recruiting add with the slogan "Join the Navy and feel a man". It was a tough three years settling in!

During my last two years there, it suddenly dawned on me that if I did no work at all, I was going to be in very serious trouble. This was mainly due to sixteen years of heavy-duty training in the art of idleness. With a sense of urgency, I got stuck in the books, but it was a little too late to do more than enter the world with two Scottish highers and one C grade in A-level biology. Clearly, Oxford and Cambridge were out of the question, but apparently, becoming an officer in Her Majesty's Navy was not. Make of that what you will.

THREE

Dipping My Toe

So with the Navy behind me, once again I was in Lymington. I was definitely down in the dumps. My friends seemed at ease in their chosen professions, none of which appealed to me. We would meet at weekends at the Chequers pub and drink until we fell into the ditches. Sundays would bring get-togethers at somebody's house for breakfast before more lunchtime drinking, with many of my friends departing for London to work. This left me with Monday to Friday to fill up. It was the late spring of 1984, and during the course of this mindless weekly routine, I got a phone call from a chap calling himself Dave. He announced that he was the skipper of a full-scale working replica of the *Golden Hinde* and asked if I would be interested in joining as a crew member for summer. I leapt at the chance, and before my father could say, "What about a real career?" I was out the door.

I had taken the train to Troon in Scotland, where the *Golden Hinde* was berthed in the harbor. A quick stop at the local pub for a sandwich allowed the staff to fill me in on some stories of the *Hinde* and her skipper Dave. I made my way from the pub by foot. The sight of an exact working Elizabethan sailing ship moored alongside a visiting Royal Navy minesweeper was surreal and magnificent in the morning sunshine. I clambered aboard and was awestruck.

The *Golden Hinde* had been built by Appledore shipyard in Devon. She was faithfully constructed with original scantlings of timber and layout. She was 120 feet in overall length and drew twelve feet. With all sails set, she carried 4,150 sq. feet and had five decks. The original *Golden Hinde* had been sailed by Sir Francis Drake during the Elizabethan era and Britain's never-ending quest for fortune and glory. The original vessel, after Sir Francis had finished his voyages, was put on display in London before being burnt a hundred years later for safety reasons. For me, more impressive than the hull, topsides and deck was the mass of ropes and rigging. As I looked around, I wondered how on earth I was going to find my way around this confusing mass of rope.

The deck layout was reasonably simple, with a high quarter deck aft from where the steering was done and a set of steps leading down onto the main deck. A walk forward about twenty or thirty feet led to another set of steps up to the foredeck. Roughly speaking, a single mast shared each of these three decks, making three masts in total.

As a crew, we had been gathered together from all walks of life within the British Isles. The guys and girls were hired for the following three tasks: First, to help with the considerable maintenance; second, to assist with delivering the vessel from port to port and third, to get aboard and show around as many paying members of the public as possible to help offset the running costs.

Our quarters were on the gun deck, just below the main deck, where we could either sling hammocks or sleep in sleeping bags on deck between the cannons. I chose the hammock. Without boring the reader with tedious details regarding my sleeping habits, it will suffice to say that generally, I find I tend to roll over onto my stomach during the night. This task my subconscious mind managed to accomplish while I slept soundly during my first night, and I awoke to the screaming agony of a back bent ninety degrees the wrong way. During the course of my semi-conscious writhing, I managed to eject myself out of the hammock onto the deck, much to the amusement of my fellow crewmates. Needless to say, I decided that the sleeping bag option was, going forward, infinitely preferable.

Little time was wasted in getting underway, and with the supplies loaded, we slipped lines and left Troon. The foremast and mainmast carried two yardarms, the main yard on each mast being essentially fixed in space and the sail let go or furled up beneath it. Above the fixed yards on each mast and above the fighting tops, or crow's nests, as they were often incorrectly called, were a single topsail on a yard that would be hoisted to the top of the mast as required and the sail, which when not used, was lashed within the confines of the fighting tops. With an additional spritsail set below the bowsprit on a yard-arm and a small triangular sail set on the aft-most of the three masts, there were six sails in total. Once set, all sail trimming could be completed from deck with the prodigious supply of running hemp rope rigging. However, to get these sails set and put away was an exciting undertaking in itself. During our first sail, Doug, the bear of a first mate, took one look at me and said, "You look fit, get up the foremast and set the foresail."

I had not the faintest idea what he was talking about, so I just stared at him blankly. He correctly sensed my confusion.

"The rigging on the forward mast," he said. "Climb up the outside of it and crawl out on the yardarm and undo the rope lashing the sail to the yard. Go!"

Did he think I was nuts? Hang off the yard in mid-air? I would have no April fool's jokes at my expense. I stood my ground.

"There's a special rope hanging from the yardarm for you to stand on while you undo the lashing holding the sail," Doug said. "Get moving!"

Still, no action came from the disbelieving crew. So without missing a beat, he leapt up the outside of the rigging and onto the yard. He shimmied out to the end, and with his upper body draped over the yard and his feet balancing on the rope below, he began work on releasing the lashing holding the sail to the yard. Clearly, he hadn't been joking, so I leapt up the portside and, with much awkwardness, clambered up. The main vertical shrouds were as thick as my wrists, while the horizontal "ratlines" were about the thickness of a finger, which provided a ladder system to get up and down. Everything was covered in a thick black tar paint to help preserve the natural hemp fiber. I made a point of not looking down, but as I made my way out onto the yardarm, it all began to feel very precarious. While I stayed close to the mast on the yard, the motion was not too bad, but things were quite different once I moved out onto the yard. With the peculiar action of a rolling, pitching, yawing vessel magnified and sent out to the poor idiot suspended on the end of the yard, I was beginning to think that this was a better training ground for NASA astronauts than an inexperienced landlubber. Somehow, I managed to release my side of the sail and duly made my way back down to deck level, which despite being adrift upon the ocean, felt surprisingly rigid after my time aloft. Much time was spent by Dave and Doug patiently teaching us how to set, trim and put away sails, as well as how to safely release a sheet through a belaying pin when under the considerable load of a half gale. As the days and weeks drifted by, we went from utter confusion to a crew who could rapidly undertake the task of setting and securing sail at speed and with little prompting.

Life aboard the *Hinde* was split into two distinct varieties. The first was tied up alongside, and the second was time spent at sea on delivery between ports. The crew numbered around ten or fifteen, depending on who had been fired or departed or what new positions had been created; for example, there was a need for a chef. As I mentioned earlier, the personalities on board were fascinating, but one particular lad took the biscuit. He was from Glasgow and short with a crop of thick black hair. He spoke in rapid-fire Glaswegian with such a thick accent that nobody had the faintest idea what he said, but we were too afraid of him to ask him to repeat himself. So, in unison, we would throw our heads back and laugh furiously, hoping it was the correct response. Every now and again, it wouldn't be, and then, all hell broke loose. He would jump and down, unleashing a torrent of swearing and verbal abuse. Once again, because we couldn't understand a word, we would try our laughing and head throwing. This brought on the next phase, which involved a purple face and bulging neck veins. It was at this point that we would all beat a hasty retreat and hope for the best. He became even more entertaining around the women. He tended to start with the same verbal abuse and ranting before resorting to grabbing them by whichever body part was nearest to hand. He was reminiscent of a Jack Russell dog with your vicar visiting on Sunday. You knew it was only a matter of time before the dog leapt on the vicar's leg and went at it like, well, a dog on a vicar's leg! Anyway, that dog on a vicar's leg is one thing, but a crew member trying to maul girls after a few beers was quite another. So with little ceremony, he and his bag were dumped on the quay, and we bid adieu to our Glaswegian Jack Russell!

We visited Liverpool, Manchester, Belfast and the Isle of Man. Life at sea was tremendous. It was very relaxed. We were more or less on a volunteer basis for watches, which regardless of the time of day or night, were fantastic. Nights were often warm and utterly romantic, ghosting along under a starry canopy. The days were spent mastering the sails and ropes. We became proficient at scaling the rigging at speed, never using the lubber holes, as we referred to the cutouts in the middle of the fighting tops, but instead hanging upside-down as we clambered around the outside and into the top. The view down over the vessel as she danced along sending billowing, rolling bow waves foaming away from the ship's side was magnificent. The great bellies of canvas strained under the running rigging, heaving the vessel along. When we had had enough of the view, we would show off by climbing down a piece of fixed rigging hand-over-hand with our bodies dangling dangerously in midair to the deck. The days of the politically correct health-and-safety-conscious workplace had not yet arrived, and there was barely a glance from those on deck at whatever stupidity went on aloft, of which there was plenty. Somehow, there was not one injury of any description during my time aboard, but it was not for want of trying. There was always maintenance to do, which involved splicing new ratlines, fixing tears in the canvas sails, painting and the myriad work that goes into keeping this type of vessel in good working order. I never tired of our time at sea, which was always busy and fun. When not on watch, our nights were spent on the gun deck, listening to the wood and rigging working to the rhythm of the sea as we drifted off to sleep.

Most of our port visits went off without too much incident. However, Belfast was for me the most interesting. This was at a time when the troubles in Ireland were in full flight, and when the *Hinde* showed up, I got the sense that there was utter delight among the local population in a visiting attraction for a place that did not see a lot of this kind of thing. I seem to remember that we were there for a week or two, at the end of which some members of the local community decided they wanted to take us ashore for a few beers to say thank you. There was just one problem, and that problem was me. I had one of those English accents that were just not welcome in that part of the world, and they could not quite decide what to do about me. After much head-scratching, they told me to come along and not say a single word in the couple of the pubs that we visited. With a healthy sense of self-preservation, I was happy to comply, and so we were taken around some of Belfast's finest drinking establishments. It was the only time in my life I got plastered without ever uttering a syllable, which I consider to be no mean feat under the circumstances.

All too quickly, our summer was over, the *Hinde* returned to Troon and the crew was paid off. It was time to return home to Lymington.

Having returned from the *Golden Hinde* and loafing around at home in Hampshire, my mother heard that a yacht was departing Lymington for Cyprus and suggested that this was something I might enjoy. I was intrigued and set out to find the skipper, Ken. Having tracked him down, I was surprised to find a rather elderly gentleman, who agreed to take me on as part of his delivery crew.

So on September 17th, 1984, when all preparations on the Rhodes 39-foot sloop had been completed, food bought and stowed, crew assembled and tanks topped up, I walked down the marina docks towards the *Mahjong*, as she was called, with my gear slung over my shoulder.

At the last moment, my mum turned to me. "He's gay, you know!" she said.

"Who is?" I replied, now only feet away from the yacht.

"The skipper," she whispered. "Do watch out, won't you!"

As I clambered over the guardrails, I couldn't help wondering why, as Mum knew me to be a very red-blooded, women-loving male, she couldn't have passed on this piece of vital information earlier. Having eyed the skipper suspiciously, I stowed my kit and helped get underway. As we departed, I couldn't be sure, but I could have sworn that Mum was giggling as she waved us farewell.

It is one of the quirks of life, but despite being one of my first major forays to sea in a small vessel, very little of the early part of this voyage proved noteworthy. The skipper proved competent, as did the rest of the crew. The *Mahjong* suffered no failures. The food, prepared by the owner's wife, who had decided to come on the delivery trip, was adequate. The weather cooperated all the way down the English Channel and across the Bay of Biscay as far as Gibraltar, where we refueled and replenished. After departing Gibraltar, Ken decided to stop over in Annaba, North Africa. This, too, should have been a brief footnote in the story, except for our departure day.

While moored stern to, Ken had used one of the dock lines attached to the key that could be picked up with a boathook and brought to the bow hand-over-hand before pulling it through one of the fair leads to hold the yacht off the quay. However, upon departure, and with a touch of overexuberance on the engine throttle, Ken managed to foul the mooring line around the prop, and our voyage came to a grinding halt. It was at this point that I glanced over the side and looked into the inky depths. To be more precise, I was looking at the lumps, chunks and brown soupy mess surrounding the vessel and wondering how we were going to resolve this little crisis. When Ken took me on, he did so as his number two, and at this particular moment in time, as he called for volunteers, all eyes rested upon me as the man for the job to go overboard! There was nothing for it but to put the knife between my teeth and head for the depths. Having entered the water, I was immediately struck by the fact that unknown objects were bumping into me, not just at head level but also throughout the depths. Clearly, Annaba, at the time, did not have particularly strict environmental rules about what went into the harbor, and apart from the obvious raw sewage component, this "soup" was beginning to irritate my skin. So it was to the inky depths that I dove and found the tangled mess around the prop. With a series of dives to gasp for air, I hacked through the line and began to unravel the mess—not an inconsiderable feat with zero visibility and the nagging sense that each and every second was introducing my bodies to toxins and parasites as yet unknown to mankind. After some fifteen or twenty minutes, the task was complete, and despite a thorough washdown with soap, endless brushings of teeth and spitting, I still spent many days wondering what entities had entered my body and were roaming free. The wind from Annaba blew in our favor, and our trip down to Malta and then to Larnaca was, despite a broken engine twenty-four hours prior to arrival, uneventful.

I have kept the story of this delivery short for two reasons. First, it really was quite uneventful. There were no desperate storms, no gear failures and no crew issues, and the boat performed perfectly for the most part. Second, it is one of those quirks of age and time that despite my brief notes on the occasion, I can remember almost nothing of it. However, the delivery may have been without too much difficulty or excitement, but this trip was important in my life for one reason: it cemented my love for the sea and the possibility of adventure and excitement it could offer. I now knew that the usual careers available on land were not for me. I returned home with a new sense of purpose and a determination to continue on the path of life at sea. I was to have little idea, at this stage, of how quickly things were going to develop or that my quest for adventure and excitement was indeed heading my way at full speed.

FOUR

A Developing Career

Alistair Easton seemed straight off a movie set, not in looks but more in manner. A tall man with rather washed-out pale blue eyes and a receding hairline, he was in his mid-seventies and ran a yacht brokerage at Bucklers Hard on the Beaulieu River in Hampshire. During the war, he flew with the Fleet Air Arm off British aircraft carriers, and he was the only man I knew who could make wearing a cravat look cool. Presumably, years of listening to noisy engines while flying in open cockpits and no doubt the odd bullet flying past had made him deaf as a post. He could always be found talking in a loud voice at the bar, ordering and consuming huge quantities of whatever alcohol was at hand, with apparently little or no effect. Everybody was addressed as either "Hello old boy" or girl, depending on who he was talking to, and he often got this the wrong way around, depending on how far he was into depleting the bar of stock.

Alistair lived in Lymington with Kitty; I lost count of quite which wife this was, but she would have undoubtedly been a stunner in her younger years. He had four passions as far as I could tell: women, including Kitty; work; drinking and sailing. It was his fourth passion that involved me because on the Lymington River, he kept an X boat, which could best be described as about twenty feet long with a deep open cockpit. It was constructed of wood, including the mast and boom. He seemed to have run out of friends and colleagues to sail with in the often cold and damp conditions of spring and autumn racing in the Solent. So I found myself on the phone with him one day, being asked if I could crew for him in the upcoming race.

"We best get supplies," said Alistair.

I naturally assumed we had to dash to the chandlery to load up on rope and fenders. Quite wrong, I found myself with armfuls of beer at the liquor store. Once back at Lymington Yacht Club, Alistair and I gathered the beer from the back of the car and headed down the river in his tiny rowing boat, with the "supplies" precariously balanced on our laps. No sooner had we got on board his X than out came the beer. The racing was soon lost in a haze of alcoholic confusion as we tried to work our way around the Solent racecourse while peeing into the bailer with increasing regularity.

Having returned to the mooring, we secured the boat and rowed back to terra firma. Alistair inquired as to my plans for the future. With uncharacteristic silence while listening to my response, he finished up with, "Thanks for coming out old boy." With that, he was gone.

It was not many days before the phone rang. The man I found myself talking to introduced himself as Peter Haward and said that Alistair, an old friend of his, had rung. He asked if I would be interested in helping on his next delivery. I never had a chance to thank Alistair for his introduction because the next day, I was off to Goole.

This is an appropriate moment to introduce Peter Haward. Peter was tall and gangly with large round eyes and a face to match. There was both a mischievous gleam in his eye and a steely resolve. At the ends of his spindly arms were two massive, calloused hands with fingers as thick as sausages, an indication of the hard life he had led. He was quick to laugh and very slow to anger, a disposition borne of much difficult time spent at sea, which either develops such a personality or deflects the individual elsewhere in life.

Peter had started his yacht delivery business rather by accident while in the British Army in northern France at the end of World War Two. While loitering about, he was asked to deliver various small naval vessels that had been purchased by private individuals across the English Channel, from France back to England. During the intervening years from 1945 to 1985, when I first meet Peter, he, by his own reckoning, had done over one million miles at sea, including in excess of thirty trans-Atlantic voyages. The vessels he had delivered ranged from, funnily enough, a delivery of the *Golden Hinde* halfway around the world to the small open naval launches across the channel mentioned above and every type of motor and sail yacht in between. There are not many people I would say this about, but what he didn't know about small vessels at sea was probably not worth knowing. He became without a doubt the finest instructor of small vessels at sea that I ever sailed with, and this first trip was to be an instruction indeed.

So in March of 1985, I found my way to Goole, just inland of Hull on the Humber River. Much to my surprise, when I arrived at the predetermined location, I found a hundred-foot river barge, named *Tyke*, tied up alongside and no sign of anything else. Now, bearing in mind we had to deliver this vessel south to the English Channel, traveling along the south coast of the U.K. across the Irish sea and around Fastnest, skirting the North Atlantic to Limerick in Southern Ireland, surely I had the wrong place and wrong "barge". Since I was clearly lost, I thought I had better rouse a crewmember and see if I could find out where I was going. There was no mistake, and having been welcomed aboard, I found myself in the cavernous empty hold, which was entirely free of bulkheads from the bow to three-quarters of the way aft. The hold was covered by loose-fitting deck planks, but in the middle of this enormous space was a large pile of sand. It was my first meeting with Peter, who was hunched over a shovel, moving the sand around. He stopped briefly for introductions and hellos, and then, it was back to work. I grabbed a spare shovel sitting in the middle of the sand pile and started shoving the sand evenly around the bilge. 2″ x 6″ pieces of wood about ten feet long ran the full length fore and aft, each placed end to end. Running athwart ships about every fifteen feet were further 2″x 6″ pieces of wood, all of which combined to neatly box the sand off into sections. This, it was hoped, would prevent the sand ballast from shifting as a whole in rough weather. I was glad Peter's knowledge was at work here because despite my total lack of experience, one thing I felt fairly confident about was that a narrow barge might not be fair game for the fury of the North Atlantic in March.

Above deck, there was more work to be done. As mentioned, the hatches over the cargo hold consisted of wooden planks laid flat, side-by-side, resting upon a central support that provided about five degrees of angle to ensure that water ran off to the side decks. However, they were not watertight. A shore party was organized to head into town to buy a number of tarpaulins and seemingly endless lengths of rope for lashings. The tarps were then laid tight over the hatches, and to secure the tarps, wooden chocks were hammered into place on the metal housing at the side. On top of the tarps, the lashings were then secured into place in a criss-cross pattern that by the time it was completed, looked far in excess of what was required. While I and the other crewmember were undertaking this, Peter was buried in the engine room, giving a thorough going-over to what looked to me to be a completely filthy shambles. Peter seemed unfazed, and following a trip into town, he returned with one huge cardboard box full of fuel filters. Interesting, I thought. Again, he must have known something I didn't. Peter eventually became satisfied that all that could be done to prepare the vessel for sea was complete. It was time for a final visit to the supermarket, where Peter's simple attitude towards catering became apparent. He would not cook for us, nor did he expect any of us to cook for him or each other. As such, he would buy whatever supplies we requested for a week at sea. I was at that youthful age when tea, toast, sausage sandwiches and Jaffa cake biscuits seemed to keep me feeling fine and energized. So it was with the vessel loaded and considered ready for sea that we left Goole for the coastal confines of the North Sea.

The barge looked, upon deck, as one might imagine, with a high vertical bow and then three-quarters of the vessel from forward aft covered with deck hatches, as well as two small side decks allowing access fore and aft. At the aft end of the barge was a small accommodation area, which included a bridge, behind which was the galley/open cabin area where we ate and slept. In one corner, a few steps led down to a rather flimsy door and the engine room. She was no speedboat. Little more than five knots could be achieved, and that was without headwinds or seas. The start of the delivery was uneventful as we made our way south past the Wash and Thames estuary and into the English Channel. Indeed, our passage along the south coast of the U.K. was also uneventful, with the three of us splitting the watches equally and, in my case, eating sausage sandwiches and sleeping in-between. Peter had decided he wanted to pull into Penzance Devon to gain up-to-date weather information from the meteorological office.

I suppose there may be some curiosity as to wages in this yacht delivery world. I would love to describe the complex hierarchical system related to experience and qualifications for remuneration, but it was really quite simple. There were no wages. You did it for experience, the love of it, getting away from the wife or quite possibly, although I have no specific examples, the Inland Revenue. You did get fed, and you got a free ride home. Thus, food was quite important to the delivery crew, and any decent captain spared no expense, within reason. Peter was no exception in this regard, and while in Penzance, we ate at the finest pubs and all we could manage. I was in heaven—all I could eat and a life of adventure, adventure being lying in my bunk between meals and waiting for the weather to break so we could dash across the Irish Sea. Peter was in daily contact with the meteorological office. After about a week, Peter returned to the barge and announced that we had a small weather window of forty-eight hours before the next inbound depression from the North Atlantic arrived at the shores of southern Ireland, but the "window" came with a warning that the speed of the approaching depression might increase. We needed to get moving.

We slipped lines and made our way out into a light southwesterly wind and slight seas. It was midmorning, and the day progressed well. As dusk arrived, we could make out the loom of Fastnet light as it scanned across the horizon. As my late night watch finished, I was aware the sea was getting up, as was the wind, but it was certainly nothing to alarm us. With a final glance out the bridge windows, I turned in.

I was awoken by the violent motion of the barge and Peter's request to get up and lend a hand. Upon arrival on the bridge, I found Peter repeatedly moving the engine control from full ahead to full astern and then to neutral. While the control was full ahead or full astern, he would dash to the bridge wing door and hang off it while looking over the side to check for prop wash. I enquired as to what he was doing.

"Just checking the propeller hasn't fallen off. We can't seem to make progress against the wind or sea," he said.

Now, I was alarmed.

"Where the hell are we?" I yelled above the din of the full gale blowing outside.

"Well, to the south of Fastnet," replied Peter. "I didn't want to hit it."

Very commendable, I remember thinking. A quick glance at the compass told me we were hove to heading roughly due west, at which point the engine quit. The bow was blown down until we were port beam onto the finest the North Atlantic and accompanying southwesterly gale had to offer. The wind had risen with great speed in a short period of time and was continuing to do so. It was obviously a system moving fast to the east and north. Peter got to work on the engine and quickly diagnosed a blocked fuel filter. In no time flat, he had changed it out, bled the fuel system of air and gotten it going.

Fifteen minutes later, it stopped again. Once again, the fuel filter was blocked. Clearly, the weather was stirring up the fuel tanks and the filthy mess lying within. This process continued on while the storm raged and kept Peter busy as he kept intermittently dashing to the chart table.

The wind continued to build until by Peter's own estimate, we were experiencing a force ten gale. Despite full power, the barge would not maintain a direction, so Peter had us put about by bearing away downwind and come up on the other tack, heading away from land. Once on the other tack, a new problem arose. The roof over the bridge was trying to peel away under the violence of the gale. By sheer good luck, there were two eye bolts screwed into the deck head about a shoulderwidth apart just aft of the helm station, and so I put two fingers through each eye bolt and hung from them. This was how we spent the next hour: one crewmember on the helm, one crewmember holding the roof on, Peter changing fuel filters ever thirty minutes or so and navigating, all of us hoping nothing else would go wrong. We had no more spare hands. In the early hours of the morning, the wind swung round to the northwest with the passage of the cold front and began to abate. No longer did I have to hang from the ceiling, and as the seas calmed slightly, Peter was not changing fuel filters with the same regularity.

Peter altered course for land, and by late morning, we were making our way into Crookhaven and a quiet anchorage. As we squared away the vessel at anchorage, I remember reflecting upon my utter youthful stupidity. There I had been, dangling from the ceiling hooks, barely restraining the roof from flying away with an intermittently stalling engine on a river barge in a severe gale of Fastnet, and my only thought had been *Whoa—this is fun!* What I failed to realize was that we had only stayed out of trouble thanks to the very great experience of Peter and his preparation of the vessel, including the sand ballast, spare fuel filters, secure lashings and tarpaulins over the deck hatches, as well as a healthy respect for margins of safety with regards to land and navigation.

Our arrival in Crookhaven had us experiencing Irish hospitality firsthand. Residents up on the hills surrounding the anchorage came down to look and insisted we stop by their house for drinks and meals. The local pub made us very welcome and plied us with pints of Guinness. It really was a shame to ever leave. Our short trip up to Limerick was engineered to be uneventful, with careful planning around weather. Our arrival, while unexciting, was no less welcome. Having arrived and met the owner, we were dispatched back home, ready for the next trip.

Peter wasted no time, and within a week, we were in Lymington aboard a Nicholson 46 that had to be delivered to Kip Marina in Scotland for a refit. I was struck by this vessel's muscular sense of purpose. Beamy and sleek with little structure above deck and a pronounced tumblehome, I loved the look of the boat, but her looks were not just for show. She felt solid and determined at sea. Very little frustrated me about deliveries, but there was just one thing that did. We were duty-bound to look after each vessel and absolutely not push any vessel, motor or sail, outside sensible boundaries with good margins of safety. In other words, no sailing or motoring to the max. This was a shame because this was one vessel that I would have loved to have put a full suit of sails on to test her mettle. Despite a brief force eight of Holyhead, this trip proved easy and, relatively speaking, rapid. However, we were not finished with this yacht. She was to provide possibly the worst night at sea of my life, but more on that later.

Upon completion of this delivery, I now had 4,568 nautical miles logged in only three trips, not including the *Golden Hinde*. I knew my future lay at sea. How things were going to develop, I did not know, but I was loving every minute.

FIVE

The Atlantic

Les Powles was out of money, and so he found himself employed as skipper on a Rival 41 that had to be delivered from Lymington Yacht Haven in England to Boston, USA for its new American owner. He asked me to come along as his number two. It was late in April of 1985, and as I sat opposite Les with a cup of coffee, I couldn't help wonder who this man was. This healthy dose of curiosity was entirely motivated by self-preservation. I wanted to get all the way across the Atlantic and not have to swim half of it. I asked him a little about his background, and his story almost made me choke on my coffee. Following his wartime exploits and failed marriages, he suddenly came up with the idea of building his own yacht in his backyard, despite having never sailed in his life. Having built it and built it "solid"—he was a man who believed in good safety margins—the boat was launched. With zero sailing experience whatsoever, Les failed in the simple task of moving the vessel from launch site to berth. He decided to rectify the situation and dashed out into the Solent to give himself eight hours of on-the-job sailing experience. He returned alongside the marina loaded up with supplies and decided he was now ready to sail around the world. Having crossed the Atlantic and thinking he was well on the way to the Caribbean, he forgot that during the process of sextant navigation, which he also taught himself en route, you have to allow for a change of declination in the calculations from north to south or vice versa, depending on which way one is crossing the equator. In any event, this failure led him to wash up on the beaches of Brazil, instead of arriving in the Car-ribean, much to the excitement of the local nuns who took care of him. Once he gathered himself, he continued on round the world. This trip was completed in 1978, after almost three years. He was not satisfied and, feeling he had to make up for the mistakes of the first voyage, decided to sail non-stop around the world from west to east single-handedly and out of sight of land. He was too poor even to afford a radio transmitter and was quite literally out of touch in every sense of the word from July 9, 1980 to June 3, 1981. For the last months of this voyage, he was even running low on supplies and survived on half a cup of rice with a little milk powder and sugar. He shed 76 lbs. of bodyweight and completed 28,496 nautical miles during this second circumnavigation by the time he returned to Lymington Yacht Haven. This was the man who sat opposite me over our cup of coffee. *Right*, I remember thinking, *if he can survive that lot, I guess we have half a chance.* I was in.

On the 3rd of May 1985, with Robin, a young Lymington lad; Les; myself and provisions for fifty days, we departed down Lymington River out of the Solent on an ebbing tide and past the Needles into a messy English Channel. As late afternoon came and I could see the white cliffs of the Needles receding, I felt utterly isolated and lonely. As night fell, I began to wonder about watches, but Les, with his unique experience as a single-handed sailor, announced that he felt nervous around land and shipping and would stay up all night. I looked all around me as we stood in that tiny cockpit and could see neither land nor shipping. Odd decision, I thought. Still, what was on offer was one full night in my bunk. I was not to enjoy many more of those for a while.

The Rival 41 could probably be described as a traditional Bermuda sloop of the era, with a cockpit and helm at the aft end. At the forward end of the cockpit, steps led down into the saloon and galley area. The galley was to the left, and the navigation station was to the right. Just forward of these two was the open saloon area, with seating port and starboard and the usual offset table, from amidships, with opening leaves for mealtime. The salon seats could be converted to bunks with lee clothes that could be secured to the deck head eye bolts in heavy weather. My bunk was to port, and Rob slept to starboard. Further forward was a small head and v-shaped double berth capping off the bow area. Les slept in the navigator's berth, just aft of the chart table.

Descending the steps that first night with a couple of bunk lights on, it felt cozy, a pleasant escape from the cold enveloping darkness up on deck. I rolled out my sleeping bag, crawled in and was soon asleep. The following morning, Les woke me, so he could get some sleep. As promised, he had spent the whole night on watch. We were dancing along on 240 degrees, with the wind 60 degrees of our starboard bow and making six knots, which was very respectable. This was a piece of cake: a cooperating breeze, sunshine, good sailing and a happy crew. What could go wrong?

At 1.30 a.m. on the morning of the 5th of May, a fatigued Les woke me as the wind was increasing to gale force. We had to reef the main, at which point we discovered a couple of the mainsail slides had disintegrated. We had no spares, so we now had to put in a single reef and take the good slides from below the first reef to above this point to ensure that we could keep some main flying at all times. For now, though, this would not be necessary. The main was securely lashed down. By dawn, the gusts were holding the anemometer needle on the stop mark at fifty knots. We were in the area of Ushant off the northwest coast of France, and in my limited experience at sea, I had never seen seas like this. The confused seas were large, with the tops periodically breaking and spray being torn away to leeward, leaving long foaming trails behind them. Occasionally, a breaking sea would deposit itself into the cockpit, and the watch keeper would find himself waist-deep in water until, some minutes later, the cockpit drains took care of it all. We did pass one ship, which was heading northeast, but I could not tell who was having a worse time of it all. The pitching and rolling as she clambered up and over those vast mountains of water looked rapid and violent. For us, with the steadying effect of the storm canvas, it felt more like an elevator ride. Up, up up, down, down, down. When the waves were not breaking on us, I felt we had the better deal. By late night, the wind had eased to twenty-five knots, but it was still blowing from the west and driving us deeper into Biscay, with Ushant by now astern.

Rob, the poor fellow, was incapacitated by severe seasickness. On the 7th of May, Les received a double dose of bad news. Rob told him that if his severe seasickness persisted, he might have to get off at the Azores, where we were heading. My problem was a little different and, in hindsight, quite amusing. Following the storm and our continuing journey southwest towards the Azores, while taking a piss one day, I noticed I was discharging puss; I had an infection. As one does with too much time on one's hands, my mind raced through all the horrible possibilities: some foul internal body failure as yet unknown to man, from which I would quietly rot from the inside out before dying just prior to arrival in the Azores. Clearly I would have to be buried at sea, but I was so young! Possibly it was a venereal disease, despite the fact that I hadn't been anywhere near a women for months, quell domage! I explained my predicament to Les and told him I might not be able to continue on should it prove to be as serious as I was certain it must be. It was not a good day.

We did manage to get a curry made that evening and, as Rob pointed out, I think it was the first time we had all used a fork since leaving Lymington. The following day was uneventful, much of it spent off watch reading and playing cards. The rather pleasant afternoon was finished off with a delicious evening meal of fray bentos pies, boiled potatoes and cabbage. By the 9th of May, we were halfway to the Azores and thoroughly enjoying a superb beam reach on a direct course, hitting sustained speeds of eight knots. There followed a couple of calmer days before once again, around the 12th of May, the wind settled just aft of the starboard beam at twenty knots, and we were flying with nine knots plus showing on the log at times. By the 13th, we had a twenty-four hour run of 170 nautical miles, which averaged out at just over seven knots. Under delivery conditions, this was excellent mileage. With the beautiful sunny days and the yacht dancing along, much time on the 13th was just spent on deck, thoroughly enjoying the lovely sailing. Even Rob, despite his earlier bouts of debilitating seasickness, seemed to be settling in. The 17th once again brought excellent sailing conditions, with twenty-five to thirty knots of wind on the port beam as we passed Terceira and Sao Jorge. Now that we were close to land again, Les decided to stay up all night. When we departed the U.K., I was not conscious of the smells of land being left behind, but as we approached the Azores and sailed under the lee of the first island, the wafting smells of terra firma and humanity were strong indeed and a reminder, as if we needed it, that we had almost made it through the first part of our voyage.

We had a tedious time close to the Azores, with light headwinds and some low grey clouds. By 0900 on the 18th of May, we entered Horta. It was a very welcome refuge, with the local hillside surrounding and overlooking the port. By midday, after some moving around, we were secure alongside the jetty. Having cleared customs, I went at full speed to the local hospital to see a doctor and find out why I was alive following my infection. Having checked me over, he pulled his stethoscope from his ears and asked if I had been eating and drinking normally for the first four or five days prior to the infection. Well, casting my mind back, I didn't remember drinking anything except the odd cup of tea and even less during the storm. He chuckled and said it was probably a light kidney infection as a result of dehydration. Holy crap, I wasn't going to die. This was great news. I returned to the boat and informed Les and Rob. Even better news awaited: Rob had decided he would be fine to crack on the rest of the way to the States. It was off to Café Sport for some beers. I had escaped death, and I needed to celebrate!

While in Horta, we caught up on the usual repairs to sails, running rigging, catching up on laundry, filling the fuel tanks, visits to Café Sport and, far too many times, changing berth due to the coming and goings of various yachts and vessels. We did finally end up secured against a beautiful seventy-five or eighty-foot yacht with a dark blue hull and seemingly endless lengths of teak deck. Despite being thoroughly absorbed with my own adventure, I couldn't help but wonder about life as a crew member aboard this large magnificent yacht and all the exotic places it might visit.

Les had a schedule to keep, and loafing around in Horta Azores was not part of it. On the 21st of May, it was time to depart. Fuel and water tanks were full, and at 10.25 a.m., we let go. Once again, we confronted the emotions caused by leaving behind the security of land for the unknown of the North Atlantic.

During the course of the next thirty-six hours, we managed to get 130 nautical miles away from Horta, but by the 23rd, we were encountering strong headwinds in the thirty to thirty-five knot range. There was not much to do but take all the sails down and lay a hull because we wished to sail on a course of 270 degrees and the wind blew from 270 with remarkable regularity and determination. Although we did not know it at the time, we were to encounter a very great deal of this in the coming weeks, and it was to severely test our patience.

So what of life aboard a small yacht mid-Atlantic or, in our case, not mid-Atlantic enough? As a single-hander, Les ensured a very relaxed routine at sea, which I was never to experience again. If we were lying a hull with all sails down at the mercy of wind and sea, then it was fine to shut the hatch, read, sleep, cook, relax, navigate, play cards or any other activity the crew could dream up. Les was not particularly fussed about cleaning and left it to us to decide when to clean the heads or, for that matter, the rest of the interior. It was an interesting curiosity of human beings that one's own mess seems just fine to hang around in.

However, within the close confines of a yacht, other people's messes could easily become not-so-fine. All three of us generally kept the yacht tidy. Cooking was interesting and always provided a crucial break from the monotony of life afloat. Whether cooking or eating, food preparation was always, weather and stomach permitting, an activity I looked forward to. Upon leaving port, we had only a few days of fresh fruit and vegetables, and then, it was tinned products for us. Still, fray bentos pies, curry fixings, tinned meatballs and sausages, ravioli with tinned new potatoes, pastas and rice with tinned vegetables, including sweet corn, peas and carrots, provided ample variety for our limited tastes. We also carried tinned peaches, pineapples, pears, tangerines and creamed rice. The galley to port of the saloon steps was confined and basic. With the gimbaled cooker on the outboard side of the area and the sink on the forward side, this, apart from a small area of countertop surrounding these two and a few cupboards, was about it. The gas locker in the cockpit housed two large gas bottles that fed the cooker. The locker was sealed from the rest of the boat and had a special drain directly overboard because gas is heavier than air and, if left to its own devices, will happily accumulate in the bilges. One spark and... One wonders how many vessels went bang before that lesson was learned. Pies could go in the oven, and the two rings were free for two saucepans. For washing up the sink, we had a saltwater pump that we used for the main scrub and a quick rinse in a tiny bit of fresh for plates and cups, mainly so your next meal or cup of tea was not too salty. We tried to make a point of sitting together for an evening meal at the saloon table whenever possible, with an off-duty person subbing the watch keeper so that he could dash down and eat. Whoever cooked generally did not clean up. That was the evening meal. Breakfast and lunch were decidedly less formal. Breakfast was most definitely grab what you wanted, when you wanted, i.e., cereal, and clean up behind you. Lunch was just a quick sandwich.

So what of topsides? For me, particularly at night, one rule applied: stay safe or at least try to. Always, while on deck, I tried to remember to keep a safety harness on, but I have to admit this was not always the case. I do remember watch keeping without a harness and then having to step up out of the cockpit to reach a sheet or halyard. This was foolish, and I was always aware of it: one slip and it would have been overboard in the dead of night with the sleeping crew and, well… It was a stupid habit I tried to avoid. Our watches would be two hours long in bad weather and four hours long in good weather. If it was really bad, as I already mentioned, Les would just shut the hatches and stay below. This only applied during daylight hours. During darkness, we maintained a deck watch at all times. Rob and I did not know better regarding this policy of nobody on deck, but an incident would soon to befall us that nearly cost us the yacht and quite possibly our lives. While not directly related to this practice of having no watch keeper, it would be easy to see just how it could have been.

It was on the 24th of May that this event occurred. We had spent a very frustrating forty-eight hours with the wind out of the west and were making no progress. Adding to our irritation, we had managed to bend the exhaust valve that remained shut when the engine was off to stop the ocean waves that slap against the hull from entering the exhaust manifold and destroying the engine. This valve must be open when the engine is running. The natural pressure of outgoing exhaust gases keeps the water out. We had managed to start the engine with it closed and bent the valve. It needed to be stripped to correct the problem. Quite sensibly, Les decided that there would be no more using the batteries until we could get the engine operational again. At 03.00 a.m., I was just in the heads, having a pee prior to my watch, when I happened to look out the window and was horrified to see, looming above me, the bow of an approaching ship. With urine flying everywhere, I tried to tuck myself back in in an undignified fashion as I tore aft, yelling for the engine batteries to be put on because we were about to be rammed. Les, at the chart table, quickly obliged. Once on deck, I hit the start button and, dispensing with the usual gentle warm-up protocol, slammed the engine into full ahead so that we could turn away from impending disaster. The inky black hull slid down our side no more than fifty feet away. Lost in the sands of time are who was on watch and who failed to see impending "death" bearing down on us. Needless to say, the incident ruined both the engine valve, again, and all of our night's sleep. Way too much adrenaline! Little more was said about what had occurred, and the next day, upon waking, I could hear Les hard at work fixing the exhaust valve. This task took him the better part of the day.

The 27th of May brought a small celebration. We had crossed 35 degrees west or, in layman's terms, by longitude, we were half-way across the Atlantic. Prior to departure, we had been given a package by well-wishers to mark this occasion. With great excitement, we gathered around the saloon table to open it. Inside, we found an assortment of chocolates, a bottle of whiskey (none of us drank!) and a book of logic problems (of no interest to me). All in all, a very nice thought, and the chocolate was much appreciated.

The final days of May produced sporadic but steady progress westward. By the 30th of May, we were some ten days out from the Azores, with 600 nautical miles between Horta and us as the crow flies, while the log showed 770 nautical miles. This discrepancy of 170 miles was the distance we had to sail north or south of our rhumb line due to headwinds to try and fight our way westward. On the 31st of May, Rob and I decided to take stock of our food and water. In the end, we concluded that there was food for twenty-five to thirty days, but water could easily become a concern. We were going to have to be careful.

On the 1st of June, I managed an impressive display of eating. Quite what brought this on was a mystery, but while I made bread rolls, around 11.30 am, I consumed four bowls of cereal, and as soon as the bread rolls came out, I downed a couple of them. An

early dinner followed, consisting of three sausages, five roast potatoes, cabbage and baked beans. To follow, I had rice pudding and
mixed fruit. As I lay in my bunk that evening, I felt a bit full!

Navigation remains the paramount concern of all sailors, not
only for safety of location in relation to land but also the "are we
there yet" factor, from which I tended to suffer from rather badly.
We had a sat nav system aboard this vessel. This was the precursor
to the current GPS system, and it used the same satellite-based technology. There were two problems with this system. First, when we
turned it on, we had to wait for one or two of the limited number
of satellites to pass overhead in order to get a fix. This could take
some time. The second problem was, of course, that it consumed
power, which on a small vessel crossing the Atlantic, was in limited
supply, there often being periods of a few days between running the
engine. Les was proficient in sextant work, but as a result of his time
working with radios in the R.A.F during the war, he had brought
with him a radio direction finder, which could lock onto radio bea-
con signals. While mid-ocean, it was not particularly accurate, but
when closer to land, we would find Les with his peculiar T-shaped
direction finder, earphones plugged into the side, slowly weaving
it back and forth. With intense concentration, he would slow his
"weaving" until he zeroed in on a direction before taking the bearing on the small compass on top of the device. In my fearful, youthful ignorance, I took little interest in navigation on this trip and left
it all to Les. He had gotten us from Lymington to Horta, so he must
have been doing something right.

I awoke on the 4th of June and could feel the listless movement of
the boat. I felt it would be another washout waste of a day becalmed
somewhere in the North Atlantic, but I was in for a pleasant surprise.
Upon arriving on deck, I was greeted by a beautiful day. The sun
shone with not a cloud to be seen. As I stood on deck, holding the cap
shroud and surveying the oily calm ocean framed by the bright blue
sky, a whale of some description popped up and seemed to survey us

as we did him. This lifted my spirits, and so with renewed vigor, I returned below and set about making some bread. Soon, the smell of bread permeated the boat. Satisfied by the results of my baking, I returned topside and set about some idle sunbathing. With my hands clasped on my chest and my feet crossed at the ankles, I was soon awash in warm, dozy contentment. The loud splash woke me in a hurry and sent adrenaline coursing through my veins. I was vertical in a second and ready for whatever emergency was building.

"Whoa, it's fantastic. Come on in!" yelled Rob.

I couldn't help but laugh. Rob had decided that being becalmed presented a perfect opportunity for a dip, and why not? I stripped down to my underwear and leapt over the side. The water felt fantastic. I splashed around a bit and kicked my way through the water until I found myself about a couple of boat lengths away, lying on my back and looking at the boat, ocean and sky while blowing fountains of salty water up into the sky. At this point, I suddenly realized the nearest land was about a thousand nautical miles away and that there was a mile of ocean below me. I had just seen a whale earlier, and God knew what else lurked below the surface. The theme from "Jaws" leapt into my head. That was it. With all the speed of an Olympic athlete, I sped back to the boat and got out of the water as quickly as I could. While dripping and panting on deck, I couldn't stop laughing. I did manage to pluck up the courage to get back in, but I did not stray far from the boat. Rob and I spent the next few hours engaged in this wonderfully child-ish activity of leaping in and out, and in between, we would lie in the sun, heating up to get ready for the next plunge. It was one of only two times in my life that I stopped in mid-ocean for a dip. By the end of the day, I sat thinking about the strange feeling of being so far from land and leaping in and out of the ocean. It was definitely not an entirely comfortable emotion. By evening time, suitably exhausted from the day's frivolities, we managed to hail a passing Norwegian ship en route from Galveston Texas to Antwerp for an updated forecast. He informed us the high pressure system two or three hundred miles to the west of us was moving slowly due east. In other words, it was coming right over our heads, and light winds looked to be the order of the day.

Life at sea is nothing if not unpredictable. So much for the previous evening's forecast; by the next day, we had a wind from the east, blowing a steady force four to five. It was very nice indeed. The only problem was that with the wind dead astern for some reason, the wind vane autopilot could not handle it, so we had to maintain steering watches, a shocking hardship we had become unaccustomed to!

The 6th of June was my twenty-first birthday, and despite my happiness at turning twenty-one, I could not help being a little nostalgic for my friends and the Chequers pub in Lymington. That pub was host to many a fun evening celebrating everything from birthdays and Christmas to absolutely nothing at all. However, I decided to celebrate the previous day's run: 160 nautical miles on a day that according to the passing tanker, should have been spent under flapping sails, becalmed. Today, yet again, it was hot. The wind shifted around to the NNE and was light. Les decided to set the ghoster, a huge sail that is basically a cross between a headsail and spinnaker, but by the end of the day, the halyard had chafed through. Still, there were some good milestones to celebrate. By 1800 hours, we were 1050 nautical miles from Horta, with 1030 to go to Newport, Rhode Island. Our position was 36° 55′.0 (N) and 51° 00.0′(W). We also managed to pick up a radio station on the Eastern seaboard, but it was very faint. However, we had made connection with land, and it felt good to our ocean-weary minds.

The only item of interest on the 7th of June was dinner and a small crew mutiny. Well, it wasn't really the crew, and it was hardly mutiny. I just decided I couldn't be bothered to do any washing up or cooking. My mutiny really didn't have any oomph to it, because Les and Rob were delighted to cook and wash up, and I was delighted to eat.

Dinner was excellent, with fray bentos steak and kidney pie, mash potatoes and peas and carrots with gravy, followed by treacle pudding and Nestle's evaporated milk—delicious. Life had been easy. Unbeknownst to us, the next two weeks were going to be quite the opposite.

By the 8th of June, the wind had woken up and got to work over the course of the day. Coupled with the rising wind was a steady decline in weather conditions. The morning's sail was superb, with fifteen knots of wind just aft of the port beam. We spoke on the VHF to a passing Brazilian ship that gave us a forecast of southeast to easterly winds of ten to fifteen knots. By midnight, it was blowing twenty-five knots from the south southeast. Fat lot of help that forecast was. It became a bumpy ride, but none of us dared complain, as we were still heading west at five or six knots. The forecast we had been given also stated that a cold front stretched north and south over Bermuda, which could give us a bumpy few days of winds out of the south southwest. This would still be manageable, allowing us to continue close-hauled on the port tack, heading west. The barometer was 1019 and falling.

The 9th brought a real mixture of weather. By early dawn, we had grey skies and winds of force six to seven, but later, we broke through to clearer skies behind. Not long after, it was pouring rain, with winds straight out of the west, so we took the sails down and lay a hull. The last few days brought good mileage. The distance to go on the chart was about 660 nautical miles, and Les estimated that we had enough diesel left to motor the last 250 to 300 miles. We were all down below around midday when we were disturbed by the blast of a horn. We dashed up on deck, and there before our eyes was a monumental container ship. Contact was made on the VHF. He said he had just come by to see if all was well. *Very kind*, I thought. He gave us a forecast that indicated a low-pressure system was right on top of us but moving east at twenty-five knots. So tomorrow, we hoped, would provide more friendly winds. It was so warm I was able to stand on deck in a full westerly gale in only a pair of shorts. Down below, it was suffocating with all the hatches closed and us trying to cook meals.

In the early morning on the 10th of June, the wind abated somewhat. Les decided to hoist a single reefed main and storm jib as we headed on a southwesterly track. By noon, it was force seven from the west once again. All sails were stowed or lashed down, and once more, we lay a hull. Morale aboard had sunk to great depths, and we were all reaching our flashpoints very quickly. I was sure this was more about Rob and myself because Les was a relaxed chap used to long periods of time at sea. However, he was used to being alone, but the pressure of a couple of surly youths fed up with our lack of progress was clearly not helping his temper. The only positive was making some fresh bread.

I had had enough of this trip and was ready for some solid progress towards our destination, but it was not to be. The 11th brought the same. The wind was thirty knots bang out of the west, and its direction just would not budge. We spent long periods of time in our bunks, reading or sleeping and doing little else; conversation was terse and brief. The 12th bought the same. The day's frustration and boredom were punctuated by my cutting a lemon in half, sprinkling sugar on it and eating it like a grapefruit. This was what our life had come down to in terms of entertainment. The wind blew thirty knots just slightly north of west. The barometer was 1008 and falling. The next day, the 13th, was spent as the previous four or five were: lying a hull with the hatches shut, in our bunks or at the saloon table, reading, sleeping, playing cards or occasionally chatting. However, by now, apart from the topic of our arrival at Newport, there seemed little to stimulate conversation. Unusually, I was up all afternoon and early evening through to my watch at midnight. I had become amazed by the persistence of the westerly winds and their enduring gale or near-gale force. Our destination still lay some 500 nautical miles to the west, and the crew seemed resigned to waiting it out for some time. Strangely, our spirits improved and conversation among us returned more or less to normal. In a few days, some food items would be in short supply, but generally, there should be no great problem for a week to ten days. We had used a quarter of a tank of water since the 31st of May, some thirteen days before, and a quarter remained. As with the food, we would be fine on the water front for ten days, but then, we were going to have problems. During these days of lying a hull, Rob and I made it a habit to sleep in until eleven or twelve o'clock. This was lazy and perhaps care-lessly relaxed on Les's behalf, but it was a blessing because it ate up large parts of the day.

On the 13th, the wind was blowing with increasing strength and at a steady gale force eight with gusts over fifty knots. I decided to put on my foul weather gear and go topsides for a look around. The scene that greeted me was spectacular. After so many days of blowing so hard over the ocean, a powerful swell had built that created a landscape of rolling hills of water, all marching eastward. Every so often, a crest would build upon a wave until the top ten to fifteen feet broke uninterrupted for three to five hundred feet downwind. The spume from the breaking seas was gathered up by the gusts and carried downwind ahead of the advancing walls of water. The ceaseless advance of the overcast grey skies above made for a majestic backdrop to the angry seas. To stand and watch this entire landscape marching eastward was spellbinding. I had been in storms at sea, but this was different. As I looked north and south, as far as the eye could see, there was the orderly eastward advance of the large ocean swells. So often in storms, there is some confusion among the waves. I settled down on the weather seat of the cockpit with my back to the wind to watch nature at its finest. It was not long before I could hear the crashing roar of an approaching sea, and with a quick glance behind, I tucked myself deep into my hooded foul-weather jacket, locked my feet onto the leeward cockpit seatback and waited for the impact. The force of water was impressive and threw the boat onto its side until the mast was more or less horizontal. Tonnes of water enveloped me, but my grip was firm. I could feel the weight of water rippling over my foul-weather jacket and cascading past the open front of my hood. It was a wonderful sensation to remain dry as the liquid chaos did its worst, and I peered at the foaming maelstrom fighting past the material at the sides of my face. The boat bobbed back upright with water cascading off the coach roof and side decks. The cockpit was waist-deep in seawater, and the drains slowly did their duty to rectify the situation. This whole process kept repeating itself until I grew tired of being dumped upon, and so, during a suitable gap in the mayhem, I returned below.

My bunk was on the weather side of the saloon, and having removed my foul-weather gear and hung it up in the locker, I lay down. The low-pitched whistle of wind through the rigging was, for me, always a comforting sound. This was probably because it meant I was inside and able to listen to it rather than being outside with all the other noise of the storm drowning it out. As I lay in my bunk, the rising and falling pitch was a reminder that I was warm and comfortable. However, this was intermittently interrupted by a faint rumble and then a roar as the next wave slammed into the side of the boat. As the vessel fell over to leeward, I would fall into the lee cloth, secured tightly to the deck head, and wait for the boat to return upright. There was the usual sound of items moving around within lockers, but we had been at sea too long for things to fly around the cabin. There even seemed to be a certain organized rhythm to this chaos, but it was still hot, and the exertion of returning from up top and removing my foul-weather gear, despite just wearing shorts, caused me to lie in my bunk sweating. In these conditions, Les decided to leave the masthead light on at night, but it was draining the batteries, and they would have to be recharged within the next couple of days. At midnight thirty, the wind was a steady force eight from the WSW. We were lying a hull, with the barometer at 1004 and falling. Cooking in these conditions became a problem because it turned the cabin into a real sweatshop.

The morning of the 14th brought a very clear signal from the radio station in Halifax, Nova Scotia that we spent a little time listening to. It was a nice break in our dull routine. The station was forecasting westerly winds during the next few days around their area, so we saw little reason why it should be much different in our location to the south. There was little to report for the day. We did try to sail, but we made almost no progress, doing little better than north. This, combined with the effects of the Gulf Stream, probably meant our true course would be northeast or NNE. Our latitude was not far enough north to make the other tack any better, so we lay under storm jib for most of the day but gave up around midnight and once again lay a hull. By the early hours of the 15th, the wind was blowing out of the west at a force five or six with a rising barometer.

The 15th and 16th brought little change, except for one little piece of excitement. The 16th brought some unscheduled maintenance that involved someone being nominated to go up the mast to help effect some repairs. I was nominated. I strapped myself into the bosun's chair. It had a hard plank base encased in canvas material, with a high seat back up to the kidneys and a kind of seatbelt arrangement around the front. All in all, as I sat down at deck level, it seemed a very snug and comfortable arrangement, which led me to believe my job should be a piece of cake. Now, for those of you who haven't sat in the middle of the Atlantic on a typical Atlantic day, with all the sails down, bobbing around on a relatively small yacht, it is fair to say the motion is quite lively, but something one becomes very accustomed to. However, as Les and Rob began to wind the handle on the main halyard winch, with me progressing skyward, the movement became increasingly wild. To understand this motion, hold a pencil between your thumb and forefinger with the base on the table whilst you flick it back and forth. Now, look at how far back and forward the pencil moves at the top compared with the much slighter motion at the bottom. By the time I got to halfway up, I was straining just to hold onto the mast as we accelerated back and forth. I was beginning to feel ill, much to the amusement of those below. There was no sympathy, and they kept winding until I was at the top. By this stage, I was experiencing greater accelerations and decelerations than any park or plane rides I had encountered, and I knew that if I let go of the mast, I would be smashed and severely injured. Both legs and arms were wrapped firmly around while I tried to figure out how I could release my grip long enough to grab hold of the offending halyard that needed to be recaptured. This task was taxing my atrophied muscles to the limit. Each time I thought about letting go with one hand to grab the rope, we would accelerate at great speed on the next arc before slowing at the outer limit to violently recoil back before starting all over again. After a couple of minutes, I couldn't take much more and was about to yell for them to lower me down when the briefest of lulls gave me just the gap I needed to get the offending line between my teeth. Once more, I grabbed hold of the mast with both arms and legs while yelling between clenched teeth for them to lower me back to deck level. The deck that had before felt like a yacht at sea now felt as steady as dry land. I was never to go to the top of a mast with all the sails down mid-ocean again, and I was very glad not to do so.

The 17th started with great promise. I was awoken at 09.00 a.m. to go on watch. We were under a storm jib and triple reefed mainsail. As I surveyed the scene, I thought about how pleasant it was to actually be sailing again. I disengaged the Aries wind vane autopilot and took on the motion of the boat against the quartering wind and seas. It felt great to be sailing, helming and making good progress. I was loving it. Before long, black scudding clouds were fast approaching from the south, and then, bang, it hit us. With gusting winds and driving rain, steering became hard work as the seas picked up our stern and slammed us down on our starboard beam. It became too much.

By midday, we lowered the main and continued under storm jib. The winds continued to veer, and by 15.30, we were up once again against westerly winds driving us almost north, at which point Les quite sensibly decided to call it quits and lie a hull. The barometer began to drop rapidly for the next five to six hours. By 2100 hours, the wind built to a force nine, gusting ten. Unusually, the boat lay in these conditions with no commotion at all, and I was able to cook with little trouble. The rapid change in temperature was of interest. By 3.30 in the morning, I had on a pair of socks, a T-shirt, a sweatshirt and a jersey, but at least by this hour, the wind had decreased to force six or seven, with a rising barometer. We had clearly passed out of and to the north of the Gulf Stream, hence the cooler temperatures. Halifax, 180 nautical miles to the north, was forecasting easterly winds for their immediate area, while we were encountering westerlies. We deduced that the centre of the low pressure lay between us.

I awoke on the 18th with a dreadful depression, feeling that the world was against us and that we would be locked out in the Atlantic forever. However, not all was lost. We hailed a passing tanker, who promised he would report us to Lloyds of London. Quite why this improved our morale I have no idea. We hoisted a triple reefed main, a storm jib and a third of the genoa and started sailing on 290 degrees. Having gotten everything set up, the wind decided our company was no longer good enough and departed. At 17.45, Les started up the engine, and a debate ensued about a course for Halifax or Newport. We were low on fuel, food, water and morale! Still, course 285 was set for Newport. During the late afternoon, we heard the double boom of the sound barrier being broken by some aircraft—possibly a Concorde. My mind drifted up to their high altitude as they relaxed and sipped on champagne and canapés. *They're probably wishing they were down here, cold, running low on diesel and supplies, wondering why they can't remain bobbing out on the Atlantic forever*, I thought! By 21.45, the wind had returned from the south. Up went the sails; off went the engine. As the night wore on, the winds increased until by 0600 on the 19th, we once again lay a hull.

By the time I awoke on the 19th, we were in thick fog. This was a new experience for me and an eerie one. We became closed hauled on the port tack, steering 300 degrees by compass. With leeway and the outer fringes on the Gulf Stream current, our progress was little better than northwesterly. I checked the gas supplies for cooking and was concerned by how little appeared to be left. There would be no more teas and coffees. Only evening meals could be cooked. After the last month or so of relative warmth, the cold waters off the coast of Nova Scotia were quite a shock, and to be immersed in cold, thick fog was weird indeed. While on deck during my morning watch, I suddenly became acutely aware of the risk of collision in this misty soup. My normally relaxed senses were now on edge. As I stared ahead with intense concentration into the mist, I began to see all sorts of potential shapes looming in the tumbling fog. Equally important as sight, I found myself straining to listen for the slightest sign of fellow mariners. Our location was most definitely on the great circle routes from the Altantic seaboard to Europe, and it was not long before I heard the intermittent muffled moans of foghorns. Sighting ships normally brought pleasure and excitement, but now, I cursed their presence. I looked up at the diamond-shaped radar reflector secured to the fixed rigging and dearly hoped it was doing its job, portraying us as a very bright blob on other vessels' radar screens. As the foghorn got nearer, I desperately tried to figure out from which direction it was sounding. However, fog has a strange habit of destroying the directional information of sound, and I gave up. I gripped the wheel tighter as the horn grew louder. I peered into the gloom for the first sign of impending disaster. I was looking all around as we ghosted along with no more visibility than a boat's length in front, but I saw nothing. No collision ensued, and slowly but surely, I became aware that the horn was no longer getting louder but beginning its gradual fade out until it was gone. By the end of my watch, I was exhausted, glad to return below and let somebody else struggle with imaginary collisions dancing out of the mist. Les decided that some time during the next twenty-four hours, if the wind remained in this current direction, we would put in a tack and head south to a point where we could motor the final stretch into Newport. While this should have buoyed our spirits, we were just too used to being messed about by the weather to believe we could be on the final stretch.

By the 20th, our time trapped in the fog banks off Nova Scotia was over. It was bitterly cold with some scattered clouds that allowed the occasional bursts of sunshine through. I guess because of the cold water surrounding the hull, it was not long before the cockpit became a warmer place to linger than the cabin. We continued our westerly progress on the port tack at about four knots. Little of interest occurred until around 1700 hours. I was glancing out of the cabin window and suddenly found myself staring into the face of a passing pilot. I dashed on deck to see some sort of military surveillance aircraft banking hard before making one more pass down our side at very low altitude. Obviously satisfied nothing was afoot, he sped off towards land, gaining height as he went. It was a nice reminder that land was indeed close by. Despite my protestations about using our limited gas supplies, Les and Rob persuaded me that a cup of tea was in order. We treated the tea with great reverence, and Les even managed to bring out a few biscuits he had been saving up. During the early part of the evening, a fishing boat had passed by our stern, with their crew waving and yelling cheerily; however, this only reignited Les's worry about being near land and potential trouble, so he decided to stay up all night.

So it was I awoke on the 21st after having had a whole night in my bunk. At 07.30, I took the watch, and Les went below for some well-earned rest. To the west was the advancing bank of a dark, ominous cloud. *Here we go again*, I thought, but no. The cloud slid overhead without rain or wind and slipped gently eastward before allowing the sun to pop over the top of it all and make for a glorious day. To me, it felt as if the Atlantic and its tempestuous weather had final given in and would allow us to make landfall. Most of the day was spent motoring at four knots westward and having a never-ending discussion of our fuel situation. We had concluded that there was enough for about 120 nautical miles of motoring, while Newport lay 200 nautical miles to our west. We had some sailing to do. Our sat nav would not fix, and upon investigation, we found a fuse had gone. As we ghosted along, the log kept telling us we were doing between five and ten knots, so that wasn't working either. After supper, we decided to have some rice pudding for dessert, and I managed a rather disgusting concoction by mixing in marmalade, UHT milk and sugar! I must have been getting bored. Around 2300 hours, a fishing vessel was sighted heading towards us with all lights blazing. By the time he had closed in to about fifteen or twenty yards, we asked if he had any spare diesel. No luck. The wind, what little there was, had come round to dead ahead, 225 T, so we continued to run the engine at very low revs to conserve fuel, giving us about four knots. At midnight, watch complete, I went to my bunk and slept.

The 22nd of June turned out for the best. The local radio stations on land promised a fine day, and indeed it was. From morning right through until 1800 hrs, I only saw one cloud in the sky. We had become a curiosity. Fishing vessels, which were becoming increasingly numerous, altered course from their task to come over and look at us. We tried to sail throughout the day and made about twenty-four miles, but began to head east of south with the cool westerly winds, so at around 1800 hrs, on went the engine. We hoped it would last. An interesting moment occured around 2100 hrs. During a break in dinner preparations, I went up on deck and, while gazing out over the ocean, a fin slowly appeared, running parallel to us a short distance away. Just below the surface, I could make out the rather menacing shadow of the owner. It did make me grab the cap shroud rather more tightly than usual. The seas had become a beautiful light green color. We were definitely closing in on land.

It was difficult to sleep much. Shortly after midnight on the 23rd of June, we sighted a buoy that Les couldn't recognize on the chart, but we altered course and headed due west. By 0800 hours, we turned onto the last leg to Newport at 315 degrees compass and made superb progress. With the wind just aft of the port beam, we put up the ghoster with the main and made great progress: seven, sometimes eight knots. In these relatively flat waters, we had not experienced such easy good sailing for a very long time, and with us all laughing and in high spirits, we thoroughly enjoyed it all. Les had initially planned to enter Newport on the 24th, but with such good progress, we aimed for late afternoon. I don't remember sighting land, which is strange after so long at sea, but I do remember, for the second time, the powerful smell of "land" as we approached.

We now became quite busy because Les was concerned with the safe passage of the vessel as we entered between the headlands guarding the waterway into Newport. Contact was made with the marina regarding a berth and the need to clear customs. Sails were stowed, and sheets were neatly squared away. Rob and I finally dug out the fenders and mooring lines as we entered the marina. With great care, Les brought us to a halt in our berth. We had crossed the Atlantic.

I immediately decided to celebrate by getting, more or less, the last of our food. Two cans of rice pudding were opened up so everyone could enjoy a few spoonfuls. We had to wait to clear customs, but I couldn't resist a quick walk on dry land. I stepped off the boat onto the concrete pier and took a few steps but immediately halted with my legs spread wide in a half-crouch, desperately searching for something to hold onto. Dry land was rolling up and down like a rough day in the English Channel. I tried a few more steps but experienced the same sensation. Anybody watching me must have been very amused at the sight of a drunken idiot trying to walk, but I wasn't drunk and could understand why land wouldn't stay still. I didn't enjoy this sensation at all and headed back to the boat. As soon as I got back aboard, the world was once again steady as a rock. It became obvious that my inner ear had adjusted to life afloat and was not quite ready for the demands of dry land.

As I pondered this mystery, it was time for the next. Our customs man arrived and leapt aboard. Following brief introductions, he proceeded below and began work at the saloon table. It was not long before he appeared in a certain amount of discomfort and decided he would finish things off in the cockpit, where we sat and answered his questions. Having waved him off, we scratched our heads as to what could have been bothering him and shrugged our shoulders before returning below. Then, it hit us. The boat stank. We stank. We had not washed since the Azores. The smell, beyond our well-trained noses, must have been disgusting. We chuckled to ourselves and set about getting things cleaned up. For numbers, we had spent forty-nine days at sea and logged 4,342 nautical miles, and I had spent 141 hours on night watch.

There is one final footnote to this story and that relates to the return trip home. The return flight aboard a British Airways jet was the usual eight-hour tedium. After landing, I found myself at the fringes of the airport, waiting for the underground to take me into central London. It then hit me. I had just spent the best part of six weeks fighting my way across the Atlantic, with all the trials and tribulations involved. At the end of this voyage, thanks to modern engineering, I had sat at 38,000 feet for seven hours, enjoyed a delicious meal, a glass of wine and a good snooze before landing right back where I had started. It was, for a little while, hard to make sense of. Still, time to move on.

SIX

The Desk Job At Sea

It was July of 1985, and Peter Haward was on the phone.

"I think I may have a job in about six weeks. Are you in?" he asked.

"Are you kidding me? The chance to be cold, wet, miserable and not get paid! Of course I'm in," I replied.

He chuckled. "Good, I'll get back to you once things firm up."

During the course of the last year or so, I had become aware of my lack of professional qualifications. Within the U.K. yachting world, whether for pleasure or for people such as myself looking to make a living delivering yachts, there were the Royal Yachting Associations (R.Y.A.) certifications. The courses started at the "competent crew and day skipper/watch leader certificate" and ran right up to "Yachtmaster Ocean Certificate". I was interested in the top two certificates, the "Yachtmaster Offshore" and "Yachtmaster Ocean". Now, for both the Yachtmaster Offshore and Yachtmaster Ocean certificates, the course was split in two. First, there was the classroom work, which was to be studied and examined within the confines of four walls and central heating. Second, there was the practical exam. This was either an exam on a yacht in real conditions at sea, as was the case for the Yachtmaster Offshore, or work completed while on a passage to be examined by an instructor at a later date, as was the case for the Yachtmaster Ocean. For the R.Y.A Yachtmaster Offshore Certificate, the experience requirement for the final practical exam at sea aboard a yacht was to have spent fifty days living onboard a cruising yacht in commission and to have logged 2,500 nautical miles at sea in tidal waters, including at least five passages over sixty miles. Candidates for examination must have been acting as skipper for at least two of these passages. Furthermore, two of these passages must have been overnight. Now, these were requirements for the examination. I still had to do the classroom coursework and exam before I even began to worry about the final eight-hour practical exam at sea with me as skipper.

Tucked down one of the side streets in Lymington was a small nondescript house with a small sign announcing "RYA course instruction". I went in to be confronted by a chap who introduced himself as a retired Lt. Commander from the Royal Navy, a powerfully-built man with thinning straw-colored hair and a naval background aboard submarines. I got the feeling he knew what he was talking about. Yes, he ran the courses. Yes, there was room for me to start the next week on the shore-based Yachtmaster Offshore coursework.

The following Monday, I reported with sharpened pencils and a dull wit, prepared for action. As I sat at the desk, I was expecting the usual Dartmouth onslaught of information coupled with my increasing disconnect as I failed to keep up. However, I was in for a pleasant surprise. First and foremost, I was paying for the course, and apparently, as a paying customer, it was no problem to ask the instructor to slow down or go through something again. Secondly, as a result of being at sea on the various deliveries to date, apparently some little bits and pieces here and there had sunk in, leaving me a tad wiser. Thirdly, I was motivated.

If one buys an R.Y.A logbook from the early 1980s, it is possible to find, halfway through it, the "shore-based course for the RYA/DoT Coastal skipper and Yachtmaster Offshore certificates" syllabus. It is comprehensive and lists some twenty-four items, each of which is further divided into up to seven topics. Listed below are the twenty-four major topics taught during our two weeks of coursework:

1. Definition of Position/Course and Speed
2. Navigational Drawing Instruments
3. Navigational Charts and Publications
4. Dead Reckoning and Estimated Position
5. The Position Line
6. The Magnetic Compass
7. Position Fixing
8. Basic Coastal Navigation
9. Tides
10. Tidal Streams
11. Buoyage
12. Lights
13. Pilotage
14. Echo sounds and Lead Line
15. Radio Direction Finding
16. Logs (Speed and Distance Measuring)
17. Deck Log
18. Meteorology
19. Anchoring
20. Rule of the Road
21. Safety at Sea
22. Signals
23. Navigation in Restricted Visibility
24. Passage Planning and (Passage) Making

It was a comprehensive list. Little time was wasted during the day, so we could cover as much ground as possible. Our time was spent, as it would be at school, with a couple of hours of instruction followed by a quick coffee break, then another hour or two and lunch. After lunch, depending on how people felt, the instructor might run straight through the afternoon, stopping around 4.30 or 5.00 p.m. It was hard work to not only understand the elements of the course but also take comprehensive notes and keep up with the practical questions, which came tumbling down upon us during the day with regularity. The evenings were no picnic either. Having returned home for a quick dinner, we spent many a late night not only completing homework but also going over the day's content and making sure we had a firm grasp of the subject. We would be struggling with tidal calculations and plotting an imaginary cruise around craggy headlands on our practice charts. We would scratch our heads, trying to work out from all the relevant nautical publications our constantly changing tidal situation. At the same time, our fictitious passage would require us to use the bearings of objects and headlands while making the correct conversions from our imaginary compass bearings to true bearings by using the appropriate variation and deviation adjustment as we laid them on the chart. The moment it had all been calculated and drawn up on the chart, the question would move you onwards, and the whole process would start again. When questions arose, we gathered them together and tackled them with the instructor first thing the next day.

Without a doubt, the most taxing thing of all was mastering the intricacies of secondary port tidal calculations, coupled with the interpolation of tidal diamond information, and then trying to accurately use it in real time aboard a moving yacht with constantly changing time and speed paramenters. These changes instantly affected calculations and meant they more or less had to be done again. If I am completely honest, I am not sure I ever fully mastered this skill. I certainly could not manage it at the speed I noticed among some very smart and effective navigators that I did manage to see in action during later years.

We moved through the course content until it was time for the final exam. I was delighted when informed, on the final day, that I had passed. Into my logbook was glued my certificate of satisfactory completion of the shore-based course for the coastal skipper and Yachtmaster Offshore shore-based course. As I was about to skip out the door with logbook and certificate in hand the Lt. Cmdr. called after me.

"You would be well advised to do the practical course now," he said.

Practical course? What was he talking about?

"Ah, yes! We run a practical course aboard our yacht, where we put all the classroom work into real time action. You get a chance to skipper the yacht on different legs of a local voyage. In between skippering, you act as navigator, crewman and helmsman. We all sleep aboard, and there is the usual cooking, cleaning and maintenance to consider as well. At the end of it, we issue you a certificate, which goes in your logbook and is definitely favorably considered by the examiner during the final practical exam," he replied.

It didn't sound like much fun to me. I was used to not getting paid to not have much fun at sea, but to pay to not have too much fun at sea was a whole new experience. As usual, I was in. I had to grab hold of any advantage I could gain before my final exam, however small it might be.

I and the other students who had signed up for the week at sea all met on Monday morning in Lymington aboard a rather cramped 32-foot Contessa sailing yacht. True to his word, he kept us busy. During the course of five days, we sailed from Lymington to Cowes, Newport, Poole, Swanage, Bournemouth, south of the Isle of White to Beaulieu, Yarmouth and finally back to Lymington. We did indeed take turns at everything, but my most vivid memory is sitting at the navigator's chart table with my body wedged to avoid being dislodged as this rather small yacht bobbed around in a bumpy English Channel and I tried to put to good use all the classroom work of the previous couple of weeks. Trying to lay out a chart and all the tidal publications on this tiny chart table while controlling the movement of parallel rules, pencils, rubbers and most importantly the rather sharp dividers, all with a nervous chef to leeward looking on, was taxing to say the least. At the same time, the helmsman would yell down for instruction or, if unlucky, a request along the lines of "Do you want me to sail around this buoy or keeping heading straight at it?" These requests were normally followed by panic from the chart table while I tried to figure out why a buoy was in the way when I had thought we were in perfectly clear water. At about this point, a small rogue wave would then dislodge me, and my entire chart, publications, pencils, dividers and parallel rules would all slide onto the cabin sole only to be anointed by a hot cup of soup that slipped from the chef's hand as he tried to pass it up into the cockpit!

However, the trip was useful, not only for instruction but also for providing the first of two voyages of over sixty nautical miles acting as skipper, which I had to do prior to my final exam. Without a doubt, it was a very real opportunity to put the coursework into practice in a small busy yacht under the scrutiny of colleagues from the course and a very vigilant and knowledgeable examiner. I learned a lot. Anyway, I was signed off, and another ticket was glued in my logbook.

Peter Haward, true to his word, had the next trip lined up. It was across the Atlantic again. It was a brand new yacht, an Oyster 46, which was to be delivered from the builder in Ipswich across to Essex, Long Island Sound in the U.S.A. via the Azores. The rather dilapidated state of some of the yachts we delivered had never been very apparent to me, but as I walked towards the gleaming new hull of the yacht we were to call home for the next seven weeks, I decided I liked the look of brand new. She gleamed, and the space inside seemed cavernous. She had a central raised cockpit with the usual instrument panel just in front of the wheel. At the forward end of the cockpit were the steps down into the saloon. I had become used to the damp smell of salt and mould, but they were not here. The smell was a combination of new car and varnish. To port was a galley with loads of counter space. The entire galley space, which was considerable, existed in a "corridor" running down to the aft cabin. This cabin had a large double bed against the aft bulkhead with its own "bathroom" en suite. Going forward once again to the saloon, to starboard was the navigator's chart table with the instrument panel, where everything was in perfect working order. Forward of the saloon was a double bunk bed cabin with a further V berth right at the bow. I simply couldn't believe this beautiful brand new yacht was our home for the next month and a half.

There was, however, a caveat. The owner had decided to join us for a short leg to the south coast of the UK, while his son would be with us for the entire trip across the Atlantic. Peter, I think, had mixed feelings about all this. He well understood his duties towards the yacht and crew. However, playing "entertainment and moral officer" to owners was not his thing. I wasn't concerned; I had a new yacht to play with. It was a sentiment I would pay for dearly quite shortly.

Unusually, we had to help conduct acceptance trials with the new owner. It was soon apparent that the Oyster organisation had its act together, and before long we were back alongside completing the final paperwork and loading the yacht for the voyage ahead. Shortly thereafter, we departed for our short leg down to Littlehampton on the south coast. This yacht was a whole new animal and just ate up the miles with no hassles at all. Whereas we had become quite used to sailing at four or five knots, this yacht seemed unable to do less than six, even in the lightest of airs. We had a greater range of fuel, so when speed dropped below the six-knot mark we could put on the engine and get cracking. The sails were another delight. Both the main and headsail were roller-furling. It was fantastic. If it was getting windy, one could just wind them in. If the wind was fading a little, one could wind them out. If the wind was gone, on with the engine and six or seven knots. Everything was reliable. Everything was easy and without fuss. It was great. We made Littlehampton in no time and soon secured alongside the dock at Hillyard's boatyard. It was a rather tired and rundown affair, but somehow, it looked exactly as it should look.

Peter; the third crewman, Ian, and I set about the usual business of getting fresh supplies loaded aboard. Within a day, we had loaded all the supplies, filled up with fuel and water and done a complete check over of the vessel, including running up the mast and giving a final look following our small shakedown cruise. Satisfied, it was time to say farewell to the owner, who was flying back to the States. As he clambered over the side onto the dock with his bag and son, who was going to accompany him to the train station, he shook hands with us all and wished us luck.

As he turned on his heels, he looked back at Peter and said, "There seems to be something wrong with the heads in my cabin."

"Funnily enough, the forward heads have a problem to," his son said.

With that, they disappeared off to the train station.

Peter and I looked at each other, both thinking the same thing. How could there be a problem? Both heads were brand new and for them both go at the same time seemed strange. When we got below, there was a problem all right. They had both been blocked solid with yesterday's curry and way too much paper!

"Time to earn your money," Peter said, looking at me.

"But I'm not getting paid," I replied.

"Yeah, sorry about that. Never mind, get cracking" was his chuckling reply.

While contemplating my future as a toilet cleaner, I could think of no satisfactory way to get this sorted until my eyes landed on an empty milk carton lying in the garbage. There was nothing else for it. I cut it in half, made my way to the first of the two blocked heads and started bailing. It was damned difficult not to throw up and add to the general filth I was bailing through, all the while thinking I had another one waiting for me. It was a disgusting hour. By the end, I couldn't stop washing my hands, and Peter couldn't stop laughing!

"Not so easy dealing with the boss on board, huh!" Peter said while catching his breath.

I was still gagging too much to respond. When the boss's son returned, I eyed him with suspicion. Peter began laughing again. No more was said, and it was time to go.

Peter ran a very different ship than Les. There were formal watches from the moment we departed port, but this trip had two benefits: a brand new yacht and the owner's son, who made for an extra watch keeper. With Peter, Ian, the owner's son and I, each twelve-hour block of time was split four ways. With a three-hour watch, we managed to have nine hours off. It was blissful. This was as good as it got in yacht deliveries. Having just completed my shore-based Yachtmaster course, I found myself paying closer attention to Peter's hard work at the chart table.

Before long, we had once again cleared Ushant for the deeper waters of the eastern Atlantic. The trip from Littlehampton all the way to the Azores was uneventful. The watches ran smoothly, the yacht performed flawlessly and even the weather decided to turn out and cooperate. Before long, we found ourselves moored alongside in Horta, once more dealing with the usual minor running repairs and replenishment before sampling the delights of Café Sport. As usual, there was a schedule to keep, and Peter needed to get moving. However, our routine was about to be shattered by a quite unexpected source.

The first day out from Horta was the usual "settle back in" period, but by the late afternoon of the second day, we were on a close reach port tack, enjoying a thoroughly pleasant sail and ready to settle in for the evening. Dinner was complete, and the clearing up was done. I happened to be up on deck in the cockpit, doing nothing particular, just enjoying the sail. Peter was at the chart table, and Ian had just finished his usual tapped-out rhythm on the bottoms of a couple of saucepans held between his legs, which was really quite good. With a steady few degrees of list, the yacht rode steadily up and over the slight seas, making, as usual, light work of it all. With the wind ruffling my hair, I stared lazily ahead.

The bang felt explosive, and the yacht shuddered under the shock. In a surreal movie moment, I was amazed to see the entire furling genoa with its track and forestay lift over the leeward rail and fly away downwind while the top was still secured at the masthead. Like a piece of laundry, the entire mess flailed about in a slow but powerful fashion at masthead height, causing the mast to whip fore and aft in an alarming fashion. For the briefest of moments, we were mesmerized. Then, I realized it would only be seconds before we were dismasted.

"Bear away," I yelled. We had to get the load onto the intact backstay and off the unsupported forward side of the mast.

By now, Peter was on deck taking charge. He grabbed the helm and kept us sailing on a very broad reach but was careful to avoid any risk of gybing. At the same time, he got us to wind in on the starboard sheet to get the flailing mess under some degree of control. We sheeted in until the sail had almost reached the winch. By now, the entire genoa was under the lee of the main and the shaking throughout the yacht, from the whiplash of the mast had ceased. Without the forestay, there was little support to stop the mast from collapsing. Peter ordered the spinnaker halyard, attached at head height on the mast, to be released, taken forward and secured on the now-available forestay deck fitting. Once attached, the halyard was wound around an available mast winch and tightened up. We had stabilized the mast. Now, we had to sort out the Genoa mess lying behind the mainsail. How were we going to get the Genoa off its track and onto the deck? We assumed the furling track had been damaged, precluding us from lowering it onto deck in the normal way. There was no choice; we had to try. If it was damaged, we might have to cut it free, but first, we had to get the whole mess to a position where we could try.

Now that all ropes were clear of the water, Peter decided to put the engine on and motor at full speed almost downwind to make sure there was as little wind over the deck as possible when we began to wrestle with the sail. We decided we couldn't do it in situ, because the furling drum was currently secured outside the rail almost to the water line. We would have to heave the entire drum, forestay and genoa, forward, up over the starboard rail and back to its correct position so that we could have the best chance of lowering the sail onto the deck. While Peter steered and gently released the starboard Genoa sheet, the three of us struggled forward with the bottom end of this mess. The task of lifting the drum over the rail/bowsprit was exhausting and took many attempts. After much colorful language and more than a little sweat, the task was complete. We wasted no time in securing the drum in place with an excess of rope so it could not blow away again.

We now had to get the genoa down. The track was damaged, but luck was with us that night. It was not so bad, and after much tugging and struggling, the sail was off. It was now dark, but the yacht and, equally importantly, the mast were now secure. We folded the sail and took it below. Finally, we set about making absolutely sure that the mast and forestay were safely juryrigged and would allow us to set a course back to Horta, Azores. While using a torch to check all our lines around the deck fitting for the forestay, we found, nestled under the forward-most deck cleat, the cleavice pin and split pin used to secure the forestay to the deck. Upon examination, we found the split pin was brass; it should have been stainless steel. It appeared that under the minute motion of a working forestay, the cleavice pin had moved over hard against the securing split pin, which because it had been soft brass, had given way and allowed the main pin to work free until it was so far out and ... bang!

If you are going to have this mess at sea, do so near port. In this regard we could not have been luckier. We had only just left Horta and had ample fuel to steam back at full speed.

Our time back in Horta was busy. We had to disconnect the forestay at the top of the mast and lower the damaged track with its stay onto the quay alongside the yacht. The whole track consisted of a number of interlocking sections secured by small screws. Whilst a small team was working on this problem, another went off on a rather nebulous search for some aluminum welder/roller furling track repairman! A tall order, but much to all our surprise one was located who agreed to come and look at the problem. We had indeed been lucky. The damage was minor and involved a couple of twisted sections with a small tear in the aluminum track. It was all well within this man's ability. Within twenty-four hours he had returned, and we began to get the rigging back together. Needless to say, we did a meticulous search of the entire mast from masthead to deck. This was not only to identify any damage as a result of its whiplashing, but also to make sure all pins securing the rigging were in place and stainless steel.

After a couple of days, Peter pronounced himself satisfied. Once more, final tank top-ups and fresh food were purchased before we departed, almost a week behind schedule. We were all extremely nervous using the sails during the first few days. We constantly checked and worried about every sail trim and every wind gust. The yacht had been damaged on our watch, perhaps through no fault of our own. However, we were mindful of our duty to get the yacht safely to its destination.

The rest of the delivery across the Atlantic proceeded smoothly, rapidly and uneventfully. Peter had decided that we would clear customs in Newport, Rhode Island, and so as we hove into view around the headland of Newport, we were a little stunned to find the marina empty. It was a calm but slightly overcast day with a watery sun trying to show through the grey high-altitude clouds. Perhaps that should have piqued our interest. Without a single vessel in sight, we felt very smug about being able to choose our berth unhindered by other yachts. As we secured our mooring lines and gazed around at the silent emptiness, I realized I had never been in a marina without the white noise of endless ropes tapping on masts. It was all very peculiar. Out of nowhere, some fellow came down the quay.

"What are you doing here?" he asked, panting.

It seemed odd to ask what a boat was doing in a marina, but we answered anyway.

"We have just crossed the Atlantic and want to clear customs," Peter offered up.

"You just cleared, now get out. There's a hurricane coming," the official replied and legged it down the quay.

Well, that explained the empty marina, but my next thought was, get out to where! Peter was thinking the same. He rang the owner, who seemed delighted to hear we had got in ahead of the storm. He was right on the ball, having organized a hurricane hole for us. He gave all the details to Peter, who returned and pulled out the chart. He scanned it for a short time before his finger came to rest on a spot that he studied for some moments.

"Right, let's go," said Peter.

On went the engine, and off went the mooring lines. We only had to motor a couple of hours west of Rhode Island before we entered an inlet that as we progressed inland, became narrower and heavily wooded. Peter was creeping along with no chart information and only the promise from the owner that there was plenty of water for our depth right to the top of the inlet, where we would find refuge. True enough, we arrived at a small basin perhaps 150 feet by 150 feet that was completely surrounded by trees. By now, the skies were filled with grey clouds scudding along and gusts already getting the treetops to work. We wasted no time and first set bow and stern anchors. We then, using our small inflatable dinghy, assembled every mooring line we carried and ran them ashore before securing them to the largest trees we could find. We were careful to make sure antichafe material was strategically placed around trees and fairleads to avoid any of the lines chaffing through. Secured as we were, surrounded by a large dense forest, we felt well-protected. The intensity of the wind and rain kept building until the height of the storm, when the wind sounded like a freight train through the treetops, which remained leaning at twenty or thirty degrees, from upright, under the barrage. I was amazed at the steady velocity of the wind. The yacht bounced and heaved around on her lines like a restless stallion, and despite our protected location, the wind found its way down, causing us to heel over and leaving us rushing to grab hold of something to keep our footing. We kept a constant check on the lines, with the engine ready for immediate action in case we broke free. The rain was impressive and did a wonderful job of getting a month and a half's salt washed away, only to be replaced by a deluge of leaves and small branches torn from their homes further upwind.

I thought we would be able to sit idly by with a cup of tea in our hurricane hole, but the violence of our motion kept us all moving about nervously, constantly doing the rounds inside and out making sure all was well. During the course of the night, the wind rapidly swung round and began to abate. By dawn, it had passed, and we began to clear the mess of foliage off the decks. What was impressed upon me was the power of the storm. We had been secured deep in a forest surrounded by high trees with very little open water for the wind to make its way down, but even so, the amount of motion made us feel like we were at sea. In slow time, we removed, one at a time, the spider's web of mooring lines and began our slow exit from our hurricane hole. It was not long after when a very grateful owner met us at the dock and the yacht's new home. Our duty was done; now, it was back to England.

The statistics produced by my two trips across the Atlantic were interesting. The first had taken 49 days, while the second had taken 48. The first had logged 4,343 nautical miles, and the second had logged 3,722, despite the second starting with a couple-hundred-mile disadvantage in Ipswich on the east coast of the U.K. as opposed to Lymington on the south coast. The second trip was even more impressive, bearing in mind we sailed the extra distance and lost a week of time with the forestay damage. This, coupled with the start disadvantage, still managed to produce a 620 nautical mile log advantage over trip one.

I now had 12,847 nautical miles logged. It was time for my Yachtmaster Offshore exam.

In autumn of 1985, the R.Y.A confirmed the date of my exam and told me to provide a boat, crew and provisions for a day out and be ready in all respects by 0800 on the day in question. Yikes! If there was one thing I hated, it was exams. The only thing I hated more was being examined not by pen and paper but by having some official eye my every move for six hours. There was nothing else for it. I would have to use subversive tactics. I managed to persuade Mum to be one of the crew for the day, with explicit instructions to overdo it on catering. Her "leave it to me" response left me wondering how this would all turn out.

Dad had been lucky enough to inherit a little money from a rather distant and not very well-known relative, and with the proceeds, he had acquired a slightly middle-aged Nicholson 38. He was good enough to let me borrow it, which as far as he was concerned, was tantamount to lending your newly-licensed son the midlife-crisis Porche. I did manage to persuade him that despite his reservations, which were well-founded, we did have an experienced R.Y.A. examiner on board, who I felt would be unlikely to let me thump into the Needles lighthouse. Suitably calmed, he handed over the keys and, kindly enough, a full tank of fuel. A local friend provided the second crewman. He was an excellent sailor, and I knew could be counted on with regards to all that would be required of him. Prior to the day, I stared at every tidal book and chart to make sure I was fully aware of all things nautical for Lymington and the Solent area. I went over the boat again and again to make sure I was satisfied she was ready above decks and below. At the chart table, all charts, dividers, parallel rules, nautical publications and any other miscellaneous equipment I felt would be remotely relevant were neatly laid out. I checked and warmed the engine and checked it again.

Finally, down the dock came a rotund, balding man with prerequisite yacht club red trousers and sailing shoes, swinging a leather briefcase to the rhythm of his gait. He knew the berth number and caught sight of the waiting crew and myself and slowed. His examiner's eye took over and I could sense he was giving the vessel the once over. I met him at the side of the boat, welcomed him on board and made the introductions. At this point, we were all standing in the centre cockpit, shuffling around nervously and wondering what to do.

"Excuse me, but what would you like me to do?" I asked, wondering if the question had just destroyed the image of me as a skipper in the making.

"Ah yes," he replied. "If you could get underway and depart the marina into Lymington River, I shall give you instructions as we go."

Thank goodness I had survived the first verbal encounter. Once the moorings lines and fenders had been stowed, Mum got to work on her clandestine "operation distract". With the small gas oven loaded beyond capacity, a never-ending supply of delightful snacks passed through it to the salivating crew above. As he peered over my shoulder to concoct the next tricky navigation exercise, Mum would lean in politely with some delicious delicacy and a "Could I tempt you?"

Poor fellow never stood a chance. Even I was distracted and barely able concentrate on what I was doing. Slowly but surely, he broke free from the galley temptress and began to get into the exam. Much of the early part involved me at the chart table, plotting courses between buoys to see if I could correctly interpret the published tidal information along with the tidal diamonds. This was never my strong suit and not a part of the exam I enjoyed or excelled at. The exam was thorough and covered not only the necessities of navigating around a tidal area with some accuracy, but also a period of one-on-one questioning. This was conducted while we anchored under the Lee of Hurst castle. The questions were wide-ranging and covered everything from vessel lights at night to Morse code and flags.

As the day wore on, I became more comfortable and understood what he was trying to achieve. He, I felt, wanted to make sure that if he passed me, I would spend my time at sea making sensible decisions, with the safety of the vessel and its occupants as my primary goal. If I got a technical question wrong, he would probe around and see if I could arrive sensibly at the correct conclusion or answer. He certainly made allowances for the general stress of the day. By mid-afternoon, whether from exhaustion, hopelessness or satisfaction, he signaled the day was over and that I should set course for home. I relinquished my spot at the chart table and took the helm as we entered Lymington River. With all the "captainly" dignity I could muster, I issued crisp orders to prepare all mooring lines and fenders as we made our sedate way towards our berth. As we approached, I made our ninety-degree turn to starboard with a combination of helm, paddle wheel effect from the prop and gentle ahead and astern use from the engine control lever next to the helm. We glided into our slot and secured all lines. With a quiet sigh of relief, I shut off the engine and felt I had done all I could. I turned to face the examiner, wondering if he had any final tests or questions.

"I would like to inform you…." the examiner began.

I held my breath.

"That you have met the requirements for the final certification of Yachtmaster Offshore."

I was too elated to remember what else he said. I had always tackled exams with a sense of dread and usually failed. It felt good to get this one tucked under my belt with a positive outcome.

SEVEN

Then There Were Three

I was beginning to realize that the secret to controlling expenses was really very simple: just stay at sea. When I was soaked to the skin and plunging through the waves of the North Atlantic or the English Channel, I had no opportunity to spend money. Back on dry land, it was a different story altogether. My "working" mates charging down from London at the weekend seemed to have inexhaustible supplies of cash dripping from their wallets, which kept both the local pubs and the women happy. I did not seem quite so able to do so. The yachtmaster courses had been expensive. I either had to get a "real" job or get back to sea, where bank managers could not get hold of me. Very lucky for me, Peter once more came to the rescue.

I was to do three more voyages with Peter, and each of them was to be interesting, but all were interesting for very different reasons. One of them was to be one of the most rapid and exciting journeys at sea I would ever experience. Another was to provide arguably my worst night at sea, and the third was to continue my education in an unexpected fashion.

"Gus, wonderful opportunity for suffering and misery. A 35-footer from Gibraltar back home. Can you make it?"

"Sure. Where and when?" I replied.

It was mid-October of 1985, and within twenty-four hours of Peter's phone call, we were on a jet bound for Gibraltar. Gibraltar was a rather interesting place: a little chunk of Britain, including an airport and port, smushed onto a tiny rock, most of which is vertical. The place reeked of history, and if one climbed the rock and surveyed around, two things came to mind: firstly, the commanding geographical position of Gibraltar and why various countries, through their navies, so continually clobbered one another for possession and, secondly, because it was so small and mostly vertical, why on earth anybody would bother fighting over it! However, we were on no history tour, and having disembarked from the plane, we found ourselves wandering down the quay towards our yacht. Before you conjure up gleaming hulls and scrubbed sandy-colored teak decks, the reality was a rather sad and dilapidated antique that looked like it had been left by Admiral Nelson on his last visit.

"What is it?" I asked of no one in particular.

"She's a rather beautiful 35-foot Hilyard cutter," replied a nostalgic Peter.

Clearly, beauty is in the eye of the beholder, I thought. I think I preferred our last yacht, the Oyster 46. It had hot and cold running water. I bet the only running water this yacht had came through the deck into the cabin below, but apparently I was showing my ignorance in failing to appreciate the beauty of true wood yacht construction from a bygone era. In this regard, she was indeed a beauty, if in need of a little TLC, which was why we were here: to return her for a refit. It's an odd aspect of the job that owners seem only too delighted to take the helm of the vessel after the shipyard has lavished its finest tradesmen's attention on it, but they leave it to the "professionals" to get their leaking, broken, dilapidated and generally unloved wrecks to the refit. Looking at the yacht, I was beginning to realize just how sensible they were. She was filthy from masthead to waterline. Her mast and rigging looked antiquated and tired, with rust streaks from the rigging down over her dingy yellow hull. Varnish peeled from all the bright work, and goodness only knew what condition the sails and engine were in. Peter unlocked the hatch cover and slid it back. She smelled as only a wooden vessel can: a strange combination of damp canvas and aged varnish wood.

We threw our bags on the nearest bunk and slumped down on the saloon seat. I remember thinking about how much I admired Peter. He never flinched or complained. Despite the state of this yacht, he set out on the business of getting her ready for sea with energy and enthusiasm. The question of where to start was simple: anywhere. Wherever you start will simply lead onto the next item needing to be looked at. For instance, lift a floorboard and see if there is water in the bilge. If there is, check the seacocks, stern glands and any general damage. Then, check the bilge pump, both manual and electric (if available). During the course of trying to get the electric bilge pump working, invariably you find yourself staring at the instrument panel that leads you all over the boat, including the engine room. We removed the sail covers, hoisted the sails in the calm conditions and established that they seemed fit enough for action. We worked together and independently, going over the boat making lists, fixing things, sorting and organizing. Peter always put particular effort into engine checks, and whenever in doubt, he would summon the local engineer to give it the once over. Peter would try to establish the condition of fuel tanks and shut-off valves. In this case, everything seemed passable, but only just. Invariably, there were the usual runs to grocery stores, chandlerys and customs before it was time to depart.

I was not looking forward to this trip. I felt that with the tired state of the yacht, it would not be easy, but how wrong I was. In fact, the trip was completely unnoteworthy. It was slow but safe. When the wind failed to blow, the engine chugged along just fine. My one prediction was correct: water dripped onto the bunks whenever the seas broke over the decks or it rained. There seemed to be no rhyme or reason to where the leaks would occur, and the poor off-duty person would find himself playing musical bunks, without the music, to escape the newest development of drips.

While the delivery may have been routine, I did get a chance to find out a little more about Peter. He had a real thing about safety. When

I met him at a train station or airport, the largest item he carried was a suitcase-sized life raft. At first, I thought it odd, but he did not want to rely on the unknown service history of whatever life raft each individual yacht carried, if indeed they had rafts at all. Whenever I went on deck at sea, he would always say, "Where's your safety harness?" During one of our quieter moments headed north through Biscay, I pushed him on this point, and the story he told was sobering indeed. It was well-documented in Peter's book *All Weather Yachtsman*, with the relevant chapter titled "Tragedy". To read the tale is sickening. It's every mariner's nightmare.

He had been delivering a vessel from Southampton to Sunderland. It was December, and the wind was a strong northerly with a touch of west in it. The yacht was sailing under tough conditions of wind and snow in the Humber estuary area. There were three of them on board, splitting the watches. Riding up the steep waves before crashing into the troughs was giving the helmsman on the tiller plenty of hard work. On one particularly heavy crash, Peter poked his head out only to be reassured by the first mate on the helm that he was fine. As Peter put it, "Three minutes later, he was gone." There followed the usual frantic efforts to get the vessel turned about, and as they sailed back and forth, they had to endure the agony of hearing a weakening voice in the dark hailing them until it hailed no more. It must have been a shattering experience, but Peter decided to learn from the tragedy, and vowed no crew of his would be on deck at night in bad weather without a "safety belt", as he called it. So he set about designing one, and some years after the tragedy, a number of professional organizations began to stipulate that one must be on board for their organized events. Today, during offshore cruising or racing, one would be hard-pressed to find a sailor who does not wear a safety harness at all times, even if on occasion they are not clipped on. All this is thanks to Peter's loss and subsequent ingenuity.

The story had been humbling. I knew that on occasion, I had

been cavalier about roaming around the deck at night without a harness. It was an important lesson that Peter was trying to teach me: never ever compromise safety. As usual, I was always learning. As he departed below, perhaps sensing the dark mood, he turned to me.

"Hey Gus, do you know this one?

There was a fellow named Crighton,
Who said to his girl you're a tight 'un
Well upon my soul,
You're in the wrong hole
There's plenty of room in the right 'un."

I immediately started laughing. A smile spread across his face as he disappeared below. I was left to ponder what a fine man he was. To deal with all the variables of humanity, yachts and location over so many years and to be still going strong was a fine example indeed.

On the 2nd of November, we pulled into the Hamble River and secured alongside. From start to finish, with only two brief stops, the voyage had taken seventeen days to cover 1,302 nautical miles, which is averaging little better than three knots. I can't say I was sorry to be off this tired, leaky, wooden example of yacht construction from a bygone era, but I was glad for the experience, and Peter was right. When the shipyard finished with her, giving her clean paint and fresh varnish, she would be a fine example of how things were once done "properly"!

It wasn't long before Peter summoned me for the second voyage. It was late November, and the trip was to be from southern Spain back to the U.K. I had been planning to be home for Christmas this year, but Peter could make no promises. The 25th of November 1985 found us greeting each other at the check-in for our flight to Spain. As the check-in assistant dealt with the paperwork, Peter informed me that we would be delivering a ketch-rigged 48-foot centre-cockpit Nicholson from Jose Banus, Spain back to Portsmouth, England. As usual, I really didn't know what to expect. After the last trip, I didn't have my hopes up, but when we finally arrived at the berth, I was impressed. She looked neat and tidy. The yacht had obviously been washed recently, the sail covers over the main and mizzen were secured and everything topside was ship shape. We unclipped the side screen and stepped into the roomy centre cockpit, which was dominated by a huge white leather-clad bucket helm seat offset to port. Next to the helm was access to the interior through a couple of neatly varnished cockpit doors. The interior was clean. The saloon curtains were drawn to stop the fading effects of the sun on the interior. This vessel had been loved and looked after well. As we made our customary rounds of the interior, we could find nothing amiss. Engineering, electrical, spares, sails: everything was easily sorted and brought quickly up to speed to make ready for our departure. Peter did his usual engineering overhaul, and although he never complained, he now had me as a shadow, trying to learn as much as I could. I was aware that one day I would be in Peter's position, trying to get a crew and vessel ready for sea.

After the usual scurry around the local supermarket, we were set, and on the 28th of November, we set sail for Gibraltar. Our first day at sea allowed us to get to know the vessel, and after a quick stop in Gibraltar to top up the fuel tanks, we moved on. The trip to Cape St. Vincent, on the southwest corner of Spain, was mostly motoring with fluky winds. With the Cape in the distance, it became flat calm, but I was about to encounter a most unusual weather phenomenon. It was an almost-unheard-of freak of nature. It was something most mariners dream about but rarely encounter. It was total cooperation from the wind! As we made our turn to the north around the Cape, a gentle zephyr of wind stirred the water from the southwest, and minute by minute, it gently filled in until by the following morning, we had a nice breeze of force four or five blowing on our port quarter. We had all sails set and began to wonder how long our luck would last.

The Nicholson yachts were all well-built, and having sailed the Nicholson 55 while in the Navy, the Nicholsons 38 and 46 and now the Nicholson 48, I had become accustomed to their solid feel at sea. They dealt with wind and waves well, and I enjoyed being aboard them, but this trip just kept getting better and better. It was almost as if someone was sitting in a control room for a wind test tunnel with the dial in hand, turning it up ever so little, hour by hour and day by day, but always from the same direction. The boat was just romping along at a steady eight knots, and with seas that were beginning to pick up, she occasionally began the odd surf. Watch after watch, we came up into our protected centre cockpit, settled into the bucket seat and enjoyed sailing along at speed, in comfort towards our destination. With the sails filled out to starboard, she listed nicely in that direction and barely rolled or pitched as we tore along. We opened the cockpit doors and attached them to the fasteners. Cups of tea and biscuits were regularly handed up to the helmsman, and the crew of three were like kids. Whoever was in the galley delighted in cooking and cleaning up. Navigation was a pleasure, and our foul-weather gear remained in the cupboard. Twenty-four hours since rounding the Cape, the wind and seas continued to build to a steady force six gusting seven. The yacht was flying on a broad reach, and Peter decided, despite the joy of sailing so well and fast, that we must begin to shorten sail. It was the first time since rounding the Cape that we had had to unzip the cockpit side covers and step outside, but Peter was right as usual. Safety must come first. Peter decided to triple-reef the main but leave a substantial amount of headsail unfurled. This meant that if we had to shorten sail further during the night, it would only require winding in and releasing lines from the cockpit to reduce the amount of headsail.

The reduction of sail barely reduced our speed. We just seemed to be a little more upright and in control, and we had less of a sense that the boat was working hard. The night continued as the day had, with a steady increase in wind. The log never fell below eight knots of boat speed. By dawn, the skies had cleared, and the wind was blowing a full gale-force eight. Without a doubt, I was enjoying the easiest, most thrilling sailing I had ever experienced. Even the Atlantic seemed to be playing along, with great rolling seas that had picked up considerably in the steady winds from the southwest. There was no confusion, just great lumbering masses of rolling North Atlantic seas gently picking up the yacht and sending us flying down the front before leaving us pointing at the sky as we fell down the back side of the departing wave. However, in the cockpit, we began to concentrate on steering. While fun, we were aware if we lost control on a surf or broached, things might not be quite so amusing. There were no more cups of tea for the helmsman. He needed to concentrate. Nothing changed throughout the rest of the day and night, except for the very gentle increase in wind. By the next morning, we had cleared the northwest tip of Spain. In around two and a half days, we had done a little over 480 nautical miles, averaging around eight knots. This was a remarkable feat on a delivery, and it was achieved in safety and without overworking the standing and running rigging.

The best was yet to come. I sat down in the helmsman's bucket seat to the most enjoyable watch I could remember. Due to the southerly nature of the wind, despite being early December, I was able to wear a t-shirt and shorts. We had been blasted up the coast of Spain and Portugal into the Bay of Biscay in spectacular fashion. The wind, by Peter's estimate, was now a steady force nine. The skies were clear, except for some spectacular "mare's tails" that stretched away into the distance and framed the commotion below. The seas had, not surprisingly, grown, with the top five or ten feet breaking occasionally. However, because of the steady direction of wind over so many days, there was order to the advancing waves. I had my work cut out on the helm. By now, we were sailing under storm rig. With our slight turn to starboard after having rounded the northwest tip of Spain, we were now sailing almost downwind.

We had a triple-reefed main out to port with a preventer running from the outer end of the boom to the forward-most portside fairlead and then made up on the cleat. The headsail was held firm out to starboard using the spinnaker pole, which was also secured with lines fore and aft to keep it steady in case we broached. The pattern became familiar; under sail in the trough of the wave, the boat speed never fell below eight knots, and it felt as if we were standing still. Slowly but surely, I would feel the aft end rise as the next advancing mountain of water approached. I found myself looking not at the horizon but at the trough we had just been in. As we rode up the approaching wave, the sails would be exposed to ever-greater wind until where there had been a hint of slackness in sail and line, there was none. I could feel the power of the wind transmitted through the sails and rigging into forward acceleration, which combined with our downhill angle, started us flying down the face of the wave. The log, which was dial and needle, kept climbing through to the stop mark, beyond twelve knots, where it jammed. We never did know our true speed on these surfs. Tearing up from the sea on either side of the bow were huge bow waves breaking and flying high up over the guard rails and arcing almost as far aft at the cap shroud. The helm was responding like a dinghy, with barely a twitch port or starboard getting a nudge left and right from the bow. The sensation of flying at these speeds on such a large yacht was magnificent. All the while, I sat in bright sunshine in a t-shirt in our centre cockpit, with the side screens zipped shut. Without doubt, they were the easiest, most fun sea miles I had ever done. For hour after hour, we continued the pattern. Whenever we only surfed down a wave at ten or eleven knots, there was a groan of disapproval. Before we knew it, we had blasted past Ushant and were flying up the English Channel.

During the course of our transit through Biscay, the winds had subsided, but we were still enjoying downwind sailing with reduced seas. The winds continued in our favor all the way into the Solent and our eventual tie up alongside in Portsmouth. We felt like a water skier who, having enjoyed a fast ride, accelerates out to the side before letting go and, with graceful deceleration, arrives at the beach and steps onto dry land: no fuss, no bother. We simply could not believe the trip we had just made. Even Peter, who had seen it all, was amazed at the easy and rapid nature of the delivery. We had just done 1,150 nautical miles in eight days, bearing in mind that the first day, we had been doing barely five knots down to Gibraltar and stopped overnight in Gib with a slow transit over to Cape St Vincent. For a delivery, it was as good as it gets, and I had loved it. I was not only home for Christmas but I also had no excuse not to shop!

I mentioned earlier that we had delivered a Nicholson 46 from Lymington to Inverkip Marina in Scotland and that later, it was to provide one of my worst nights at sea. Well, it was time to return to Scotland to get this yacht down to the Mediterranean. The refit did not seem considerable, but she was most definitely ready for sea. That made our usual few hectic days of rushing about and trying to create order aboard rather muted. It was a pleasant way to start. There was a shop very nearby, which also made stocking up a simple task. On the 19th of February 1986, we slipped lines with Peter, as usual, at the helm. Nowadays, if somebody told me they were heading out on a delivery in February in Northern European waters and crossing the Bay of Biscay, I would tell them they were mad. Back then, we did not think anything of it. Indeed, we considered ourselves lucky to have the work on such a well-founded yacht. Not all of them were.

Our next stop was to be Penzance. We secured all lines and fenders and enjoyed the beautiful rugged scenery of the Firth of Clyde. Normally, we would settle quickly into our watches, but under the wintry grey skies, the rugged landscape of Scotland was magnificent and menacing. With hot cups of tea, we watched it all slide by.

Having become aware that Peter was a walking encyclopedia of all things nautical, I was even beginning to take note of his eating habits. It seemed that sausages slammed between two great chunks of white bread and washed down with endless cups of tea and Jaffa cake biscuits several times a day, as well as very little exercise, did not seem to be creating the regularity I would hope for in the bowels department! Peter had a different approach that was based on age, experience and common sense. He enjoyed fruits and vegetables as the main staples of his diet. At the beginning of the voyage, he would enjoy fruits such as bananas, and after a few days would to a switch to apples, oranges and tangerines. However, it was his main meal selection that was most impressive. He would select a variety of vegetables to cut up, the greater the variety the better. The list would include, but was not limited to, potatoes, carrots, turnips, leeks and onions. He would boil them down, often adding rice, marmite and/or Bovril to create what I can only describe as a hearty vegetable broth. While staring wistfully at his food, I kept up my poor eating habits and continued to regret it. Ah, the stupidity of youth!

So it was as we slid down North Channel, with me munching on my sandwich, Peter sipping his soup and the third watch keeper on the helm. We maintained good speeds. With this being a short hop to Penzance with a recently refurbished engine and full fuel tanks, when the wind failed and speed crept below the six-knot mark, on went the engine. If we couldn't sail in the right direction, a small amount of main was left up for stability, and the engine stayed on. This approximately 400 nautical mile leg down to Penzance was no great effort. Sailing and motoring proved routine, with no great wind, no heavy seas and no drama. By early afternoon on the third day, we had the distant silhouette of Lands End in sight under an increasingly grey sky. The February sky was rather magnificent. Despite the high-altitude grey cloud cover, it was crystal clear. Interestingly, the weather situation was the opposite of what one might expect. Generally speaking, in this region, it would be normal to look to the west and see thickening clouds from systems rolling in from the Atlantic. What we were looking at was, despite the clear visibility, rather thicker clouds to the east and clearer skies to the west. This should perhaps have put our senses on alert, but with Lands End drawing rapidly closer and Penzance only a fifteen or twenty nautical mile jog eastward up the coast, I certainly felt we were home and dry and would be getting last orders in the local pub that evening.

As darkness began to envelope us, I did not like our last glimpse of the thickening skies in the east. It was cold too, somewhere around the freezing mark. Peter plotted a course that kept us well offshore. As we continued south by west and the silent sweep of the Lands End light drew abeam to port, we began to notice that while its light was lost to sea out west, to the east, it was beginning to reflect back, almost as if it were passing over a fog bank. The wind that had been essentially calm began to fill in from the east. It came in odd puffs that made us feel uneasy. Peter had been altering course every twenty or thirty minutes a few degrees to port on a wide arc around the Lands End light, but as the light drew aft, he decided to keep heading south, feeling that distance between us and land might be necessary.

It was now late evening. Quite suddenly, despite the good visibility around us and to the west, the Lands End light disappeared, and nothing more than a muffled flicker swept occasionally out to us. Peter became quite concerned and took as many bearings as possible to ascertain our position, thinking it might be his last chance. The wind had rapidly filled in, and Peter decided to shut the engine off and sail under a heavily reefed main and headsail, which while not enough sail for speed now, would, he sensed, mean that there would be no need to adjust them if the wind got up. It was a good call. The wind kept rising, as did the seas. The speed at which this happened was a concern. Within an hour, we were laboring to windward in a force six. It started to snow. I was off duty until midnight, but the demands of sorting the boat and navigation in our rapidly changing circumstances kept me in my foul-weather gear and stationed on the saloon berth, ready to help. The weather continued to deteriorate. It was snowing hard, and the yacht was pitching violently. Peter's call to set storm canvas was an excellent one because by the time my watch came, it was blowing a full gale force eight from the east and snowing hard. The motion inside, as we beat to windward, was tedious, making the smallest of tasks difficult. The demands of putting on clothing and foul-weather gear to get ready for a watch, coupled with holding on, made me feel seasick. I took a quick scan of the chart and headed up top. It was a miserable night. As I stood in the cockpit with my back to the wind and snow, hot from the effort of getting sorted below, I stared out over the helm and stern into the inky blackness beyond, and it didn't seem so bad. However, as I took the helm and faced the onslaught, I realized I was in for a long watch. I immediately put the hood of my foul-weather jacket up over my wooly hat and secured it fast around my neck with the Velcro strip.

We were now pitching violently over the oncoming seas and sending spray high into the dark night before it was taken by the wind and hurled down into the cockpit and onto me. Almost immediately, I could feel the spray make its way around the seal of the hood and trickle down the side of my face onto the narrow towel I had around my neck for just such a purpose. The snow impacting the eyes and face in the full gale was painful indeed and made looking to windward for any length of time impossible. It dawned on me that should any vessel bear down on us out of the murk, we would have no chance to avoid it. Visibility was zero. You might think that a man who had spent the best part of the previous year and a half at sea would be well-prepared, clothing-wise, for any weather. I had no such luck. I had the thinnest of leather gloves, and within minutes of gripping the wheel, my hands lost all feeling. By now, snow mixed with spray was accumulating on the spreaders and rigging. Periodically, chunks would break off, and if I was lucky, fly right by me.

Occasionally, a piece would strike my face without warning. Not only was I trying to stay warm but I was also trying to dodge flying ice. Within thirty minutes, I was cold and utterly miserable. The constant trickle of water around my hood and down my neck had started to soak my clothes inside. The routine became monotonous: we would pitch over the wave, with the whiplash of the stern following the bow, throwing me into the helm. Clouds of spray, from the bow, mixed with snow buried me, followed shortly thereafter by the relentless trickle down my neck. My eyes hurt from the snow flying into them, and every second I was wondering when the next chunk of ice would strike me. I began to give up trying to look ahead. I could barely make out the bow now in the heavy snow, and missing land or ships would be an impossibility if they loomed out of the darkness. Still, even as I was sliding into an idle attitude towards my watch keeping duties, I could hear my grandfather's voice in my head, "Come on, my boy, do your duty." He had been an officer in The Royal Navy and had survived on active duty during both World Wars, rising to the rank of full Admiral by his retirement. Among his many achievements was leading North Atlantic convoys through to Northern Russia during the most frightful of North Atlantic winters, all while under the threat of attack. My evening out would have been like a pleasant Mediterranean cruise to him. I kept reminding myself of this and trying to pull myself together, remembering that the lives of those below were in my hands.

After about an hour, I found myself checking my watch every minute, staggered to find only another minute had gone by; it felt like an eternity. I stopped looking at my watch. I could see a crack of light through the cockpit saloon hatch and knew it was relatively warm inside. I was desperate to leave the helm and get below. As I sunk into the second hour, I was soaked to the skin and shivering hard. My hands would not operate, and I had taken to operating the helm with the crook of my arm wrapped around a spoke instead of holding the wheel. My stance left me hunched over, with my left shoulder leading into wind and my head looking down and behind, leaving the covered back of my head to take on the snow, spray and occasional chunks of ice. I would make a very conscious effort to look up and to windward at regular intervals to keep watch and was rewarded by another barrage of snow and spray. As we continued on port tack, sensibly taking us away from land, I knew my coursekeeping was poor at best.

Just when I thought I could take no more, Peter slid the hatch back and came up on deck. Having closed the hatch behind him and surveyed the night, he turned to me with a serious look on his face.

"There was a mathematician named Hall,
who had a hexahydraulical ball,
the cube of its weight,
plus his penis times eight,
was three fifths of five eights of fuck all!"

I immediately burst out laughing. Despite the serious nature of our situation, here was Peter at his finest once again. I know he had been at the chart table, busy with the task of dead reckoning, and the motion must having been making him feel ill as well, but once again, he was concerned about his crew and keeping up their morale. I was amazed at his coolness under the most trying of circumstances. He took the helm, and as he did so, I collapsed onto the cockpit seat for a brief moment, with my back to the wind. I used each hand to slowly work the other, but there was no feeling. I was cold and soaked and decided to head below. I slid the hatch cover back and stepped inside, but before I disappeared below, I glanced at Peter. He was also wearing the scruffiest of gloves, but even more concerning was the state of his foul-weather gear. He wore the cheapest thin plastic variety I had ever seen. The hood had the feeblest of draw strings with two white plastic toggles on the ends, which when pulled, tightened the material around the face in the smallest possible way. The sleeves had no ability to close down and left his jersey hanging from them, getting instantly soaked. Down the front of the jacket, there was no zipper, only four or five poppers spread out to keep it closed. Even as I looked on, the spray covered him. I could see the water make its way between the poppers and begin the task of soaking him through. Even now, he was teaching me a lesson. In the most trying of situations, keep your eye on the ball, keep positive and, despite your own uncertainties and difficulties, remember that you're the skipper and act like it. It was most impressive. He gave me a huge smile and wave as I sunk below and pulled the hatch shut.

I slumped down in front of the chart to eye Peter's work. The situation was not as I hoped. It was now 2.15 a.m., and by the look of Peter's last dead reckon fix, we had barely made eight nautical miles easting from the longitude of Lands End. So in the last eight hours, we had barely been making good one knot. The motion inside was making me ill again. I began to peel off my foul-weather gear and wet clothes before finding a dry top and underwear and climbing into my bunk. Never have I been so glad of a warm refuge in my life. Peter decided, after his watch, that we should all do only one hour on deck in these conditions. We all did our bit through the rest of the night, and by the time the weak wintery sun was beginning to shed light on our new day, the conditions had improved. The wind was dying down, as was the snow. Even better, Peter was satisfied that we could close land again, and as the visibility improved, it became possible to make out headlands and lights. Peter established a fix, and by 09.00 a.m., we were able to make our way in towards Penzance. It had taken the entire night to get from Lands End to Penzance, a distance of only about fifteen or twenty nautical miles, depending on how one sails the course. I did, however, come to a conclusion. I did not like beating to windward in February in Northern European waters during a snowstorm and force eight headwinds from the sanctuary of an open cockpit. It was most disagreeable! However, as Peter had shown as a skipper, difficult situations were going to arise, and one had better be prepared to deal with them. Once in port, I pressed him on this point and asked him if he had been in "survival storm" situations. In other words, a situation in which he felt seriously that his very survival was threatened. He was very clear on this point. No! He felt it was the duty of every skipper to make absolutely sure that the yacht and crew are prepared in every way for any situation that could be encountered at sea. He felt no need to elaborate and he was, of course, quite right.

Arriving in port had never been a better experience. The sanctuary of harbor and a hot cup of tea were most welcome, but after a fantastic pub dinner and a good night's sleep, it was back to it. Peter had decided that an up-to-date meteorological forecast was in order. He was determined to make sure that our passage across Biscay, at least, was uneventful. Peter did such a good job that not only did we have an uneventful crossing of Biscay but also an uneventful trip all the way down to Gibraltar, where we secured lines and Peter announced we would be heading ashore for dinner. As we navigated along some of the back streets of Gibraltar, we eventually found ourselves in a particularly dimly lit alleyway with the feeblest of lights by the door. Peter turned the handle and entered. Inside, it could not have been more different. With the dim lights, it felt cozy and familiar. The tables were all covered by red and white checkered tablecloths and a central candle. The oval bottle covered with wicker next to the candle completed the look. The restaurant was full.

Over the dinner chatter, we suddenly heard, "Peter, great to see you!"

The man who had hailed did so from the far side of the room. He was the owner and strode through the crowd to reach us. They embraced each other like long-lost friends before he guided us to a table. Clearly, Peter had frequented this place numerous times on his stopovers in Gibraltar. For some reason, I got lost in the menu and failed to keep up with their story of times gone by, but he departed and, without us ordering, there followed a never-ending supply of food and drink. It was a wonderful evening, and in the warm glow of full stomachs and plenty of alcohol, the evening melted away into a very late night that was not remembered by any of us the next day. However, the hangovers were. Apparently, we had agreed to stop by the restaurant owner's house for coffee the next day, and so we scrubbed up and duly followed the directions. We began a steady march uphill and came to a spot with the correct number and name and knocked. We were once again greeted like long-lost brothers and ushered into the sitting room at the front of the house. The view, over the harbor directly below out to the Straits of Gibraltar and Africa beyond was breathtaking. Once again, a sense of naval history began to invade my imagination. I found myself lost with Nelson and stealthy U-boat commanders, finally wondering how many lives had been lost in the scenery I was surveying. I wandered around the room before, like a good sailor, my eyes came to rest on the photograph of an exceptionally beautiful young woman.

"That's my daughter," the mother told me. "She would love to meet you, but she is at university in England."

I was about to add that I would love to meet her, but I didn't think she needed to hear that piece of information! I could have happily relaxed in the living room and consumed coffee and biscuits all day, but Peter, as always, had a schedule to keep. We got ourselves back to the boat, and having topped up the fuel and food supplies, we were ready for the final leg down to Palma Majorca. I would love to write about the harrowing conditions and heroic actions of all involved, but it was, like the trip from Penzance to Gibraltar, remarkably dull and routine. I was also well aware that my time working with Peter was rapidly drawing to a close. I felt the need to move on in life to gain new experiences. So it was that after we secured lines in Palma and handed the keys into the marina office, we found ourselves in the taxi to the airport for the last time. We landed in London, and the awkward moment came to say goodbye to a man who had introduced me to a way of life that I hadn't even known existed, one that was so very right for me. This man had never lost his temper and had always, at any time of day or night, been happy to impart his considerable knowledge of all things nautical. I left with some considerable miles under my belt in a variety of vessels and a variety of conditions and felt quite ready for what lay ahead, although at that moment in time, I was not quite sure what that would be. Peter promised that he would get a letter of reference sent on to me as soon as possible. We did the usual awkward farewells and promised to stay in touch. With that, we turned and headed in opposite directions. Not only did Peter forward a reference, but unbeknownst to me, he was to be responsible for securing my future. I charged off into life, but Peter had yet another surprise for me. Quite undeservedly, he was to pay me the ultimate compliment. I received a letter asking if when he published his latest edition of *All Weather Yachtsman*, I would mind if he put a photo of me at the helm of the Nicholson 46 on the front cover. I was delighted and a little embarrassed. After all, I knew of the man and his experiences, and I did not feel worthy. Shortly thereafter, a copy arrived in the post with a kind inscription:

"To Angus—With all best wishes & in appreciation for an excellent crew."

It was not to be many years before Peter would be struck down by a degenerative nerve condition that very quickly killed him. Peter was undoubtedly one of the finest men I ever knew. He was dedicated, often to the shoddiest of vessels. As to his knowledge and experience, I think I can safely say that I have never found his equal, but more importantly, his tolerance and kindness for the wide spectrum of humanity with whom he sailed was extraordinary. I liked Peter immensely, and as I am sure is so often the case, when his death came, I felt an enormous void and sadness that we did not get to spend more time together on voyages and in the pub. I would always miss his wisdom, humor, knowledge and friendship.

I was a little over twenty-two years old, a qualified Yachtmaster Offshore with a little over 17,000 nautical miles behind me. Somehow, I still felt lost and quite unsure about what to do next. I knew I had thoroughly enjoyed my yacht deliveries, but I wanted to get away from the demands of small yachts on the open ocean, with their unknown maintenance histories, which so often only came to light at the most inopportune of moments.

EIGHT

The Bright Lights

So my future lay at sea. That much was clear, but in what capacity, was not quite so clear. I mentioned that Peter was responsible for what happened next. While back at the parents' home in Lymington in early April of 1987, the phone rang.

"Hello, my name is Paul. Could I speak to Angus please?"

"Speaking!" I replied.

"Ah, good. I'm the captain on a 100-foot Benetti in the south of France, and I need a deck hand for the upcoming season. Would you be interested?" he asked.

"You bet!" I replied. "When do I start?"

"As soon as you can get down here," Paul replied. "You may be interested in how I got your name. I was walking down the street and quite literally bumped into Peter Haward, who I had crewed for many years ago, and we got chatting. As a result, he recommended you if ever I should need a deckhand."

Once again, it seemed I was indebted to Peter.

Paul informed me I would get paid one thousand pounds a month, along with all the food I could eat and a place to sleep, free of charge. I couldn't believe what I was hearing. After the tough financial discipline I'd had to endure for the last year or two, I was a little stunned. Now, I would be paid to be on a large private yacht in the south of France. I would have warm water, sunshine, free food and money. I was excited. I was also told not to bring too much, as my uniform would be provided. I would have free clothes as well! This just got better and better.

I packed my old naval kit bag and made my way across the channel down to Paris. Once there, I picked up the TGV train to Antibes, where I had been told to get off. I clutched the rail timetable and checked off the stations. I had no intention of missing my stop. I was mesmerized as we approached the French Riviera and I caught glimpses of the blue Mediterranean Sea between gaps in the rugged sun-drenched landscape. Eventually, the train pulled into Antibes Station.

It was late afternoon as I exited the station. The sight that greeted my eyes I shall never forget. Spread out below was one of the largest concentrations of yachting wealth in the world. This seemed to be a place where size most definitely mattered. From where I stood just outside the front of the station, I could survey the entire port, which was dominated by a large fort. The inner harbor contained a huge number of yachts, ranging in size from tiny up to about 120 feet, but the outer harbor had the real monsters that were moored up stern-to one after the other and ranged from about 150 to 250 feet in length. From a distance, they looked spotless. I had never seen anything like it. My yachting had been done on small vessels sleeping up to six or eight, bobbing around the Atlantic or Northern European waters in often revolting conditions, with spray and the elements as my main companion. Before me was a whole different game. These vessels were a statement that this person had arrived and was putting it on show. It struck me that not only were these people and their yachts dedicated to the pursuit of leisure in the most beautiful and warm of places but that if they needed to do business, watch out: they had a proven track record of success right in front of your eyes.

It was a lovely late spring afternoon, but the promise of a warm summer was in the air. I had to make my way down to the harbor and find the yacht. The easiest thing, I thought, would be to head to the harbormaster's office, a mushroom-shaped structure in the middle of the inner harbor. I was in awe at the sight of yacht after yacht, all over a hundred feet in length, moored up stern-to and all absolutely gleaming in the sun. I had a certain amount of trepidation, but I knew I was in the right place. I just loved what I was looking at. As I walked passed each yacht towards the harbormaster, I checked each name just in case. Just as I was about to give up and make a beeline for the office, I suddenly sighted my new home.

This was not a yacht in the sense of what I had experienced to date. For me, she was enormous and seemed more like a small ship. At a hundred feet, she was well over double the length of anything I had sailed on before. She was one and a half decks and a beautiful off-cream color, with acres of varnish work at the aft end of the main deck. She had portlights just above the waterline and wide side decks you could walk down comfortably, all covered in teak. Above the main deck was the bridge deck, at the aft end of which was the ship's tender, a small open speedboat, and a crane horizontally stowed above it. Above it all was a final small sundeck, at the back end of which I could just make out the covers over the cushions that covered the area. Sticking out of the sundeck was a mast, upon which was mounted a magnificent brass triple foghorn. I stood for a moment at the gangway, wondering how to let anybody know I was here. I was not sure of the etiquette but decided to just clamber aboard and hope I wasn't upsetting anyone. Halfway down the port side, a side door popped open, and a large man with a huge barrel chest and shorts stepped out. He had short black curly hair and very dark brown eyes with just a hint of humor in them. He was tanned from years in an industry that stuck to the sun.

"Get those shoes off my deck!" he roared.

I was wearing my metal-heeled brogues, which at the time, didn't seem a problem, but with the benefit of hindsight, I cringe at the thought of it.

Sensing a rough start Paul, the captain, tried again.

"Angus, you made it. Good to see you, and welcome aboard."

We shook hands, and he took me forward, now in bare feet, past the side door amidships leading to the interior and up a couple of steps to the focsle, at the aft end of which was a hatch leading down to the crew quarters. The yacht felt enormous, and I was still astounded that one individual could own and operate this. Paul went first, and I passed my belongings down to be confronted by my crewmates. The focsle living area housed four of us, twin bunks to port and twin to starboard, all sharing one heads. It was all very neat, clean and quite clearly well-maintained. I stowed my stuff on the bunk and set about meeting everyone.

The first hand I shook belonged to the ship's engineer, Peter, a neat and tidy kind of chap with few words but personable. I sensed he would be an easy fellow to work with. Sally was our steward-ess. She was tall with long shapely legs, a good-looking face and medium-length brown hair. She smiled plenty and also seemed an easy person to get along with. The fourth bunk, at the moment, was free because we currently had no chef on board. Introduc-tions complete, I was free to roam around my new home. There was a door leading aft from the crew quarters directly into the guest areas. The first thing that struck me was the paint color. Everything was a shade darker than pea green, but off to port and starboard were two guest cabins with their own bathrooms, all in the same green theme but beautifully clean and tidy with the beds made. The ceramic sink and shower had shiny lacquer-covered brass fixtures, so they shone brightly without the endless cleaning brass usually needs. Towels were neatly folded, and new soap, in its wrapper, sat in a spotless soap dish. Nothing was out of place, and there was not a hint of dust or dirt. I backed out, not wishing to be responsible for disturbing anything, and closed the door.

At the aft end of the guest corridor was a small flight of stairs leading up into an athwartships corridor. There were six exits off this small corridor, two at the starboard side, one leading to a for-ward saloon used for TV and lounging around and one leading aft into the spacious main saloon, which had a dining area at the forward end. On the port side of the corridor was an access forward into the galley and small crew mess. On the aft side amidships was a small spiral staircase leading up into the bridge, and finally, there was a door at each end of the corridor, one port and one starboard, leading out onto each main side deck. The bridge had beautiful teak floors with gloss varnish that gleamed in the very late afternoon sunshine. There were bridge doors port and starboard that led outside onto a full teak-clad deck, which allowed you to walk right around in front of the bridge windows and gave excellent visibility over the ship's side for stern and side maneuvering. The bridge wings were dominated by two gyro repeaters. There would be no more converting compass bearing to true for me. This little ship had a gyrocompass on board, giving true bearings for course and objects. Aft of the bridge on the starboard side was the radio room and captain's office, where Paul spent much of his day running the ship. At the aft end of the radio room was a door that led to an outdoor dining area with a large open deck aft of it that was home to the ship's tenders: jet skis to starboard and a small speedboat to port. A small flight of stairs just to port of the outdoor dining area led up to the sundeck, which was covered in cushions and had a commanding 360 degree view. Back into the bridge, one could turn left and left again, walk down the spiral staircase, turn right and right again and walk into the main saloon that covered fully one half of the vessel's main deck. It was well-appointed, with chairs and sofas and, as previously mentioned, a small dining table at the forward end. The windows were large and tinted, making looking in during the daytime impossible. Everything was green or lacquered brass and, particularly at night, very welcoming. Halfway down the saloon on the starboard side was a flight of stairs leading down to the owner's quarters. These were comprised of a huge cabin running the full width of the vessel. Needless to say, the bathroom was equally large, and there was also a ladies' dressing room.

The engine room occupied the space below the forward half of the saloon and was accessed through a noise-suppressing door and a steep vertical ladder amidships on the port-side main deck. It was cavernous and had two main engines and two generators. At the forward end on the bulkhead was a switchboard covered in numerous switches and dials. As with the rest of the yacht, everything was very neat and tidy. I had had enough for one day and turned in early. I suspected the next day would provide a steep learning curve.

The next day, Paul summoned me to the radio room and went through the dos and don'ts, just like any boss covering all the introductory stuff on a new job. He made clear to me my responsibilities: to maintain the exterior and keep it spotless, to assist with watch-keeping duties on passage and to generally be available to help out in any way required. Sally had fixed me up with uniform, and having finished with Paul, I leapt out onto the deck, ready for action. I came to a shuddering halt and realized I had not the faintest idea what I was supposed to be doing. What did the deckhand/first mate do to maintain a yacht of this size? Paul had told me that Martin would be arriving around 09.00 a.m. Martin was the day worker who had been hired during the winter months to assist with all general repairs and cleaning duties. He would be my best source of information. This practice was not uncommon among the yachts in Antibes. It meant costs were kept down because there was no need to feed and house a full-time crewmember. Captains using so-called "day workers" only paid for their labor on an hourly basis, as required. Day workers lived ashore and housed themselves wherever they could find cheap accommodations. Martin, a large fellow with a cheerful disposition who looked like he enjoyed his food, arrived punctually. I introduced myself as the new deck hand/first mate and then somewhat apologetically informed him that I hadn't the faintest idea of what was required to maintain the yacht. Martin laughed and promised he would get me up to speed over the next couple of weeks.

True to his word, we went through all the storage lockers and identified all the cleaning products to keep paint, metal, windows and wood looking brand new. I realized that the best way would be to empty out all the lockers and rearrange them according to how I felt they should be. Martin had a myriad of small paint projects around the boat, and I followed him like a hawk, watching as he tackled a particular blister of paint with a pointed hammer to dig out the offending filler and rust. This patch of metal was then sealed with a coat of metal sealer, followed by filler, and sanded smooth. Then, the undercoat and finally several coats of topcoat were applied with a brush and maestro's blend of paint and thinner in just the right quantities so that there were no brushstrokes.

There was, of course, varnish work to complete, and there was plenty requiring a final topcoat. The entire bulkhead around the saloon doors at the aft end of the main deck, including the table and cap rail around the canoe stern, were all varnished wood. The outdoor dining table on the boat deck was also varnished teak. By the time I arrived, Martin was down to the final sanding and topcoating. We were using 220 grit wet and dry sandpaper and getting the previous fresh coat of varnish sanded until there was no hint of the shiny coat beneath. The entire surface, whether it was table, bulkhead, door or handrail, would then get a full washdown with soap and water before being left to dry overnight. The next morning, a clean cloth soaked in thinners was used to clean the surface of all traces of grease and dust before a final sticky rag, called a tack rag, was used to wipe the surface of the final traces of dust. Then, once the risk of early morning dew had past, with masking tape, we would isolate the areas to be varnished. Martin would mix the varnish with a little thinner and apply the coat with careful brushstrokes, working rapidly so the varnish could settle, hopefully leaving no hint of the brush that had applied it, but only a bright mirror finish.

At the end of the first week, with the yacht looking filthy, we decided to start pulling her together before the boss arrived in a couple of weeks and the season got underway. We needed to do a full washdown. The decks were a very dark grey from a couple of weeks of our chipping, sanding, painting and varnishing, and the filth from these operations helped generate the look of unloved disrepair. In addition, as the season approached, endless people had been on and off the boat while failing to take their shoes off, adding to the mess. Cleaning teak decks was new to me, and Martin happily showed me how. We informed the rest of the crew that we would be cleaning decks and closed all doors down on the boat deck. We hosed the entire deck down until it was saturated. Next, Martin bought out a liter-size bottle of dark liquid, opened the restricted pour nozzle and squirted it back and forth over a patch of deck. The already dark deck became even darker under the influence of the chemical sprayed on it.

"Right," he said. "That stiff-bristled brush in your hand. Get scrubbing across the grain, the harder the better."

I got stuck in. I went back and forth, back and forth, producing a light foam. When Martin pronounced himself satisfied, he rinsed the area with the hose, expertly directing the filthy mess away from where he was standing, down the slight run of the deck and into the scuppers. We continued this pattern until the entire boat deck was done with part one. We then got hold of the bottle labeled part two, which was a light straw color. Once again, Martin opened the nozzle and, as before, with a squeeze of the bottle, directed the stream onto the clean but black surface. The effect of the bleaching agent was instantaneous: the wood miraculously turned a beautiful sandy color. Using a soft brush, we spread the liquid around before once again spraying it off with a hose. The rest of the boat deck was finished off and left to dry in the rising sun. We moved to the focsle and main deck, giving them the same treatment. Once all decks were completed and the sun had dried them out, they were a beautiful sandy color. Martin then led me through the washdown procedure. From the top of the mast to the waterline, we worked methodically. First, spray an area with water. Second, with a bucket and soft brush, wash with detergent and water. Third, rinse off with the hose, and finally, before the sun dries the area, use a shammy cloth to dry it thoroughly to a "new car" mirror finish. By the time we had finished, the decks and topside paintwork looked fantastic. After I had been on board for two weeks, Paul decide to pay Martin off, and I was pronounced fit for service. Personally, I felt I still had only had a rough grasp of what was going on with regards to maintaining the exterior of a yacht of this caliber, but one thing was for sure: I loved every minute. Even better, I was getting paid for it, and we hadn't moved a foot.

We were now busy six days a week from dawn to dusk, with the looming summer season soon upon us. The final preparations for both the exterior and interior were being completed.

The boss rang Paul one day and announced that he would be sending his personal chef to cater for both the crew and himself for the upcoming season. We had no idea what this meant, but for me, having somebody concerned about my stomach three times a day, seven days a week was too good to be true. Sure enough, Pino, as he was called, arrived. Where his name came from, we never did find out. He could only be described as an elderly gentleman, almost portly. He walked with a pronounced limp and was absolutely charming. The women on board fell in love with him, as they would their grandfather, and fussed over him constantly. We chaps weren't far behind and couldn't do enough for him. Whenever he had to go ashore for shopping, someone made sure they could help him out. Upon return, it was all hands to get things aboard and stowed where he wanted them, but in the galley, this guy was a genius. His repertoire of both exotic and simple cuisines was extraordinary. After a few meals, we began to see why the boss had employed him. He was exceptional. As crew, we could eat indoors in the small crew mess in the galley or on deck at the crew table rigged up over the anchor windlass under the shade of the focsle awning. Evening meals were a fantastic experience: salads or vegetables, lobster or beef, shepherds pie or roast chicken. Sauces of incredible flavor would appear to accompany meals where appropriate, and all the while, we realized Pino was just warming up and getting used to the availability of local produce. He never served the same meal twice and always served them in a variety of cooking styles and presentations. Lunches would always be salads, and never just one, always two or three. There was no restriction on alcohol, and on weekends prior to the boss's arrival, plenty was consumed. I was in heaven. I was being fed regularly, paid regularly and had plenty of physical labor of interest, even though the boat hadn't been up and over a single wave since I had joined.

Inevitably, the boss arrived, and I was nervous to say the least. I had no idea how to conduct myself around him and the guests. I decided that the Dartmouth approach would be best. I would keep out of the way and, if confronted, resort to a lot of "sirs" in the conversation. As the car pulled up, the crew was arranged on the aft deck in smart uniforms of starched short-sleeve dark blue shirts with white collars and cuffs. Paul had his captain's four gold stripes on each shoulder. I had been given two, and the engineer had been given three. It was a smart group and matched the gleaming yacht that I had spent the best part of three days cleaning. The boss stepped out and looked every inch the multimillionaire that he was: tall, elegant and with just the right amount of immaculately groomed graying hair. His clothes looked expensive, and he looked relaxed in the carefree way that only a wealthy man with few concerns could. He was followed out of the car by his wife. Wow! I hadn't come into contact with multimillionaires' wives before, and from top to toe, she was magnificent. They came aboard, and Paul greeted them before introducing us all. They were obviously tired from the flight, but with their apparent delight at being on holiday aboard their yacht in France, they managed to put us all at ease. I retreated and left them to Paul's wife Martha, the head stewardess, and Sally to take care of their needs. I found myself roaming around the foredeck once again, not sure what to do next. Within twenty minutes, Paul found me and let me know we would not be going anywhere that night. The boss just wanted a light dinner and an early night. The atmosphere on the boat became very different. It was very businesslike, and all on board realized it was time to earn our pay cheques. It was up to the stewardesses and chef to take care of things. I retreated to the sanctuary of my bunk for an early night. The next day was going to be busy.

With guests on board, I would be up and on deck by 0600. The biggest challenge was to conduct my morning chores in absolute silence. No more clumping down the deck and dropping buckets. It was barefoot and placing things down with the upmost of care. First off, I would clean the scuppers right round the boat deck, main deck and focsle. Once complete, the entire upper deck paintwork would get a shammy-off from the morning dew. All covers over the exposed sundeck and boat deck cushion would be removed, and the sandy-colored decks would get a sweep around the tables and chairs. Finally, I settled in front of the main windlass and started to polish the brass drums that protruded from either side. It was not something that had been done before I arrived, and to get it sparkling took hours of effort, but once done, like this first morning with the boss on board, it just required a quick application of brasso, a little elbow grease and a final polish. They gleamed in the early morning sun. I would get to know this routine well with guests on board, and it changed only when we were at sea or it was raining. Once it was complete, I was resigned to waiting until the boss got up. I stood on the bridge, waiting for things to happen. I was ready to go, but apparently the boss was not.

Finally, around midmorning, Paul summoned me to the bridge. It was time to go. I quickly went from cabin to cabin, checking that all the waterline portlights were shut and dogged down. Then, it was time to single up the lines. To moor the yacht stern-to, we had port and starboard bowlines that disappeared down into the water to where they were anchored on the bottom. At the aft end, we had our own port and starboard quarter lines attached to the quay. Under

Paul's instruction, we slipped one of the lines and, in its place, rigged up a slip line running around the bollard and back to the boat through the fairlead and made up on the bollard. We let the other quarter line go until we were lying on the slip line only. We now had to get the gangway aboard. I released the handrail line and then lifted the stanchions out one by one and stowed them in a locker. The gangway itself was rolled along the quay to the edge, and then, using the metal cap rail runner, the gangway was quickly pulled inboard three quarters of the way. Then, with Paul at one end and me on the other, we tipped it on its side and carried it down the port-side main deck, hung it on its hooks and swung the latches in place.

Paul returned to the bridge. He had a small VHF radio, as did I, and having checked that they were working, he told me to let go aft. I removed the figure of eights from the bollard and pulled like hell to get the slip line back on board. Then, as the yacht drifted forward, I legged it to the foredeck to remove the final bowline from the bollard, dropped it through the fairlead and watched it disappear below the surface. I informed Paul that all lines were gone. With a little ruffle of prop wash, Paul nudged us forward until we were clear of our neighbors and in clear water between the two lines of stern-to yachts moored in the harbor. I was busy running around the main deck with a spare fender, making sure we did not bump into anything. Once clear, Paul instructed me to get all the fenders inboard, which I did. Then, I stowed them in the chain locker, along with the slip line from aft.

With everything stowed and secured, I was free to watch our exit from the harbor. The sun was high in the sky, and it was hot in the inner harbor, but with our forward motion, there was just a hint of refreshing breeze across the deck. As I stood at the bow, I began to stare in awe as one after the other large yachts in the outer harbor slid by. They were huge, and like little ants, the deck hands moved about their exteriors, busily engaged in their own cleaning and maintenance operations. All too quickly, they slid by and we were at the harbor exit. I walked up and over the foredeck saloon windows between the gap in the awning and stepped into the bridge deck surround. I walked around to the bridge wing door and into the bridge. Paul stood at the helm with both engine controls in hand. As we cleared the breakwater, he pushed them forward. The yacht trembled at the demand for power, and the props dug in. Before us lay a beautiful day with clear skies and flat seas that were as blue as the sky above. It was wonderful to be underway with a warm breeze flowing over us. Here I was, yachting on the French Riviera. We made a long, slow, wide sweep around to starboard at our ten-knot cruising speed, leaving the entire Cap d'Antibes to starboard. For a brief few moments, I stood in front of the bridge windows, looking out over the bow at the beautiful blue Mediterranean sliding under the yacht and just plain enjoying the moment. It felt wonderful to break free of the shackles of port and maintenance to get this yacht to work, but time for daydreaming was limited. We needed to get ready to arrive at our first destination. The boss wanted to anchor at the Cap d'Antibes Hotel. As we circled around the Cap to the far western side, it was not long before we arrived at our anchorage. It was not much of a bay, but what there was was dominated by a short, steep vertical rock face, atop which stood a swimming pool and waterside restaurant area. This was the millionaires' and film stars' playground. It was one of the places to be seen, and my boss had a tennis appointment. Paul nudged close into the bay, and with a splash, the engineer lowered the anchor as Paul reversed out, laying a good length of cable on the sea floor. I was able to stare at the pool and waterside club as the occupants lazed in the sun with waiters buzzing back and forth, fulfilling their endless wishes. Above them, the beautifully manicured gardens, lined with palm trees, stretched away from the pool club up towards the majestic hotel in the distance. Even from here, I could sense that not a piece of pea shingle or a blade of grass was out of place.

Paul snapped me out of my daydreaming. We needed to get the

ship's tender over the side. First, we had to get the boat boom swung out to starboard. This was a long pole, sticking straight out from the side of the yacht about ten feet above the water on the starboard side, which was supported by three strops to stop it swinging down aft or forward. On it was a pulley system to which you could attach the tender's mooring line and pull it out to the end of the pole. This kept the tender, when in the water, away from the ship's beautiful paintwork. Once the pole was out, we got to work up top. Paul swung the crane arm up and lowered the hook back down into the tender. I attached the stainless steel ring, to which were attached four steel strops, one to each corner of the tender. With the steel ring and its strops hooked up to the crane, I jumped out of the tender, and Paul hoisted away. Fore and aft painters were used to control the swing of the tender as it was swung out and lowered to the waterline. Once it had been lowered to the main deck level, I hopped back in and got the outboard lowered and ready to start. Once finally in the water, I started the engine and disconnected the four cables, and I was free to take off. Paul told me to take the tender for a quick spin around to get used to it. I needed no second invitation. I headed slowly out to sea, and then, when well clear, I floored it.

Having had a short burst of great fun, I headed back and, with great care, brought the boat to a halt at the ladder now hanging from the open gate amidships on the starboard-side main deck. I passed up the mooring lines fore and aft and leapt up the ladder before Paul attached the bowline and ran it out to the end of the boat boom. It was late morning, and we now waited at the boss's pleasure. While waiting, I checked over the yacht and was a little peeved to find a very fine salt coating on everything from the waterline up. I couldn't figure out where this salt had come from. We had only just set out from the harbor barely half an hour ago with immaculate topsides and deck. It dawned on me that the very fine mist, kicked up from the bow wave, had been carried up in the draft generated from our own forward motion and coated much of the yacht. I was infuriated that so much hard work could so quickly be undone. To date, I had never given a stuff about saltwater. After a delivery, I had quickly thrown a hose over the topsides and thought no more about it, but here on the French Riviera that new car look sparkling in the sunshine was all that mattered. Not only was it a competition among owners in terms of "mine is bigger than yours" but, just as importantly, in terms of "mine is shinier than yours." It was the creed all captains and deckhands lived by. It was all that mattered in the glittering competition of French Riviera yachting. No longer was the sea my friend. In the space of one short twenty-five minute trip, we had become enemies! I was beginning to realize that the price of cruising in these beautiful yachts is that days of hard work could be undone in a heartbeat and that it would be necessary to start the washdown and clean up all over again at the earliest opportunity.

I set about with a bucket and fresh water to clean all the windows at least. Then, I used fresh water to clean off the brass drums of the anchor windlass before once again using brasso and considerable elbow grease to bring back the shine. I also noticed the clean and shiny metallic bollards were coated in salt and provided another source of irritation to my newfound "clean yachting eye". They too needed attention. The scuppers, which barely an hour ago were sparkling and clean, now, with a fine coating of moist salt, seemed to attract the finest dust and dirt in the atmosphere. They were an abomination and, like the rest of the yacht, needed cleaning, but the boss wanted to go ashore and, as first mate/deckhand, it was my job to get him there. Paul reeled in the bowline from the outer end of the boat boom, and Sally took the stern line as I jumped in and got the outboard started. The boss clambered down the ladder and stepped in. Ready for his tennis, I delivered him to the steps of the pool club and returned to the yacht. As I circled the yacht round the bow to her starboard side, she looked magnificent at anchor, framed against the French Riviera.

However, upon return, I now had a new job. I had to tend to the VHF. I was on radio watch for the boss. He would call if he needed anything or if he wished to return to the yacht, so I clipped on the handheld VHF and carried on with the cleaning. The crew lunch was now confined to the galley and generally taken in shifts.

The afternoon bought more back and forth to the hotel for both the boss and his wife. By late afternoon, they both returned and opted for a swim and, still suffering from jet lag, announced they would not be going ashore again. We could now square things away for the evening. The tender was kept out on the boat boom while the swim ladder was lifted out and stowed back on its rack and the side door shut and secured. By early evening, I set about putting all the cushion covers back on to keep the dew off during the night. At sunset, I lowered the ensign at the aft end of the boat deck and the courtesy flags flying at the masthead. Finally, all the ship's deck lights were switched on. Pino fed the crew and worked his magic on the boss. I, along with the rest of the crew, had five areas we could hang around in with the boss on board. They were the galley, not generally welcome when Pino was cooking for guests, the port-side main deck just outside the galley, the foredeck, the bridge and the crew cabin. When not working or eating, I was quite happy to be horizontal in my bunk, which sadly, with days starting at 06.00 a.m., often being on radio watch and pick up at around midnight, was not as often as I would have liked. Luckily, with the girls looking after the boss, there were no further demands on me, and I could get an early night. We were to spend many more such days and would come to know the Cap d'Antibes area well.

With the boss on board, the morning routine changed little for me. On hands and knees and always in complete silence, I would sponge-clean the scuppers on the main deck and boat deck. Then, I would sweep around the varnished outdoor tables on the aft deck and boat deck. Finally, it was off with the cushion covers on the sundeck and time to lay out the rest of the cushions for the seating areas on the boat deck and aft deck. After this, I might start cleaning windows, first with a bucket and sponge, followed by squeegee and finally Windex and paper towel. Time in port bought forth a flurry of activity for all. The chef would dash ashore to load up on all groceries and dry stores. This was a considerable effort for him, and he would usually commandeer the services of one of the stewardesses. The engineer used the time for oil changes and spare parts purchases. With access to endless amounts of fresh water, I would set about getting the deck scrubbed and a full wash-down completed and replenish the boson's stores. Paul would conduct the entire "orchestra", including the demands of the boss, from the confines of the radio room.

As the season progressed, Paul and I developed a great working relationship. Whether at anchor or in port, he trusted me completely to make sure he could just walk to the helm, start the engines and go. For his part, he did not interfere at all with how I ran things on deck. I had never enjoyed such autonomy, and I never would again, until I became a skipper later in life.

The boss liked to cruise the entire Côte d'Azur, ranging from the Porquerolles Islands to the west of St. Tropez to as far afield as Monaco. This area was where we would spend the bulk of our summer. I loved the short hops between ports and anchorages. It kept things busy and interesting, with the endless call for lines, fenders, boat booms, tenders, swim ladders and occasional bridge watch-keeping in-between, but getting into port was always an intriguing problem. St. Tropez was an excellent case in point. St. Tropez, like Monaco and Antibes, was a place to be seen. I imagine that before Bridget Bardot and yachting arrived on the horizon, this would have been just another sleepy little port on the Mediterranean. It is very picturesque, with an outer breakwater running east west of a few hundred metres that connects to the northern end of town. The town, the front of which runs in an almost perfect semicircle, from the end of the breakwater around the inner harbor, makes for a unique port visit. The backdrop of the town is the usual sun-baked landscape. The buildings surrounding the harbor look exactly as they should for Mediterranean ports and are huddled right next to each other, containing shops, restaurants and cafés. Tucked discreetly among this array of retail activity were a number expensive shops and restaurants that catered to the wealthy clientele moored up just in front of them. Now, generally, it helped to have known George, the harbormaster from the previous year. As one progressed down towards St. Tropez, generally from the east, while still a couple of hours out, Paul would call up George and ask if a slot was available for the night, but it was always a difficult balance. If you arrived too late in the day, you probably would not get a berth. Too early, and having laid your anchors in the port, all the other late arrivals would lay their cables over the top of yours, making an early exit the next day impossible. George needed to be looked after so that he never forgot you. That meant money!

First came the problem of berthing. Having established that he had a spot available, Paul slowed the yacht down as we headed into the bay, leaving the breakwater to port. Paul turned the yacht 180 degrees round to port, now heading slowly east to enter the outer harbor. My job included flaking out the port and starboard stern lines, which were attached to heaving lines now lying over the cap rail coiled and ready to go. Peter had lowered both anchors to just above the water, and they were ready to drop as soon as Paul requested it. Finally, all fenders were lowered over the side, hanging at the same height. George and one of his harbor assistants were waiting dockside to indicate which spot he wanted us to back into. As we approached the inner semicircle, Paul had the yacht lined up perfectly and ordered the starboard anchor let go. Then, with thirty degrees of starboard wheel on, slow ahead port and half astern starboard, the yacht swung gracefully around in a tight half circle to starboard and ended up slightly offset to port from the correct angle for a straight line to our berth. This was the moment the port anchor was let go.

Now, it was my turn to help. I was in effective command of the vessel. The yacht had no bridge wing controls, and Paul had to operate going astern blind by using the main engine controls by the helm in the bridge and my directions over the handheld VHF. He needed to know the distance to the quay, as well as the proximity of the yachts and anchor cables to port and starboard. I had seen a fine example of how not to do this when I watched a poor stewardess perform the same task when the first mate was unavailable. The skipper spun the yacht around and started to reverse towards the quay when I heard the captain say over the VHF, "How far to the quay?" to which the response came back, "How the fuck should I know!"

It was honest, if a little unhelpful and perhaps not quite in keeping with VHF etiquette! When I first started out, I was hesitant, but over the two years that Paul and I worked together, we became a well-oiled machine. He never failed to act on my instruction, and I never gave him an incorrect direction. Still, sometimes, nudging into tight berths became an interesting operation, often requiring inventive methods. On more than one occasion, we would be the last yacht to arrive at a berth only half as wide as required. For Paul, it seemed no problem. He would back down onto the berth, and just as we were on the point of contact with a neighboring vessel, he would give a sharp hard blast ahead on the engine controls. The ensuing prop wash would not only stop the yacht, but as the wash jumped out from astern, it would push the neighbors apart. With another blast of astern thrust, we powered in before the gap slammed shut. In such circumstances, the fenders were often working overtime, but when we did it well, we looked like geniuses.

Still, on our first visit, it was steady as she goes. The cables were paid out, and we slid backwards under Paul's steady guidance and my faltering but steady instructions. We made it to the quay, and I threw the heaving lines and sent the stern lines ashore, making them up on the bollards. In no time, the gangway was ashore, and before long, a charming gentleman who introduced himself as George was standing on the aft deck, hoping to see the captain. I showed him to the bridge, where they greeted each other like long-lost brothers. I left them to it, but George had been paid. I never knew quite what amount he was paid on this first visit, but we were assured of a berth all summer long with the usual proviso of another gratuity on the next visit. Still, the quick math was impressive. With between thirty-five and forty-five significant motor yachts in the inner harbor for each night throughout the summer, all probably slipping George 500 francs a night for four months of the summer season, it was a good income. Suffice to say George must have been doing all right. He certainly seemed cheerful enough. It had to be the best municipal job in the world. Almost all guests liked to visit St. Tropez, although to be frank, I was never quite sure why. I think it was just one of those places that one had to "tick off" the itinerary when visiting the French Riviera. We never seemed to stay long, a night at a time, which must have said something about the place. Apart from the shops along the front and the beach on the south shore with a delightful restaurant, you could "do the place" in a morning and quite happily move on, which we invariably did.

Another of the boss's great favorites was Monaco. A couple of hours' steaming to the east of Antibes, it is a place unto its own. The small principality is governed by one of Europe's oldest royal families. It was always an impressive place at which to arrive. The outer breakwater ran, in the eighties, more or less north and south, split in the middle by the entrance way. The inner harbor was large but somehow dwarfed by the massive, steep rise of the mountainside to the north and the slightly smaller promontory to the south, atop of which sat the royal palace of the Grimaldi family. The entire amphitheatre of rock and mountain was covered in buildings and apartment blocks that just oozed money. It is, of course, home to legendary casinos and beautiful hotels, but even the boss grumbled after having been to a local hotel and paid double-digit dollars for a single bowl of cornflakes. Monaco was a unique visit and generally evoked either love or hate. Personally, it was no great favorite of mine. Once again, we never seemed to stay for long. Whenever we visited, we entered the harbor, went to port and parked stern-to along the inside of the outer breakwater, but from our berth, when on the foredeck or bridge, we always got a wonderful view of Monaco and the entire goings on. It was a noisy place, with the semicircle of mountain and city reflecting the noise back in on itself. Generally, we would only go to Monaco a couple of times a year.

Midway through the season, the boss, who must have been well-connected, announced while at anchor of St. Jean Cap Ferrat that Prince Albert would be coming aboard for a dinner cruise. We got to work preparing everything until I, along with the boss, went ashore in the tender at the appropriate time to pick him up. He duly arrived with a small armada of security. I found myself in a situation not unlike having a chicken, a fox, a bag of grain and a river to cross, in which you can't leave the fox alone with the chicken or the chicken with the grain and you can't transport more than one at a time. The tender was small, and with the boss, his wife and me, we were already fairly full. We had only expected Prince Albert. However, he had turned up with some unknown beauty on his arm and a very close-cropped, thick-necked security detail. I wasn't sure whom to leave on the dock while I transported the individuals in turn back to the yacht. The boss came to my rescue.

He turned to the Prince and said, "Do you really need this lot tonight?"

Much to Prince Albert's credit, he laughed and waved them off. The prince sat on the last seat with the unknown beauty on his lap. We set off out to the yacht, which looked magnificent in the late evening with all her deck lights on. Once aboard, we remained at anchor for the early part of the evening, but when they sat down to dinner with minimal fuss, we secured the yacht for sea, weighed anchor and set off for a short dinner cruise. The engines were barely in gear, but it was a beautiful, calm evening. With the guests enjoying themselves, we slid gently up the coast, enjoying the twinkling lights ashore and the stars out over the jet black Mediterranean sea to the south. We eventually returned to the same anchorage and, before long, returned the Prince back ashore to, I suspect, a much-relieved security detail.

The days turned into weeks, and then, we started to tick off the months. The routine remained much the same, alternating between anchorage and port, hopping up and down the coast between St. Tropez and Monaco, but one spot on the Southern tip of the Cap d'Antibes became a regular stop for us. There was a small but very beautiful, almost circular anchorage, wide open at the southern end, from which a yacht could enter and exit. The boss developed a great tennis friendship with a fellow who had a house in this most exclusive of neighborhoods. It might be fair to say that this was some of the most costly and sought-after real estate on the entire south coast of France. The neighbors were rumored to be Latsis, of Greek shipping family fame, on one side and the family that owned Mercedes Benz on the other. These were just rumors, but it shows the caliber of wealth required to own and maintain property here. Anyway, sandwiched between these two neighbours was a small but beautifully appointed beach house with a traditional clay tile roof and shutters around the windows. The garden was small and fell away to the large concrete deck area built into the rock face down at the water's edge. This housed changing rooms, showers, acres of flat with sun loungers, and finally a stepladder down to the sea. The whole house and property had clearly had a fortune spent on them to give them that just-right look so that, without being ostentatious, it fit in magnificently with the palm trees and lush vegetation. The owners of this house became good friends of the boss, and much time was spent in each other's company.

For myself, I was loving my busy days, often full of physical activity: washdowns, deck scrubbing, watch keeping and tender driving. In-between times, when possible, I would happily help out the chef or stewardess if required. From dawn till late at night, the days flew by as we alternated between ports and anchorages.

There was one place that I loved to visit that gave a real flavor of the desolate beauty of the hot Mediterranean, and that was the area in and around Porto Cervo and the Bonifaccio straits. At least a couple of times a year, we would make the trip down to this area. It was rarely a disappointment and always an opportunity for the stewardesses to fall in love at least once.

When the boss announced we should head to Sardinia, Paul called ahead and organized a berth. We would do the usual provisioning before setting off in the late afternoon. The boss preferred to sleep through the delivery, and so we departed at sunset, leaving a beautiful fiery sky over the French coast astern as we headed south and east into the darkness. There was nothing like standing out on a bridge wing on a beautiful Mediterranean night, sliding through the jet black sea with everyone asleep and just the stars and warm breeze for company. By late morning the next day, we arrived at the entrance to Porto Cervo in northern Sardinia.

Much of Sardinia looks as if it had been put through a blast furnace: hot, barren and desolate. However, carved out of it all was a magnificent millionaires' paradise. To me, it seemed a little like St. Tropez. Apart from a few shops, a nice yacht club and a good hotel, you could do this place quite quickly, but there was nothing else like it in the area, and so Porto Cervo became an essential stop over if we were visiting Corsica and Sardinia. As we slid through the entrance between rocks and slowed to a halt inside the harbor, we were surrounded by young guys flying around on zodiac rubber dinghies. The grip extensions to the outboard engine control allowed them to stand up. Their job was to direct you and pick up the mooring lines from the dock and run them out to you so your bowman could pick them up as you backed down to your 'stern to' berth. However, it was the speed at which these guys could fly round the harbor, turning on a dime and all while standing up, that was impressive. Now, add into the mixture shoulder-length hair and deep Mediterranean suntans, and it was more than the girls on board could handle. They were draped over the cap rail, watching the guys' every move as they dashed about all over the harbor, never missing a beat. It was not just the stewardesses on our yacht. The girls on the other yachts were just the same. These guys must have had a fantastic time in the bars when all these girls, having completed their duties aboard, got ashore later in the evening.

It was not the port that interested me; it was the area around the Bonifacio straits that I preferred. This body of water separated Corsica and Sardinia and was often windy, sometimes extremely so, but scattered around this strait were numerous beautiful anchorages, desolate and deserted, with golden sandy beaches and stunning clear blue water. It was the isolated beauty that appealed to me in this area, but we never seemed to stay long here, more often than not because the wind would start to blow again.

It was never long before we would leave this beautiful place and head back up to Antibes, where I was to have an amusing encounter with a guest onboard. It had been a port-bound day, with the guests doing their thing ashore. Having shut down the yacht, I had just finished crew dinner and was enjoying a quiet moment outside the galley on the main side deck. It was a particularly beautiful evening, absolutely still, which was not unusual for the time of year. The crew was particularly relaxed because the boss had declared his intention to head ashore for the evening. As I leaned against the paintwork, thinking about nothing in particular, one of the guests appeared around the corner from the aft deck. She began advancing towards me quite slowly and deliberately, but it was what she was wearing that got my full attention. From the waist down, the dress, which was bright red, ballooned out almost as women's dresses did in the late 1950s. From the waist up, it was of a skintight veil material, completely see-through, with no bra and quite a magnificent chest. As this apparition advance towards me, a raging battle began between the testosterone coursing through my veins and my own rule that guests, wives and daughters of owners were most definitely out of bounds. With every fiber of my being straining at the leash and a valiant, desperate effort to maintain eye contact, this woman came to a halt a couple of feet in front of me.

"Good evening Gus. How do I look?"

"Magnificent," I replied, "I hope you'll excuse me, I have a couple of things I need to sort out." It was pathetic, but in the heat of the moment, it was the best I could do. With that, I spun round on my feet and headed to the foredeck.

The season was fast coming to an end, and before we knew it, the boss's bags were packed. It had been agreed that I would be kept on for winter maintenance, but with the boss gone, I dashed back to the U.K. for a holiday. I had a gap, and knew that gaps might not occur with great regularity going forward. I had to use it to my best advantage. I was dreading it, but I had no choice. I had to head back to the classroom. I was now in a position to start work towards my Ocean Yachtmaster certification. This, like the Yachtmaster Offshore certificate, was split into two portions: first, the classroom course and written exam, and secondly, the examination for the final certification. However, for the final examination, the candidate had to prepare a file on a real passage, covering all aspects of the voyage from planning to execution, including all sextant navigation work, and present it upon return to the U.K. for appraisal. Should your work pass inspection, then and only then would you be presented with your Ocean Yachtmaster certification. However, that was in the future. Right now, I was concerned with taxing my limited grey matter with understanding the complexities of star navigation. I had failed this miserably at Dartmouth, and I saw little reason to think things would be much different now.

I found myself back in Lymington in early October of 1986, standing in front of the Lymington Seamanship & Navigation Centre and wondering what delights of intellectual titillation waited within. As I sat down, I was handed a sheet covering the course work, which included the following:

1. The Earth and the Celestial Sphere
2. The PZX Triangle
3. The Sextant
4. Measurement of Time
5. Meridian Altitude
6. Sun Sights
7. Planet Sights
8. Star Sight Planning
9. Star Sights
10. The Pole Star
11. Moon Sights
12. Compass Checking
13. Great Circle Sailing
14. Meteorology
15. Passage Planning

Looking through the list, you might think it doesn't look so bad. It's written in generally understandable English. However, while item one seemed innocuous enough, in the R.Y.A. logbook for 1983 under the title "broad detail to be covered" it read:

1. Definition of observer's zenith and position of a heavenly body in terms of latitude, longitude, GHA and declination.
2. Right angle relationships, latitude and co-lat, declination and polar distance. Tabulation of declination in nautical almanac.
3. Relationship between GHA, longitude and LHA. The tabulation of GHA in the almanac. Rate of increase of hour angle with time.

That was just the breakdown of item one. All I could think as I read through this was *good luck to the instructor getting me through this*. As we proceeded through the course, I found myself in the curious position of being utterly fascinated and in love with the subject I was being taught and, at the same time, totally unable to understand any of it. It really was most frustrating. Throughout my time at school, I had never understood the relevance or importance of mathematics, and here, I was dealing with a most elegant example of how it could be put to good use. I was determined, despite my feeble mathematical mind, to get my head around this problem. It required intense concentration and very late nights of study. But slowly, very slowly, I began to get just a glimmer of understanding of how it all worked together. I became anxious as our final classroom exam approached because I was by no means fluent in this complex subject. There was, however, one method of finding position that if done correctly, could produce a respectable fix. The beauty of it was its relative simplicity: the sun-run-meridian altitude. Broadly speaking, it requires an early morning sight of the sun with a sextant. Following a few simple calculations, you obtain a single "line of position", which is then plotted on a chart. At the time of doing this sight, the log reading is noted. A sight for latitude is then done at local mean time, in other words, the point at which the sun is highest in the sky in your particular location, and once again, the log reading is noted. The first sight or line of position is then run on the distance between the two log readings to provide a two-line position fix. The results are not perfect, but you obtain a position nonetheless. I liked the simplicity of this method, as opposed to taking four star sights and trying to work through the long process of looking up information and calculations with endless possibilities for mistakes. A highly competent navigator would frown upon me, I'm sure, but in later life, I became quite competent at sun-run-meridian altitudes.

The final exam was every bit as intimidating as I expected it to be, but somehow, I limped through and was presented with my certificate of completion of the shore-based course of the Ocean Yachtmaster. I would now have to find an opportunity to lead an ocean passage to complete the final exam requirements.

I returned to Antibes and the *Star of the Sea* refreshed and ready for action. The winter maintenance list was considerable, and Paul wasted little time getting me going. The cable locker below the focsle deck forward had to be stripped out and painted. While this was being done, I lowered both anchors and cables onto a floating raft before transferring them dockside so they could be taken away and regalvanised. When they returned, they looked new. I laid them out in the car park and sprayed on markings so we knew how much cable was being paid out during anchoring. In the previous season, this had been done largely by guesswork—not very scientific! I never needed to drink in the evening after work while painting the anchor locker. I was wrecked at the end of each day from the paint fumes in the confined space. The result, once complete, was fantastic. With the unused fenders stowed with their new fender covers, along with the sparkling cables, it really did look good.

There was a wealth of other activity going on around the yacht. Paul had arranged for a colorful Greek named Yanni to paint both the interior and various exterior patches. He had a wonderful, positive sense of humor and was always bouncing from one foot to the other while gesticulating with his arms. He had thinning hair with the remaining wisps going grey, and one of his eyes had a rather messed-up iris that caused you to stare at it while not being quite certain where his eye was looking. He promised the world on a shoestring budget and usually delivered woefully late and at double the cost, but he was great fun and, when on form, laid a beautiful coat of paint, all by brush. At his finest, he was a delight to watch. There was also an entirely new batch of cushion covers to have made, which kept the mobile van of Trehard well busy on the quayside. This was an impressive operation. The entire side of the van lifted up to reveal a complete cutting and sewing setup inside. The two guys who operated it couldn't have been more different. The boss was the shorter of the two, with a slight potbelly and long hair that generally hung in a mop around his face. His sidekick was quite the opposite: tall with neatly-cropped hair, bright eyes and full of energy. In their different ways, they were always keen to help, and once the fabric had been selected and measurements taken, they would be hunched over their machines, sewing like maniacs. In no time flat, they would be back with a finished product, which after so many years on the job, invariably fitted the first time round.

During the long quiet months of the winter season, we would use part-time stewardesses who lived ashore but came to work Monday to Friday and worked pretty much office hours. The stewardess we had this particular winter was very competent and pleasant to have around and equally impressive, at least as far as I was concerned, she was absolutely stunning—not particularly tall but very shapely, with an exquisite face and a short crop of mousy blonde hair. One particular lunchtime, she asked if she could have the afternoon off, and not thinking much about it, I said sure. She promised to pop back in at the end of the workday just to make sure everything was fine. Sure enough, much later that afternoon, she returned looking even more stunning than usual, with a professional makeup job. None of us were slow to notice, and I decided to jump in and find out what she had been up to.

"Whoa, you look good. Where have you been?" I asked.

"Oh," she began, "I've been on a photo shoot."

With her good looks, it didn't surprise me, but what came next did.

"Cool," I said, "for a fashion magazine?"

"Oh no, a porn mag."

She said it without the slightest hesitation or embarrassment. She even offered up which month she would be in. The news traveled up and down the quay, and I expect sales of that particular magazine on the particular month in question must have seen a spectacular spike in the Antibes area. Just in case the reader is wondering, she looked even better naked!

Having been trained by Martin at the end of the previous winter and with a full season under the belt, I was moving through the yacht's worklist with speed and confidence. One innocuous day, which I thought would pan out just as any other, Peter the engineer hailed me with an interesting pronouncement.

"Gus, we've sprung a leak. Do you want to have a look?"

I was hardly in a position to say no. Paul was off the yacht, so with Peter leading the way down into the engine room, I followed, somewhat curious. Having stepped off the ladder and turned round, I could hardly miss it. With the deck plates lifted between the engines, arcing up from the middle was an inch-wide stream that reached about four or five feet before collapsing back down onto the piled deck plates with a splat.

"Very nice!" I said to Peter, unable to think of anything more sensible to say at that moment in time. Trying to do better, I added, "How did it happen?"

"Well," replied Peter, "I was cleaning out the muck in the bilge with this scrapper on the end of the broom handle, and it just went right through."

This, I thought, raised more questions than answers. If this happened in one spot, where else on the hull might we have a problem?

We both stared at it for some time, not quite sure what to do next. I had never been on a steel-hulled vessel that had sprung a leak, but I realized that with Paul off the yacht, I had better start thinking. Clearly, we needed to plug the hole. I could only come up with one solution, and that was to fabricate two small metal plates with a bolt running through them. I summoned the port diver while Peter got to work cutting the plates. Around the plate to be on the outside, we placed a strip of double-sided, spongy foam bedded down with loads of sealant to hopefully create a watertight seal. As soon as the diver arrived, we explained the problem and our proposed solution, and down he went. He found the hole, and placed the plate over it while Peter applied the other plate and nut from the inside before tightening the whole thing down. It worked.

Now, our problems really began. I immediately tracked down Paul, who was away in the hills behind Antibes and told him the problem. He returned immediately and Peter, Paul and myself sat down to decide what was next. Despite the looming season, the boss needed to be informed that we had to arrange to go to a shipyard and be hauled out for a full hull inspection. The boss, who had been an owner for long enough, was very understanding and told us to do whatever was necessary. Luckily, being near the beginning of the season, most yachts in the area had completed their winter yard refit work, and we were able to find a slot with ease at a yard only a couple of hours' steaming up near Monaco at St. Jean Cap Ferrat.

With the yacht now hauled out, the hull sprayed off, the fuel tanks emptied and the gas freed, the surveyor set to work to investigate the integrity of the hull. We were lucky that the only real problem was isolated to the one weak spot that Peter had found. The necessary patch was cut out and repaired, and with a fresh coat of antifoul, we slipped back into the water and returned to Antibes with haste. We all dug out to make up for lost time and managed to start the season pretty much on schedule.

The season panned out in a similar fashion to the previous one. Our ports of call and favorite anchorages remained the same, but towards the middle of the season, Paul decided he was ready to move on to a job on dry land. He made it almost to the end but left with a final couple of weeks to go. There had been some talk of me taking over, but I was just not ready. So the skipper next door, whose season had already finished, agreed to take us out as needed. With Paul's departure, I too was ready to move on, and I was about to hit the big time.

NINE

Pilar

For many years, Glen had been the second in command of argu-ably the most significant motor yacht of the time, the *Nabila*. Owned by Adnan Khasoggi, an arms dealer, the yacht had a berth in the outer harbor of Antibes, and Glen and myself had met on a couple of occasions. Unknown to me, during my final year aboard the *Star of the Sea*, Glen had gotten a command of his own. He was now skipper aboard a 165-foot Feadship named *Pilar*. I got a call asking if I would come aboard as first officer. This was a huge step up for me, but I jumped at the chance.

Without doubt, during the 1980s, Feadship, or the Federation of Dutch Shipbuilders, was arguably the dominant global force in the construction of steel-hulled motor yachts of this size. *Pilar* was a testament to this.

I joined in Nassau, Bahamas, arriving at a rather rickety wooden quay to which was attached a most beautiful motor yacht. This was my first opportunity to get up close to any Feadship. She was painted white from masthead to waterline and consisted of an expansive open sundeck wrapped around a solid and angular mast, from which the engine exhaust exited. The boat deck was split in two, with the aft section, all in shade, given over to the tenders and an outdoor seating area for guests. The forward half had the boss's office, radio room, ship's office, bridge and captain's cabin. The main deck had an enormous saloon with a separate dining room at the forward end. Accessed by a small flight of stairs at the aft end of the saloon were four guest cabins. The crew area occupied the area below the foredeck, with direct access, through a soundproof door, to the engine room. Most of the crew cabins were spacious twin berths. The chief engineer and I were to enjoy the ultimate luxury of our own cabins. The attention to detail during construction was evident in the seamless and simple way all elements of the exterior and interior flowed together. There were no misfitting parts of poorly constructed elements. It was clear, as I looked her over, that great thought had been put into every part of the design and construction phase to produce this masterpiece. I never tired of standing on the bridge, staring out over the bow. Whether underway or alongside, the sheer size was a magnificent sight. Just as I had arrived aboard *Star of the Sea* mesmerized, so I was with the jump up in size and quality of finish with *Pilar*. Once again, despite my association with this industry, I was still awestruck that one man could not only buy but also afford to run such a vessel. Without doubt, this would be the finest motor yacht I would ever sail aboard.

With the jump up in size from *Star of the Sea* came a bigger crew. It was also international in flavor. The junior stewards and deckhands were Filipino; the chief steward, captain and I were British and both engineers were German. My deck department consisted of three and was led by the bosun, John. They were invariably cheerful, knew their jobs and worked hard.

Having stepped aboard in the Bahamas, little time was wasted on pleasantries because we had a minor alongside refit to conduct. The boss, on a previous visit before my arrival, had stated his dissatisfaction with the deck head in the saloon and wished to make some minor alterations to the aesthetics. To achieve the change, it was necessary to remove all the deck head panels throughout the saloon and start again. This was a major operation requiring an extensive team of professionals. The boss not only had exquisite taste in motor yachts, he also had absolutely no problem spending the money required to maintain them. His mantra seemed to be that only the best would do. He insisted that an entire team of professionals be sent out from the

Feadship shipyard. The shipyard was delighted to oblige, and once the team arrived, I began to see the wisdom of the boss's ways.

They set to work immediately. First, the furniture in the saloon was stacked up and covered before work began on pulling down the deck head. This was complicated by the presence of numerous light fixtures and smoke detectors, all of which had to be allowed for in the new deck head. With the teardown complete, work could begin on the rebuild. It consisted of the same plywood board covered with white leather, but this time, there would be a thin foam insert to give "depth" to the finished look. Before the work started, I was rather skeptical that there would be much difference. However, as the new panels went up, I began to see what the boss was driving at. As work continued inside, the outside was to be cleaned up as well.

This was a working yacht in the sense that it spent considerable time at sea. The constant working of the hull and topsides would invariable work the seams and joints, and consequently, cracks and blisters would appear in the paintwork. So at the same time as the interior work was going on, the Feadship yard, at our request, had also sent out paint specialists. They had two jobs: the rather obvious paint repairs around the yacht and recaulking some areas of the deck where the black caulking between the stripes of teak was breaking free. For John, the two deckhands and me, it was a wonderful time to watch our work be completed by some of the finest craftsmen in the world in their field. Their ability to clean, prepare and paint the exposed metal was impressive, as was their ability to fill and sand to absolute perfection, but where these guys really stunned me was in their ability to apply paint. Most of the paint systems used on yachts were derivatives of paints used in the aircraft industry. They were complex to apply correctly and most certainly required rigorous standards of surface preparation prior to painting. Done in the best of environments with specialist applicators, the effect was stunning: a new car finish for an entire 165 feet of yacht from bow to stern and masthead to waterline. It could be time-consuming and expensive to achieve such results. Despite the fact that these painters were used to the clinical conditions of their environmentally-controlled paint shed, in the dusty outdoors, they could still work magic. With decades of painting experience under their belts, they were able to adjust the mixtures on a daily basis depending on their perceptions of heat and humidity. From bare metal to topcoat, as they moved methodically throughout the exterior surfaces of the yacht, if one man was not satisfied with the previous man's work, he was called back to improve. Not one of these guys would put his name to a piece of work unless he felt it justified the "Feadship badge".

The team was a sober, hardworking and thoroughly dedicated bunch of individuals. Watching them work was impressive, and I began to understand just exactly what was required to build one of the finest yachts in the world. All this team had achieved was done in the "field". Finally, both interior and exterior teams pronounced themselves satisfied that they had completed all that was asked of them. With a deck scrub and washdown for the exterior, and a vacuum and dust for the inside, she once again looked good as new. The work was finished just in time because the boss was coming and he too wanted to see what had been achieved.

The boss arrived, and just like my last one, he looked the part. Of average height, he had acquired the usual grey hair from a life spent dedicated to the demands of acquiring wealth. He had strong features and eyes that had seen it all. He was quick to smile and seemed a man thoroughly at ease, enjoying all the trappings of his success. His wife, as befits a billionaire, had the stunning hair and looks of a voluptuous Italian. From head to toe, she was well-manicured and well-dressed. With her wonderful laugh, she seemed, like her husband, to be enjoying every minute of life.

His first order of business was to summon the crew to the bridge. We were all waiting anxiously when he suddenly appeared from his office, along with his wife, clutching a suitcase that he plunked down on the bridge seat. I was a little stunned when he opened it up and started handing out small gifts. It might be a shirt here or small camera there. Even more impressively, when handing out a gift, he would recount a conversation with the recipient along the lines off "I remember when we were talking you mentioned…" Here was a busy billionaire who was taking time out of his hectic schedule to go shopping with the memories of snippets of conversation accompanying him on his quest for gifts, but it perhaps said as much about his love of his yacht as it did about his attention to the people who worked for him.

In a quiet moment one day, he told me a little of his background. He had had a rough childhood and decided during his early teens that he could take no more of his father's abuse and left home. He made his way to the local train station, and with no money, made it to the city. Once there and homeless, he set about finding low-wage jobs. He quickly found work and accommodations. Through long hours and hard work, he gravitated towards the world of finance, and once there, as they say, the rest was history. I also remember sympathizing with him on the appalling cost of running this beautiful yacht, to which he responded with a chuckle about how right I was, especially when combined with the additional cost of running the sailing yacht and private jet, which he also owned. But apparently it was the jet that really stung as an overhead. I didn't know how to respond. My idea of cost was air flights, hotel bills and dinner out. Motor yachts, sail yachts and private jets seemed a little obscure. Still, he was, without doubt, a most interesting man to chat with, and he was still a workaholic. We had two fax machines on board with dedicated gyro-stabilized satellite communications so that at any time or place, he could maintain contact with his headquarters. It would not be unusual for him to have both faxes going at once, with a sixty or seventy-page transmission coming and going.

The boss's visit was brief, and it was not long before I accompanied him to the airport where his jet waited. His pilot and co-pilot greeted him with a combination of professionalism and courtesy borne of much time in each other's company. The pilot looked like something out of *Top Gun* with his tidy uniform, Ray Bans and easy manner. The jet was indeed magnificent and rather dwarfed the small offerings of other private planes at the field. It had three engines, one tail-mounted and two on each side. With his luggage whisked away by his attentive aircrew standing at the bottom of the ladders, he shook my hand and bid me bon voyage. He trotted up the steps to the rather beautiful stewardess at the door and disappeared inside. Now that was the way to fly. As I turned and walked away, I imagined him settling into a luxuriously appointed seat, the stewardess ready with his favorite drink and aperitifs, but for me, it was back to work and back to sea.

It was time to say farewell to the Nassau. We now had to head across the Atlantic. Our next stop was Europe, and I was sensing an opportunity. I had completed the ocean yachtmaster shore-based course and now had to complete an ocean passage as either skipper or navigator. In the back of my logbook was a very clear description of exactly what the R.Y.A. wanted in terms of information regarding a passage for final examination. It included, but was not necessarily limited to, the following:

1. An extract from the log of a yacht with details of planning, workings and plotting of a sun-run-meridian altitude.
2. The workings of the sight, including the plotting on the chart.
3. Photocopies of all relevant data concerning the information used to plot the position, the log book and all information used in the passage plan, including weather, personnel, stores and route planning.
4. Compass check.

I now had a template to work towards, but I also had a brand-new yacht and crew to get to know, and we were on the move, with the demands of watch-keeping and ongoing maintenance to consider. Glen and I were the only two bridge watch keepers onboard. During the night hours, Glen would do six to twelve, and I would do twelve to six. I never did get used to having so much of my REM sleep taken away from me during passages. The bridge of *Pilar* was almost exclusively satin-varnished teak, with leather trim around the instruments and engine controls. Amidships, among the instruments, there was a small vertically-mounted wheel for steering, which was rarely used because the gyrocompass and autopilot were almost always in use. The captain's chair sat on the starboard side of the bridge, along with a large guest sofa, against the aft bulkhead, giving commanding views out over the bow. On either side were bridge wing doors with access to the exterior side deck. It was a little disconcerting to arrive on the bridge in the dead of night to be told we were in a gale because it was totally silent. The quality of the construction around the bridge windows and doors kept all the noise out, and it was amusing trying to open the door with fifty knots over the deck as you anchored your feet and put your full weight into it. Night watch-keeping for so long was a struggle in such an environment. I was a little more used to the wind in my face and water trickling down my neck to keep me alert. The warmth and silence of this beautifully constructed bridge was not a friend to the sleep-deprived. I would constantly have to keep pacing back and forth across the bridge, and regardless of the prevailing weather conditions, I would push open the bridge wings doors and take a stroll around the front of the bridge windows. The yacht was not only a beauty to look at; she was also a great sea boat with a good average speed. On transoceanic voyages such as this, we could maintain in excess of twelve knots. We made short work of our trip to Horta Azores. The trip was completed in nine days. This was all achieved in the quiet confines of a luxurious bridge with temperature control and automation, which somehow managed to make the task of crossing the Atlantic seem a little mundane. Before, to be traveling at ten or twelve knots was confined to the exhilarating surf down the wave of an Atlantic storm, but now it was just a gentle tweak of the engine controls while sipping on a cup of fresh coffee. In crossing the Atlantic, this yacht had injected a nine-to-five quality into a task that only a couple of years previous, had felt like a cutting-edge adventure. It was a most peculiar transition. There is no doubt, particularly in reflection, that an ocean passage aboard a large motor yacht had managed to somehow trivialize the task of an Atlantic crossing. It seemed that from here on in, if I was to undertake such voyages, they would be relegated to just "another day at work".

However, in the Azores I was determined, with Glen's approval, to act as navigator for the leg up to Southampton and to try and complete all the requirements for my final exam. On the 15th of May, 1988, we set off from Horta for a four-day delivery. Being a relatively short trip with plenty of fuel, we could ring on our full cruising speed of a little over thirteen knots. It was a frustrating four days with hazy skies and poor opportunities for the sextant work that I so desperately needed. I only managed one feeble attempt, and it proved to be almost useless. Having arrived in the U.K., I realized, sadly, that I had scant material to present for my final exam. Still, I sent off what little I had and threw myself at the mercy of the examiner.

For some reason, we did not go to a local marina, where we no doubt would have quickly become a local news story. Instead, we berthed alongside in the commercial port of Southampton. It was almost deserted, and miles of empty quay were all ours. It was a lonely spot, and a dirty one. Whenever the wind blew, it would empty the entire area's dirt and dust all over the yacht. We were not particularly near the centre of town, and all in all, it was not much of a pit stop, but I did manage to get some friends and family to come aboard and have a look around. They, almost without exception, had yachting experience, but not like this. *Pilar's* sheer size was not something they had ever seen. As they wandered about the palatial decks and volu-minous interior, they clearly enjoyed getting a look at something most people would never see. Although they would never know it, the combination of visiting the U.K. and seeing friends and family triggered a chain of events that would, with the benefit of hind-sight, seem extraordinary, but for now we had a schedule to keep, and the next stop was London.

We now had the boss back on board. During passages, the boss would spend a large amount of time in his office, with views out over the boat deck and the stern. His office, which occupied the full width of accommodation aft of the radio room, was a wonder-ful space. His large desk dominated the room, but there were also a sofa and armchairs and still plenty of space to pace about. It was isolated from the rest of the ship, a quiet place with commanding views all around. He must have had wonderful moments while we were underway to just sit back and relax in the impressive silence of his office, gazing out over the wake as we slid through the ocean, but on this particular leg up the English Channel, he was keeping the fax machines going full bore. Between the skipper and me, we were busy going back and forth with a torrent of paperwork. In no time, we found ourselves at the outer reaches of the Thames estu-ary, where we took aboard a pilot. Getting the pilot aboard was no mean feat because the launch helmsman was a little more used to crunching alongside the battered, rusting hulls of merchant ships, but there was to be absolutely no battering alongside our hull! We spent quite some time fiddling with fenders and waving him off before we could finally settle the cutter alongside just long enough for the pilot to step aboard.

This achieved, I escorted him up to the bridge, where "To Pilot's advice and the Master's orders" we proceeded to enter the Thames. For us aboard, it was definitely a grand occasion. The crew lined the side decks and snapped furiously at the city as it slid gently by. As we proceeded past the Thames barrier deep into the heart of London, we were joined by a submarine and a tugboat. At last, the mighty Tower Bridge hove into view. It was clear that the boss was thoroughly enjoying himself. As a man who had spent his life involved in the tough world of finance, it must have been a proud moment to sail his magnificent yacht into the heart of one of the world's major financial centers. The Tower Bridge ramps parted and rose gently to nearly vertical as first the submarine, along with its tugboat, and then *Pilar* slid on through. The bridge closed behind us as we found our mooring buoys and proceeded with the difficult task of getting secured fore and aft in the current. Glen's prodigious experience with wriggling large yachts into stern berths in the south of France made the task of maneuvering a 165-foot yacht between two buoys in an unfamiliar tidal estuary look easy. In no time, we were secured, and now Londoners had something a little different to stare at besides HMS *Belfast* and Tower Bridge on this particular stretch of the Thames. We were not to stay long, and a day or so later, we slipped our mooring and proceeded down to Docklands, where we secured alongside in one of the quieter docks adjacent to a newly completed business and residential district.

While here, the boss had a young family member visit who was either studying or working in London. All I remember is that she was stunningly good-looking. She seemed to absolutely delight in being onboard, but she developed a particularly nasty habit. Whenever I was struggling in the bridge with some tedious piece of paperwork, she made a habit of parading through in a swimsuit that was quite clearly way too small for her. I had been at sea for far too long, and trying to maintain professional eye contact during the course of our meaningless conversations was almost more than I could bear. For her, I suspect, it was just excellent sport!

Perhaps it was youthful restlessness. Perhaps, it was seeing family members in Southampton and being in England. It may have been my endless desire to keep experiencing something new. No doubt the beauty on the bridge reminding me of what I was not getting did not help! In any event, with life going so well professionally, I was about to make a decision that with the benefit of hindsight, seems extraordinary, but I felt the tug of dry land and a peculiar desire to behave like a "normal adult" and get a real job! I informed Glen I would be leaving at the earliest opportunity to return to England. Glen made arrangements for my replacement, who would join in Gibraltar, where I would disembark. Having departed London, we made our way south before I was to experience one final reminder of all that I would be leaving behind. In Gibraltar, for my final night aboard, I was told to move to a guest cabin so my cabin could be cleaned prior to the arrival of my replacement. The beds were made up with satin sheets that were so smooth I feared I might slide right out onto the plush carpet, but before long, I was out of the cabin, on the quay and had returned to the U.K.

TEN
Aground

It was late summer of 1988, and to get things started on the right note, I got a letter informing me that I had provided insufficient information to the examiner and had therefore failed the final exam for my Ocean Yachtmaster. Well, that didn't go as planned! Still, I had an interesting opportunity appear. The yacht brokerage of Alistair Easton and Partners had been sold by Alistair, who I had previously sailed with aboard his x boat, to a fellow named Geoff, who was in need of an additional broker to man the office. Feeling that if I couldn't be at sea, I could remain attached to it by selling yachts, I interviewed and got the job. With my usual enthusiasm, I leapt through the door on day one, bouncing around and wondering how many boats I could sell before lunch. I was politely informed that that was not quite how things usually went and that I would have to park myself in a dark, quiet little corner and start to get to know my product.

The office was located at Bucklers Hard, on the Beaulieu River, to the side of a large and active builder's shed. You would be hard-pressed to find a more picturesque spot on the south coast of England. Apart from cars and motor yachts, the scene down the tranquil river, framed by a thick forest, had changed little for centuries. Nestled sporadically among the trees were some extremely expensive, tasteful properties that added to the beauty of the area. Whilst aboard the yachts, I occasionally found myself staring wistfully at the owners as they sipped champagne, staring idly over the stern. Now, I imagined myself sitting on the lawns of these beautiful properties, taking in the

English sunshine with only the wind rustling through the leaves of the forest for company.

Our products at Alistair Easton and Partners were the vessels moored along the river. Occasionally, we had yachts at other marinas, but for the most part, our domain was the Beaulieu River. I was on a small salary, small being the operative word. To boost my income, I needed commissions from selling yachts. Very quickly, it dawned on me that the successful broker was the individual who cultivated relationships over long periods of time, with a sense of trust that takes time to develop. Whenever the phone rang, quite reasonably, the caller would ask for Geoff, and whenever they got hold of me, they would find a rather useless source of knowledge or answers. Given five years, I'm sure I would have been fantastic, but sitting in a chair for hours at a time was driving me crazy. I tried my very best to remember all the lengths, widths and depths of yachts, what engine or engines they had with what horsepowers, the sails they carried, their original builders and maintenance histories, and finally the costs. The good brokers knew all about the yards at which they were built, and they had all the information on comparable yachts at their fingertips, ably directing a customer towards either proceeding with a purchase or getting a listing. I soon grasped that this situation could only by remedied with time and hard work.

Still, all was not lost. One particularly quiet day, a blunt-speaking Yorkshire man appeared at the door. He introduced himself as Bernard, and alongside him, was his wife Katie. He was over six feet with a high forehead, thinning grey hair and thick glasses. He had been inquiring about buying an Aquastar 32 and wanted to come in and proceed a little further down the avenue of investigating the process. I, as usual, was quite unable to help with the complexities of the legal documents regarding the purchase of such a vessel. However, we did get talking. His strong Yorkshire accent and bluff demeanor disguised a very keen mind and wonderful sense of humor. It was to be the start of a great friendship. He lived nearby in Lymington and promised to return to continue the discussions. True to his word he rang and arranged to come back when Geoff was there, but he insisted that I was also present during the conversation. I wasn't sure whether he wanted to improve my feeble knowledge base regarding the complexities of purchasing a yacht, or if he had some other reason.

Bernard and Katie arrived and sat down with Geoff. With no beating about the bush, they got down to the nitty gritty of price and specifications, covering everything from engine options to the material covering the cushions. I sat silently, trying, as usual, to learn all I could from the discussions. Finally, Bernard pushed back his chair and pronounced himself satisfied. Just as Geoff pushed the final document under Bernard's nose for signing, Bernard stated that he had one proviso prior to signing. He said that he would only agree to purchase the yacht if I agreed to instruct him and his wife on how to drive it. Bernard then added that he would be delighted to pay the company for my time, so this was agreed upon, and the deal was done. In short order, the yacht turned up, much to the delight of Bernard and Katie, who couldn't wait to get going. It was fully equipped with radar, a full galley, saloon, the standard heads and a V berth forward. The two petrol engines were a deviation from the more usual diesel. I arrived on day one to find a very proud pair of owners desperate to get going. I sat down and asked them both about their boating experience to date and was a little stunned to find they had never been yachting before. It was all brand new to them. Hmmm. To me, this was no different than someone buying a small plane with no flying experience and leaping in the front seat, hoping to take off. I decided we should go through some very basic fundamentals of safety before we did anything. I took them through the basics of VHF operation and channel 16 for emergencies. I made sure they knew where the flares and lifejackets were stowed and understood their correct operation. They were diligent in making sure they understood all aspects of what they were being taught. When necessary, they took notes. I taught them some knots and the basics of line handling. Then, I got them to crawl all over the boat and locate all the seacocks, fuel shut-offs, fill caps for water and fuel. We covered the safe operation of the windlass, which was electric and could be operated from the helm. Finally, I went over the engines in detail, including all fluid checks, impressing upon them that these were their safe passage home. No expense should be spared on servicing and maintaining the engines, and at all times when underway, regular checks of the instrumentation should be made, as well as frequent visual inspections, by lifting the hatches, and checking that all was well in the engine room. With regards to fuel levels, I said that they should never let them get too low and always operate with a very healthy margin for error. I told them to keep the bilges immaculate, which meant both clean and dry. This should be done for the obvious reason that a new leak, from whatever source, is far easier to spot in a clean, dry bilge than a dirty, wet one. Navigation was a long and complex subject for complete beginners, and despite their best efforts, it seemed clear that only a limited amount sunk in. It took quite a few lessons to cover some of the basics, and I felt it was time to get these guys out on the water.

Much to their delight, we finally let slip all the lines and got going. The most important thing we needed to get sorted out was boat handling. The business of putting the throttles down and going like a bat out of hell in a straight line was hardly taxing. However, spinning the yacht around in confined waters within her own length while allowing for the vagaries of tide, wind and current was quite another matter and required lots of practice.

The work at the yacht brokerage continued as Geoff tried to build business. We began trying to sell an Italian open speedboat built by the Cranchi family. They were great boats, at least for getting somewhere quick. I was dispatched to the London boat show at Earls Court to assist with trying to sell them under the bright spotlights and away from the typical English weather, which was not always conducive to open speedboat sales. Once again, it was interesting to experience at close hand those individuals who had been in the business, in some cases for decades, who could spot a potential buyer and know just how to reel him in. It wasn't just the shpiel; it was dealing with money and contracts, knowing how to adjust the numbers to suit the customer and knowing where there was financial flexibility and where there was none. Whenever I spoke with anybody and hovered around money questions, with my total lack of experience, I would invariably have to find somebody to assist. The customer would usually wander off or get grabbed by some other salesperson. The only thing I left the Earls Court boat show with was sore feet from standing all day in the wrong shoes. I was beginning to feel that I might not have the sales touch.

At every opportunity, I would get together with Bernard and Katie to continue the instruction. I loved fiddling around on boats and was always tempted to keep taking the helm, but having showed them once, I had to force myself to lay off and let them stick at it. Bernard always took the helm, and on the rare occasions Katie was let loose, she did seem to have a more natural understanding of what to do. We did it all, practicing to depart and arrive at the berth both forward and backwards in a variety of currents and winds. We would go down the river and practice picking up a mooring buoy and running a slip line through before dropping it and doing it all again. There were alongside maneuvers at a moored up pontoon on the river. They were tremendous company. He was an interesting fellow who had worked his way from the bottom to be the boss man of a large British company. They had three daughters and spoke of endless interesting exploits over the years, including a family holiday in the Rolls Royce to Paris. I informed Geoff that I had done all I could for them, but Bernard and Katie hadn't finished with me yet. They wanted to know if they could pay me independently of the company and continue the instruction. I was enjoying being out on the water with them and struck a deal that I would assist them free of charge if they provided lunch or dinner. This was Bernard's kind of deal, and with a very definitive "done" from him, we got cracking.

We began to set up longer voyages. We would meet down at the boat, where they were always waiting eagerly. They always bought a large supply of snacks, and we would sit at the saloon table and start the delights of chart work. I would show them how to plot a track and work out some rudimentary tidal information to assist with courses to steer while going there and back. On each trip, we would head somewhere for lunch, possibly over to Cowes or Yarmouth, both on the Isle of Wight, or perhaps up Southampton water but always with an excellent pub at the destination. I made sure I stayed sober, while Bernard and Katie would thoroughly enjoy the day out. Normally, on the return trip, with the benefits of an excellent lunch, I would find myself paying attention to Bernard's boat handling just a touch more than usual, but it was always fun.

After a few of these trips out, Bernard rung me one day to ask what I was up to that coming weekend. When I replied, "not much," he informed me that he would swing by and pick me up in the early evening. It was the start of an endless series of expensive evenings out in return for all the help I had given them. We would go to the finest restaurants in the area, and he would drive there and back, so I could enjoy a few drinks. It was always great fun and was his opportunity to pay me back for acting as instructor and chauffeur while out on the water.

This was all good fun, but I was not earning much money, and I was, to be perfectly honest, not really enjoying being a yacht broker. I found sitting in a dark office more conducive to sleep than the necessary task of income generation, so once again, I found myself handing in my notice and changing directions to something a little more physical. I was to join a local fencing contractor as a grunt on the end of a shovel, which I felt held every promise of keeping me awake.

Mike, my new boss and owner of the fencing company, was wiry, thin as a rake, with not a hint of any fat. He perpetually smoked, and his eyes and demeanor were those of a man on the move. He was constantly thinking of what was next. He ran his business from his dad's small farm at the end of a narrow lane in the countryside between Lymington and New Milton in Hampshire. He was married, but had no kids. The business was his life. I had wanted a more physical life away from yachts, and Mike was happy to oblige. The bulk of Mike's work, when I joined, consisted of residential repair and replacement work, in other words, your standard post-and-panel or post-and-rail around gardens. However, we were not restricted to this, and as his business grew, the range of work came to include agricultural fencing and eventually some industrial fence work too. However, when I started with him, it was a small gang of Mike, James and me. We would arrive at the yard around 6.30 a.m., usually to find Mike loading the small white pick-up truck with all we needed for the day. We had packed lunches and drinks and departed for whichever job we had on the slate. Upon arrival, Mike would introduce us to the customer with a polite good morning so that they were aware who it was destroying their garden and usually the neighbor's. If we were very lucky, we would have a clear line of sight to work with, but this was rare, and normally, as we stood trying to summon the motivation to get started, we looked upon the first post as the rest of the fence disappeared into the thick undergrowth. Mike and James would get stuck in with gusto, but with my gentle background of air-conditioned bridges and warm weather, I found myself gingerly moving a branch at a time and deeply resenting the brush of damp leaves against my face. As I moved about the worksite in this pathetic fashion, I sensed James and Mike staring at disbelief at this feeble figure doing his best to avoid getting his brand-new Wellington boots wet or dirty. They were both soon up to their necks in vegetation and mud and seemed oblivious to it all. I was going to have to pull myself together and get cracking. I decided to dazzle them with my abilities with a shovel, digging out the first hole for the new post. I launched the shovel into the ground and, just as Percy Thrower would, shoved my boot on the spade and pushed hard. Success, out came my first pile of dirt. Then, it was back in and out with the second. I was flying. Then, it was out with some more. By now, the spade section of the shovel was below ground, and I couldn't put my boot on it to go any further. *Well, it must be deep enough then*, I thought. I summoned Mike over and let him inspect what I had achieved.

"You're about ten inches down. You need at least two feet. Get cracking," he said.

Two feet, I thought, *how the hell am I going to do that?* I tried the best I could to get my foot back onto the top of the spade, now below the earth's surface, but my foot wouldn't fit in the hole. How could I get any purchase on it to break out the earth? James came over.

"Move out the way," he said patiently with a smile on his face.

He took his spade and, with a short expertly-directed jab of his arm, launched it into the dirt at the bottom of the hole. He did this a few times, directing it with accuracy from one side to the other, breaking free quite a few inches of dirt before levering the spade back loaded with muck and pulling it to the surface before putting it in a neat pile. He continued the process rapidly for a couple of minutes until to my astonishment, the handle of the spade was now at ground level and he had a beautiful, neat square hole the same size as the spade over two feet into the ground. He wasn't even out of breath.

"Got it?" he said.

I nodded weakly. Never mind. I'd have better luck on my next hole. I launched in with my newfound digging technique. This was better. I was making good progress when suddenly, halfway down, my spade hit something solid. I managed to chip away the earth using the corner of the spade until I had exposed a nice thick root running right through the middle of my hole.

"Problem, guys. We're going to have to move the hole!" I exclaimed.

This time, Mike came to investigate. With a quick glance and without pausing for breath, he crouched over the hole, pulled the spade up high and, with the savagery of launching a javelin, hurled the shovel into the hole to the root on the opposite side from where he was standing. He pulled back and did it again and again, using the spade as an axe. In no time, he broke through the root. He spun round 180 degrees and tackled the other side of the root in the same fashion. In no time, the root gave way to his barrage, and Mike bent to pick it up. He didn't even have the decency to be out of breath as he looked my way.

"Got it?" he said with no trace of emotion.

Once again, rather weakly, I replied in the affirmative. I battled on digging, furiously praying there would be no more embarrassing foul ups. Luckily, we got the holes dug out and started on the business of the new post and panels. For Mike and James, this was the easy part: mix the cement, put in the first post and, with a spirit level, pour the cement around the base, using a blunt-ended, thick piece of wood to tamp down the cement while using the spirit level to make sure the post remains perfectly upright. Using nails, mike attached the panel to the first post and the second, checked that the panel was level along the top and then sighted along the side of the first post to eyeball the second post and made sure it was in line with the last. Once done, we poured in the cement, ensuring that both the first and second post remained upright and that the panel remained level. It was an interesting process, at the end of which I derived not inconsiderable satisfaction from the sight of a clean, brand-new, finished fence.

Once the new fence was complete, we needed to clear up the filthy mess that usually resulted from our work. Not only did we have to pull back the vegetation wherever it still existed but also smooth over the soil, which usually looked like a scene from the Somme, up and down the fence line. Once this was complete, we would continue the slow retreat back to the vehicle, clean the clumps of mud from the lawn and hose down the path and driveway from all the filthy muddy boot marks of our endless back and forth to the trucks during the job. Once complete, we got back in the trucks. I was shattered, with sweat pouring down my face and alerts being sent by exhausted muscles from parts of my body that I wasn't aware had them. Apparently, Mike and James were just warming up, and as they each put a fresh cigarette in their mouths, they sat back, started the engine and headed off to the next job. We got another larger job done before the end of the day and then headed back to the yard. There were all the tools to clean up and the vehicles to empty. We had to take off the cement mixer, give it a thorough cleaning and scrape out the gravel used to make cement back onto the heap before clearing out the unused wood panels and posts, putting them back in their individual piles scattered around the yard. With a polite goodnight, I got into the car and headed home. By the time I got back to the house, getting out of the car was a struggle. I had seized up. It was all I could do to prepare a simple but huge meal and get scrubbed before collapsing in bed absolutely exhausted. It was only Monday!

Tuesday. The alarm blasted me awake at some ungodly hour that I had predetermined the night before as being the necessary start hour. I had to rise, load up with calories and get food prepared to get me through another day. I arrived at the yard to be confronted by a day very similar to the previous one, the difference being that I was so stiff I could barely move, and I now had the makings of some magnificent blisters on my rather delicate "office hands" from my endeavors the day before. The first hour or two must have been amusing for Mike and James to watch, as I moved about like an old man, hardly able to bend over. I thought yesterday had been bad, but that day was awful, as I made demands my muscles couldn't fulfill. I looked over at Mike and James to see if they were buckling under the load as I was. They had cigarettes dangling out of their mouths as they worked. Their seasoned bodies seemed to function on carcinogens and no oxygen just fine. Not a bead of perspiration was to be seen anywhere on them, but there were rivers of sweat coursing down my face and blocking my vision. How the hell was I going to make it through to the weekend, let alone deal with this as a way of life? The routine of driving the spade into the ground to dig the holes was not only tearing the skin off my fingers and palms but also causing acute pain in my wrist, especially when I made jarring contact with roots and rocks. My new boots were adding to my misery with some excellent examples of blisters joining the ranks of the previously cultivated ones on my hands. Oh boy, this was fun! By Friday, you could have put me in a nursing home, and you wouldn't have noticed my crumpled figure among the inmates! I was moving like them as well. Somehow, I made it through to the weekend, and with great relief, I headed home. By early evening, I settled into a deep coma and "flatlined" until midmorning the next day. Most of the weekend was spent trying to return some sense of normality to the functioning of my body. Just as I started to make progress, I was rudely awakened by Monday morning's alarm.

Work continued unrelentingly, and the pain followed in a similar fashion to the previous week. By the third week, however, the blisters had hardened into calluses. My permanently exhausted muscles felt both a little less painful and a little better able to keep up with the demands. I was most definitely settling in. Mike could leave us to crack on with work as he concentrated on scouting more new jobs and collecting for the old ones. Mike began to get tested out by the housing developers in the area. They started him on a small job that we did to their satisfaction, and slowly, their demands grew until we were putting up the entire fencing around all the new properties and their small gardens. This was demanding work requiring quick construction. For Mike to land the contract, he had to be competitive, and in our business, that meant speed and accuracy of construction. For each row of semidetached houses that were built, we would do all the fencing around each small rectangular garden out back. This usually entailed eight-foot long, four-inch by four-inch posts, pressure-treated to stop rot, buried two feet in the ground and about eight feet apart. Usually, they had three rails that were evenly spaced apart between posts and a vertical "feather board", overlapping each other, that were nailed to the rails to complete the fence. Each garden also needed a garden gate, which was tedious to construct and install. We would have to drill a post to the house for a landing for the start of the rails and dig in the other posts accordingly from this start point. We got good at erecting these fences at speed, so we were busy with both regular residential work and new housing construction work. Every now and then, with a new construction site, we would land a huge "straight line" project. These were normally parceling off an entire construction site from "concerned" neighbors and often agreed upon as part of the approval process to allow the new construction to go ahead. I liked this kind of work. You could really get a rhythm going. Everybody was digging holes and concreting in posts in a continual and steady stream, followed by a long and steady effort to put up the rails before all the vertical boards. There was no need to direct people. It was an opportunity to shut the mind off and enjoy just pure physical labor. This "shut down the mind" mentality was to suit me well with some of the agricultural projects that were to spring up in due course.

I was now several months in and had fully adjusted to the demands of a physical outdoor life. There were some fringe benefits. I was fit now, very fit, and my capacity for drinking and subsequent recovery had improved dramatically. My seasoned business buddies from London had their work cut out trying to recover from heavy Saturday night visits to the pub in quite the same fashion as I could. Should there be any lingering effects on Monday morning, within an hour or so of taking the shovel in hand, all was good with the world once again. I was always a big fan of eating, and in this game, you couldn't afford to stop—not for a moment.

You needed three meals a day and big ones. Snacks were no problem, worked off in a heartbeat. If there was any trace of overeating during the weekend, it seemed that the body knew what was coming up on Monday morning and stored it all away. I slept without interruption, and I was in the best shape of my life.

Things were going well at the business. Mike was doing well enough to buy himself a turbo diesel slate grey Land Rover with a soft top covering the back. He drove it around with much pride and struggled, initially, to allow it to be used for work and get covered in dirt. Following close on the heels of this purchase was a large trailer for the Land Rover to tow. This was a fantastic step up from trying to get everything in the back of the small white pick-ups. Now, we could load everything onto one trailer for all the jobs during that day. We were busy, occasionally having up to five or six guys in total now plowing away. There were two vehicles on the go. The pick-up and the Land Rover would often go to different locations, with Mike blasting around, checking jobs and getting the cash.

Mike came to me one day and told me he wanted to promote me to contracts manager. It was a tempting offer, especially when he threw in the use of the Land Rover with it, mainly because he was about to buy another one. This time, it was a hard top. Mike printed up some cards with my name and "Contracts Manager" typed neatly below. I was beginning to feel extremely important and wondered what my newfound title meant in terms of duties. It became obvious immediately. I had to make sure the Land Rover and trailer were loaded and ready to go by 6.45 a.m. in the morning. My day would start between 4 and 4.30 a.m., where despite my body's reluctance, I would eat as big a breakfast as I could stomach before departing the house by about 5 a.m. I would normally be at the yard by 5.15 or 5.30 a.m. and get started. First, I hooked up the trailer, and then, I began loading everything we would need to keep the crew busy for the day. If we were concreting in posts at new residential or commercial construction sites, we would have to make a great deal of concrete to go around the base of the posts, so shovelful after shovelful of gravel needed to be loaded aboard the trailer. This was followed by the concrete mixer, tools, posts, rails, boards, nails, string lines, buckets, concrete, generator, drills, extension cables, wheel barrow and any other particular requirements unique to the job of the day. Every day, the job was different, requiring thought and planning to make sure that if you were many miles away, nothing was forgotten. Having lads stand around for an hour or so was unpopular if you forgot something. Sometimes, I could arrive a little later if the job was a continuation from the day before and not much new was required, but the early morning load-up seemed to be part of my new job. By the time the lads rolled in bleary eyed at 6.45 a.m. or normally closer to 7.00 a.m. and often, much to my frustration, later, I had more often than not already had a full workout. Breakfast had been burnt off, and the day awaited.

Mike's fencing company seemed to go from strength to strength. The New Forest County Council had considerable lengths of road fenced off to prevent the horses from wandering over the main road, and some of the renewal work came Mike's way. The requirements of construction were very specific, and the finished product had to meet the specifications laid down. The fence needed a six-foot, round, pressure-treated post driven into the ground two feet and three meters apart from its neighbor. The fence was to be a metal netting that would be rolled out and tensioned before being stapled to the posts every three meters, with a strand of barbed wire above, also tensioned. For the most part, the going was straight and easy. About every 150 meters, we had to dig in an "end" post, which was eight feet in length and six to eight inches in diameter. It would have a strut angled into the ground to prevent the post from lifting up under the tensioned load of the netting and barbed wire, but once the next section of 150 meters was up, the tension was equalized and transferred down the line. It was good work, and the experience helped on the next job.

Mike had a friend named Pete who owned a pig farm in Somerset. Pete seemed to know a farmer who needed some work done. Mike went up to Somerset to scout around and landed a considerable contract to almost completely re-fence a farm. When we agreed to the job, we were unaware we were about to get more than we bargained for, but having agreed to do the job, we had a new problem. We would be in need of accommodation. There was not enough profit in the job to stay in hotels or bed and breakfasts, so Mike thought up a novel approach. We would take up a small caravan with a working kitchen and camp from Monday to Friday on Pete's farm. It was summertime, so weather was not really an issue, and a change in routine was looked forward to by all. Mike managed, for a fee, to have Pete's wife cook an evening meal for us. We loaded up all the tools we needed at the yard and hooked up the trailer to one Land Rover and the caravan to the other. Delivery of all materials would be direct to the site, so we only needed to make sure we had all the tools to get the job done.

We arrived at Pete's farm and found a suitable grassy mound with a commanding view of the surrounding countryside. Little time was wasted on getting tents and the caravan set up before we headed straight to the worksite to get started. The local builder's merchant delivered an enormous supply of posts, rolls of barbwire and staples. We were ready to get going. With the start point located, Mike paced out three paces and placed the first post down. Now, the fun started. To get these posts into the ground, we used a "post banger". This was a steel tube with two long steel handles on opposite sides that ran from the top to the bottom. The tube was sealed at the top and open at the bottom—simple, basic and heavy! The idea was to place the point of the post into the ground, and then, while one person holds the post, the other lifts the post banger up over the top of the post and slides it down until, with a loud thump, it lands on the top of the post. Now, the work starts. With one person on each side, they lift the steel post banger in unison before, with a combined snap down and the considerable assistance of gravity, the banger reconnected with the top of the post, which should promptly disappear a couple of inches into the ground. Once you get a rhythm going with the other person, it can be fast, satisfying work, putting up a neat line of posts in no time. We expected as much as we lifted the post banger up and onto the first post. With a grunt, we raised it and brought it crashing down on the first customer. Apart from a slight tremble, it didn't move. Once more, we lifted it up and brought it crashing down on the post. Apart from an unpleasant dispersal of kinetic energy through to our wrists, there was not a hint of downward motion from the post. We decided to skip the first post, thinking it must be on a rock or something. We moved down to the next in line, but we experienced the same result. Odd, we thought. We took a single post and went to the far side of the field to perform a test and see if things were different there. Much to our gathering shock, it was the same. We went back to the first post and decided to dig down and see what lay below. Having removed an inch or two of topsoil, we landed upon a hard, crusty sandstone. It would crumble and break apart, but with a certain reluctance. If the farmer was looking through his binoculars at us, standing at the first hole and scratching our heads, he must have been laughing his head off. He would have known what the soil was like. It had never occurred to Mike or to me to do a soil sample, but we weren't in Hampshire. We were in Somerset. That must have been why the farmer hired us: no local in his right mind would agree to the work.

There was nothing else for it. We would have to pound these posts in. Each post required up to 150 strikes with the post banger. We pounded and pounded for days to get them in. It was ball-busting hard work, and we began to develop necks and shoulders like bison. To cap it all off, in the middle of our time on the job, one of the lads decided to go on a drunken rampage around the farm, much to the confusion of the pigs. We put him on a train and sent him packing before returning to our relentless bashing of posts. We got them in, but it wasn't fun. Now, we could enjoy the relative luxury of putting up the barbed wire. This was not for the faint of heart. With the barbed wire attached at the two end-posts, up to 150 meters apart, two individuals, at equal spacing down the length of wire, would scoop the wire up in the claw of the hammer and walk away from the fence line until it was tight. At this point, they would then, with great effort, pull as hard as they could away from the barbed wire, almost leaning flat to the ground with one hand holding the hammer. This was designed to stretch out the barbwire and prevent it from coming slack over the years ahead, but when it became exciting was when it broke. With the recoil, anybody standing in the way would be shredded. For the two "hammer operators," the correct technique while straining on the hammer and length of barb wire was to keep your head turned away and, with any break, immediately fall on the ground face-first, hoping the recoiling barb wire flew harmlessly over your back. Every now and again, somebody got "sliced", but for the most part, we operated a health-and-safety-conscious workplace!

I was beginning to take note of a small voice in the back of my head asking if this was it in life. I was beginning to feel a strange stirring for an education. This notion was troubling me. I had never sought to be "educated" before, so why now? I did my best to ignore it over the coming weeks and months, but I lost the battle. With a certain reluctance, I succumbed to the urge and enrolled in a course at the Southampton Institute of Higher Education to study Yacht Manufacturing Technology and Marine Industry Management. I hung up my shovel and left my fencing career behind me.

The *Golden Hinde* alongside. Summer, 1984.

A view of the rigging looking forward aboard the *Golden Hinde*.

Tyke departing Penzance for Ireland and Force 10 around Fastnet.
Late winter 1985.

First trans-altantic aboard rival 41 with Les Powles. We are the
smaller of the two! Summer 1985.

Land sighted on First trans-atlantic!

Leo my best mate and very contented temporary 'weapons officer.' *Copihue.* Nov. 1998.

Worst night at sea aboard this Nicholson 46 around Penzance on passage from Scotland to Med. Feb 1986.

My first brush with Yachting in the South of France–*Star of the Sea*.
100 foot Benetti based in Antibes. 1986 and 1987.

First Officer aboard *Pilar*—165 foot Feadship. 1988.

I wanted change and got it. Typical residential fencing with me hard at work. 1989.

1994 and back to sea aboard *Blue Shadow,* seen here in headseas making for Antigua.

Blue Shadow looking spic and span for the Antigua charter show.

Copihue looking magnificent, at anchor, in Dry Tortugas. March 1998.

Copihue scrubbed clean and ready for the arrival of the boss.

Copihue doing what she does best. Sailing hard and fast. On delivery from Antigua to Florida via Virgin Gorda, Turks and Caicos and the Bahamas. January 1999.

ELEVEN

School's In

It was April of 1990, and before starting the course, I had the summer ahead and managed to land a job as skipper aboard a 20-meter motor yacht berthed in Antibes. I was to thoroughly enjoy this summer, when I was given full autonomy in running the yacht. She was a typical "plastic fantastic" Italian special: white in colour and rather boxy from the outside. The interior was nicely finished with expensive veneers, luxurious carpets and an interior helm station just littered with buttons and dials, making me look very skilled and important to the uniformed guest. I never liked to admit that it took me a large part of the season to figure out what half of them were for. There were two owners of the yacht, and the first came down almost immediately. He was extremely well-turned-out, always well-spoken and very well-dressed. He knew exactly what he wanted and where he wanted to go. We would do the usual "milk run" from St. Tropez to Monaco, and his time aboard was full of endless ports and anchorages. It was fun but busy. However, his partner in the yacht was different altogether. I was told that he was coming down and to get the yacht ready. The day arrived and I, along with the stewardess, was at the gang-way to meet him. It was late in the day, and he strode aboard with barely a word and disappeared down to his cabin. Having closed the yacht down, I got a good night's sleep and awoke early. I got all the weather information I could. I pulled out a chart of the area and drew up a rough cruise plan of where we might be able to go in the time he had available. It was a beautiful morning, and in due course, the boss arrived on deck and sat down to breakfast. Midway through his muesli, I apologized for the intrusion and wondered if I could go through some ideas about cruising in the time available. He nodded without pausing in his chomping. I began a long shpiel about the locations of weather systems and how these might affect this location or that and how we should perhaps go to this port and then have the wind behind us as we came home. He listened intently and continued chewing.

After I had finished babbling, he looked up and, in a beautiful Cockney accent, said, "Gus, I don't give a fuck what we do. If you want to go out, I'll go with ya!"

I was beginning to like this man. He clearly had no problem speaking his mind. I worked doubly hard to give him a fun cruise up and down the coast. About halfway through his time on board, I was chatting to him one day as we approached the Antibes harbour to refuel and restock. We were on the fly bridge with commanding views all around. I turned to the boss and asked him if he would like to take the helm and drive his yacht in. He looked stunned.

"But I don't know how, and none of our other skippers ever let me," he said.

"But it's your yacht. If you would like to drive it, just let me know. In fact, how about we spend the day sometime just messing about in the harbor, practicing going alongside and in and out of your berth?" I replied.

This seemed to bring him enormous pleasure. For my part, I was a little stunned that despite having paid for the yacht and paid the Captain's wage, he didn't feel he had the right to say "shove over, I want a go!"

The next day, very bravely I thought, he gave his wife the credit card and suggested she might find shopping preferable to ship handling. She was gone in a flash. The boss, stewardess and I settled down to a day of just messing around in the harbour. For me, it was a great pleasure to teach an owner how to handle his yacht, and I think, for his part, he was thoroughly enjoying learning to do something he had been denied in the past. We would come alongside and practice kicking the stern in with the outboard engine. We did this on both the port and starboard sides. It was amusing to see other yachts looking on, wondering what on earth we were doing going repeatedly in and out of our berth and coming alongside the fuel berth. It was a terrific day, and I think it was the only time that I have, while employed as skipper, had the opportunity to teach an owner who wanted to be taught the basics of ship handling on vessels of such size or greater.

There were quiet days too, and on one such day, I awoke early as usual. In the sleepy predawn silence, I began a walk around the harbour road that hugged the battlements to get a fresh baguette and the early morning papers. Some distance off but moving slowly from bin to bin was a solitary garbage truck. He was following the curve of the road around towards me, and while about a hundred yards away, he stopped, and the driver descended once more to empty yet another garbage bin. With his back turned, the truck, under the influence of gravity and the inclined camber of the road towards the water's edge, began to roll forward. The sleepy trucker suddenly noticed what was happening, but sadly, it was too late. By the time the front tyre had reached the water's edge, it had enough momentum to head straight in. With a godawful splash, it landed onto two small yachts, both of which indignantly sunk down by their sterns before leaping forward out of the way under their own buoyancy. What had been a dozy start to the day took on a whole new element of excitement. The poor truck driver look on in horror as the contents of the garbage truck began to spill out all over the harbour. The mess was impressive, but even more so was the speed of the response. I had barely returned to the scene with baguette and paper when the harbour came alive with special vessels with opening bows designed to scoop up rubbish in the water. Quayside, a crane had pulled up and was getting ready to pull the offending truck from the water. I walked on, feeling more than a little sorry for the truck driver, but in no need of my morning coffee. I was now wide awake.

The summer was gone in a flash, and I needed to return for the start of college. On the appointed day, I arrived at the Warsash campus of Southampton Institute of Higher Education to be confronted with what felt like a bunch of school kids. However, it wasn't them who were out of place. I was the "grey-haired granddaddy". It was official. I was a mature student. The basic concept of the course was to provide some insight into what it takes to build a yacht, whether it be aluminum, steel, wood or GRP (Glass-Reinforced Plastic). There was some naval architecture involved, but much of the course was dedicated to how the yacht gets built, how to lay up GRP in the correct fashion to account for the loads that can be expected, and what quantity is needed in any particular area. For instance, around a mast step, engine mounts or chain plates, there has to be a greater technical application of material to allow for the increased stress in these areas. In the same way when building in steel or aluminum, what are the thicknesses of material used, what are the construction methods for different areas in the vessel and how are these welded correctly? We spent a certain amount of time in the workshop, making everything from a wooden cleat, done individually, right up to a small dinghy complete with varnished wood trim, done as a group. The academic year tore by, and with summer fast approaching, I decided I would try to get some boatyard experience to capitalize on the classroom work to date.

Paul, my skipper from *Star of the Sea*, was now a European agent for Palmer Johnson, arguably the builders of the finest aluminum yachts in North America. Paul was delighted to help me get some work experience at their shipyard and contacted the head office. In no time flat, I got a positive response back, and with my visa applications complete, I was on a jet out to Wisconsin on Lake Michigan, U.S.A. I made my way up to the shipyard and set about getting accommodations. I found just the ticket with a small campsite just on the edge of town that had large mobile homes for rent. It was perfect for the summer. I now had to arrange transportation. A car for the summer seemed a waste of money, so I settled for the next best thing, a set of rollerblades. There was a supermarket near the campsite, so I was set. Getting to work was a piece of cake. It was mostly downhill, so having got up and breakfasted, I would make sure I had plenty of food for the day and strap on my rollerblades. The first half mile was mainly flat, but then, I had a downhill section towards the water's edge that I could fly down before crossing the bridge. This left a final couple hundred yards, and I was there. While the town may have had the rather usual mix of the rundown and the neat and tidy about its buildings, the Palmer Johnson shed itself was state of the art. In fact, the yard was split in two, with the old original complex on the north end of town and the brand new shed on the south. It was to the south that I headed.

I entered the building and was greeted warmly by everyone. It became apparent to me that this was a closeknit community that had worked together for a great deal of time with very little turnover in the workforce. The arrival of some strange Brit was causing a bit of a stir. I had requested, during my couple of months here, to have as much exposure to as many departments as possible. They did not disappoint, giving me a hectic schedule observing all aspects of yacht construction. I thoroughly enjoyed my time there, but in the back of my mind, I was beginning to think that I might prefer to return to sea than be involved in the building of yachts. However, I still had two more years to complete at school.

The yard time had been such a success that Palmer Johnson was to ask me back the next year, this time to their newly purchased facility in Savannah, Georgia. This was an interesting experience, not least because I was part of a squad of about fifteen guys who were tasked with opening up the new shipyard and getting it ready to conduct refits. The premise behind the purchase was simple. Owners of yachts were not terribly interested in sending their yachts north to the St Lawrence seaway into the Great Lakes to the Palmer Johnson yard on northern Lake Michigan. However, they might well be interested in the short hop from the Caribbean to Savannah, Georgia. It was a bet that paid off handsomely. We arrived and literally unlocked the padlock and chain to access the shipyard. It was utterly deserted. I made an immediate beeline for a group of buildings to the right of the entrance gates so that I could find somewhere safe to put my bags down, but instead, I struck gold. A small set of stairs on the outside of the building led up to a door. I dashed up and found it open. I stepped inside to find a huge apartment fully fitted out with carpets, sofa, chairs and table. In one corner of the large main room overlooking the shipyard was a neat but fully-functioning kitchen with a cooker and fridge. Down a small hallway were two bedrooms and a bathroom. Since most of the lads had already had accommodations arranged locally, I was the lucky winner of first-come first-serve. The apartment was mine. The skeleton crew that had come down consisted mainly of senior department heads who had to both decide what was to be done and start hiring locally to get it done. I had a more general rolling brief to go wherever I could be of use. The shipyard was basically split in two. At the entrance end was a small marina with an office and a single large shed, inside which stood some huge metal fabrication machines. Along a short section of road running alongside the harbour was access to the far end of the shipyard, which had a large covered shed with a substantial office area within it. Next to this was a tall, thin paint shed out of which tracks ran for access to the huge boat lift, which was a large platform that could sink deep into the water before settling the vessel on chocks and lifting them out. It is not often you get a chance to wander around a deserted shipyard with everybody wondering quite what should be done first to get things going. Department heads met frequently, and as the days rolled into weeks, the personnel numbers began to rise and order was slowly restored to the sleepy facility. The parts department set itself up, and orders for equipment began to roll in. The office within the shed began to fill with people, developing its own momentum. The machinery that existed was tested and repaired if it had relevance. If not, it was removed. Sheds that had been dirty, bare and filled with rusting machinery and rubbish now became orderly, neat and filled with increasingly large quantities of new machinery.

As the summer wore on, the heat increased. It was hot down here, very hot. By the time we hit early August, the heat was oppressive, but it did produce some spectacular weather. By midafternoon, the saturated hot air finally gave in and started to rise, accelerating at increasing speed skyward. The development from light cumulus to towering, threatening cumulo nimbus clouds was impressive. As this hot air rose, it dragged in a sea breeze, taking it skyward too. It must have been the perfect mix of air. Within no time, the sky went jet black with the accumulated mass of fully developed thunderstorms, and then, they let rip. Lightning forked across the sky, often striking buildings or cable poles in the area, but it was the rain that impressed me. It came down so hard that the very ground it struck seemed in danger of being pummeled further into the earth. New rivers of water across car parks and roadways would appear, cascading down into the harbour. When it seemed that there was simply no way to deal with any more rain, it would slow and stop. The clouds would drift away and break up, and as quickly as it all developed, it came to a gentle halt.

By the end of the summer, this shipyard in Savannah, Georgia was beginning to hum. There were a large number of employees, and operations were coming together. I was called in on my final day by the owner of the company to talk about my future intentions. As I sat on the seat facing him, it was obvious he was asking if I was hoping to come and work at the shipyard in some capacity. Sitting in front of him brought my thoughts to a conclusion. I wanted to return to sea. I thanked him for the opportunity he had given me and headed back for my last year at college.

The year flew by. I found myself at the awards ceremony, shaking hands with the course supervisor, who announced that he wanted a word with me afterwards. Intrigued, I tracked him down through the throng of happy students and parents to find out what was on his mind.

"Ah Gus," he began. "Congratulations on your engineering diploma. I'm not sure if you are interested, but if you do another nine months, we can give you a degree."

It must have been vanity, but I rather fancied having the initials B.A. after my name, so I agreed. This created a small problem. I had rather banked on getting back into the real world of full-time work, but being a student for another academic year meant I would have to get another couple of months' work. A yacht broker in France promised to see what he could do, and shortly, the phone rang. A very proper voice introduced himself and asked if I could pop up to Claridges in London for a chat and some afternoon tea. I had never been to Claridges for tea. I rather fancied the idea. I dusted off my feeble excuse for a suit and jumped on the train for London.

It would be fair to say that Claridges is the most distinguished hotel in London—very proper. Arriving at the hotel and feeling very out of place, I wandered over to the concierge and asked to see the gentleman who had rung me. After a few minutes, a rather rotund fellow, balding, almost elderly, came down the stairs somewhat slowly and stiffly. He halted, gazed around for a moment. Then, having caught my eye, he made his way towards me.

"Hello, Gus, shall we get some tea?" he said, shaking my hand before leading the way to the tea room.

"Nice place here, sir. Do you stay here much?" I asked.

"Oh, occasionally," he replied. "I like to keep a place here so I have a spot to keep my clothes for when I'm in London."

I couldn't think of any smart rejoinder to that one. Note to self: must remember to move stuff from barn at friend's farm, currently free of charge, to hotel room while I keep traveling the world!

As we sat down, menus were handed to each of us. He was obviously familiar with it because he snapped it shut in an instant. He looked at me and asked what I fancied. Rather lamely, I replied that I wasn't very familiar with tea at Claridges and would be more than happy to follow his lead. I sensed that despite his own reservations, he knew a bottomless pit of a young man when he saw one and ordered their full afternoon tea for two.

We began chatting, and he informed me that he owned a Fairline 43 motor yacht that he kept on the south coast of France and asked if I would be interested in skippering it for the summer. It fit the bill perfectly for me, and as we continued, the conversation tea arrived. Tea at Claridges was straight out of a movie. There was a large stacked plate stand. On the lower level were triangular sandwiches of smoked salmon and cucumber or ham and cheese. Moving up, there were scones with huge supplies of clotted cream and jam, and finally, on the top layer were some incredible-looking pastries. Tea arrived and was poured into the exquisite china cups. I looked on expectantly until my interviewer broke the ice with a smile and told me to get stuck in. He seemed a little reluctant to do much eating, so with as much politeness as possible, I tried to move gracefully through the entire contents, starting with the sandwiches. We continued chatting. I tried my best to encourage him to keep talking so I could continue through the scones. I got the impression Claridges was used to the slightly more refined appetites of a different clientele from myself, and it was with a slightly raised eyebrow that the empty tea plates were cleared away. However, it seemed not to have done my prospects any harm. With a handshake, it was agreed that I would start as soon as possible.

To get to France this time, I decided to take my car. I was convinced a convertible on the south coast of France was essential. By convertible, I mean the roll-back plastic roof of a flame-red Citroen 2 CV—a magnificent example of minimalism over extravagance. Driving down was wonderful. Having left the vagaries of a foggy English channel behind me, I settled into the highway driving of France. Driving on a highway in a 2CV is not for the faint of heart, especially when trying to maintain a good average speed or, even more exciting, trying to overtake other vehicles. The first thing to bear in mind is that this car is not designed for comfortable highway cruising. To even get close to the typical speed of the most idle highway driver requires the foot right to the floor and not a hint of release. For the more adventurous 2CV aficionado, greater speed can be attained by awaiting the passing by of a truck and diving into his slipstream. Once achieved, a careful balance must be kept between falling out of the slipstream into his turbulence or, far more undesirable, driving into the back of him if he brakes. All these maneuvers can only be attempted once the tiny two-cylinder engine has been running for quite some time and is red hot. Many a happy hour was spent getting familiar with all these techniques as I sped south, and it was with some surprise that I arrived at the Côte d'Azur alive. Once driving in the south by late morning, I could peel the roof back and enjoy the warm late spring sunshine. It felt good to be back on the French Riviera.

My destination was Golfe Juan, a medium-sized marina located just to the west of Juan les Pins of Cap d'Antibes fame. The marina was not on an inlet, but instead built out into the blue Mediterranean as a result of the increased demand for the berthing of the growing number of yachts in the area. I was quite able to stay on the yacht, but the crew quarters were tiny. Having scouted around, I found I could squat on the balcony of an apartment in Antibes. It was hardly perfect, but it was summer in the south of France, and the lads in the apartment were quite relaxed about me diving in during a rainstorm. I thoroughly enjoyed the idea of sleeping outdoors in a sleeping bag under a warm starry sky. The apartment was tremendous fun, with endless parties and activity, but for now, I had to get cracking on sorting out the yacht.

I was on my own. I was to be skipper, engineer, deckhand, chef and, God help me, stewardess! I was very unsure of what the boss would expect. I certainly hoped I would not be driving the yacht, cleaning it, fixing the engines and trying to prepare and serve a three-course meal on a regular basis, but I needn't have worried. On day one, at the appointed hour, the boss arrived at the marina, and we promptly set off to a couple of shops just across the coast road behind Golfe Juan marina. Once there, the boss introduced me to all the shops he enjoyed. We were able to get everything from breads, cheeses and salads to meats and pates. It was all very fresh and delicious. Mind you, for the price we paid, I would hope so, but whenever the boss wanted to go out for the day, this was where I would come for supplies. We never went far in the yacht— out to the islands off Cannes or an anchorage off Cap d'Antibes, always leaving around ten or eleven a.m. and coming back into the Marina around four or five p.m. When we would leave, the boss took great pleasure in driving the yacht out of the berth, but he was usually happy for me to take over for the trip to the anchorage. Once there, I would set up the table for lunch. Having cleared the meal away, he would enjoy a little swim or just laze around in the hot sunshine before heading for home. He and his wife were not young, and they demanded little of their days.

I did take the opportunity to ask him about his work, and his tale was not dull, especially the end. Following the war, he had inherited a very small tailoring business from his father. With diligent hard work and after a great many years, he had grown it into a global brand. In due course, he decided the time was ripe to sell out and made a little gentle noise in the right circles. He eventually came down to two bidders and brought them to his office for a final round of negotiations. He had each of the two parties in separate rooms and brought them in alternately with a request for their two offers. His tactic was deceptively simple. Having received the offers, the lowest bidder was brought back in and told the other party had offered more, but never how much. This seemed to put the lowest bidder on edge and forced them to offer a larger bid, which in keeping with human nature and the desire to win, was over the top but got the process rolling nicely. The first party was sent out, and the second, and now lowest, bidder was brought back in and told that he, having initially been the highest bidder, had now just been soundly beaten by a superior counteroffer. This lot now immediately came back aggressively with a new counteroffer and was summarily marched out. The boss related how he managed to eke this bidding war out all day until he felt he could bleed the winning party no more. He shook hands and signed on the dotted line, and by his own admission, a ludicrously overpriced deal was secured. He owned a beautiful apartment on the Côte d'Azur, with manicured gardens and an impressive concierge. It was elegant and luxurious in the extreme, but while he had expensive taste in real estate, with regard to cars, he owned a rather sedate Renault. It was not even top of the range. It was a gentle summer, and it was finished off by the boss asking if I would mind accompanying him with the car back to Geneva, where he lived. The journey was a chance to talk. He related his war years, how he had been on the intelligence staff of senior commanding officers during the Second World War and how fascinating it had been. He was remarkably frank about the challenges of building his company, along with the associated costs and rewards, but it was the arrival at his apartment in Geneva that I remember the most. Like the Côte d'Azur, it was beautiful. As I stepped through the door, I was confronted by an enormous sitting room. Every item my eyes came to rest on looked excruciatingly expensive. The furnishings and décor were extravagant and embraced an atmosphere of refinement and exclusivity. I was offered a seat but felt uncomfortable placing my mortal posterior on any fabric in this room. I was happy to settle for a handshake and letter of reference before retreating back to the sanctuary of the street.

I returned to finish my degree and, as promised, following a further nine months of study, I was awarded a Bachelor of Arts with second-class honours in Leisure Management. The degree looks magnificent, framed and hanging upon the wall, but I cannot remember a single significant or relevant fact taught to me during those nine months. It is with acute embarrassment that to this day, when asked what my degree is all about, I can only shrug my shoulders and reply that I am not quite sure.

TWELVE

Back To Business

I had now gathered the pieces of paper acknowledging my education, even if I couldn't remember a thing about it. I wanted to get back to what I knew best, the sea. I managed to land a job as first officer of a 165-foot motor yacht named *Blue Shadow*. Her hull and topsides were bright white with a dark royal blue strip running horizontally along the main and bridge decks. It was not a bad look, but it made the yacht look dated, which, it was fair to say, she was.

Upon arrival, the first thing that struck me about this yacht was the complete split within the ranks of the crew. The engineers were run in a wholly different way than the rest of the crew, and it showed. While the exterior of the yacht looked tired, and it always seemed a constant battle to just maintain a barely acceptable standard, the engineering aboard was quite another matter. There were four engineers associated with the yacht, two chief engineers and two second engineers who rotated three months on three months off, or six months on six months off. In other words, whatever suited them. They were professionally qualified and experienced and ran the yacht accordingly. In fact, I have seen no engineering department to its equal to this day. They ran complete maintenance schedules on every single engineering item aboard the yacht, whether it was a fridge compressor or the main engine, the ship's windlass or the gyro compass. Nothing was left out. Each item had its own computer log showing what had been done and when. It also showed what was coming due in the way of service or replacement. When they opened up their worksheet for the day, a particular pump or motor would pop up on the screen for attention, and they would get on with it. Incorporated within this maintenance schedule was a parts ordering system that ensured that whenever they undertook some service work, they had the appropriate parts. Also, when work was completed, it ensured that an order was made to replenish the spares. It was very impressive. In short, despite the yacht's advanced age, she never let us down in any way. It was a lesson in how things should be done right.

With regards to the exterior, whereas *Pilar* gleamed liked a new car and looked every bit the Rolls Royce of the sea she was, *Blue Shadow* just kind of got by like a favourite but very secondhand car that has done a couple of hundred thousand miles. She was also a charter yacht, and that meant a continuous and hectic schedule. The decks looked well-worn, and the paintwork was a constant challenge of chipping out the growing blisters over the rust and patching it up the best we could. The interior, like the exterior, was clean and well-kept but belonged to another era. The crew quarters felt cramped and well-worn and were, as usual, located forward. Malcolm, the skipper, normally fuelled by copious quantities of coffee that kept him edgy and on the move, orchestrated the entire operation from the bridge. We were constantly busy either with the boss on board or on charter. If we had nobody on board, we were full-throttle with maintenance or, failing that, at work on delivery to the next charter or a visit from the boss. We had no base of operations. We roamed the Côte d'Azur, including Italy, Corsica, Sardinia, Majorca, Menorca and Spain.

The charters weren't particularly notable, except one. It was a family from the U.K., and during the course of the two-week charter, the crew had bent over backwards to meet all the demands of two young families, with endless watersports and beach activities and numerous changes of anchorages and ports. In addition, there was the usual eating, drinking and partying that went on until late into the nights before the kids would be up at the crack of dawn ready for the next excitement. There was a certain sense of relief and fatigue at the end of the two weeks, and more than a little anticipation among the crew for the usual ten or twenty percent tip. Now, this was a charter that including fuel and food exceeded $200,000, and therefore, a tip in the range of $20,000 to $40,000, split amoung the crew, would not be unusual. Crew wages on the charter yachts, at this time, were generally lower than those on the purely private yachts, with the understanding the charter tips could make up and often exceed the shortfall. This is usually made quite clear by the charter broker to the clients, and although discretionary, the tip should generally be paid, except in unusual circumstances. It was with some surprise that a tip of about $100 was given to each crew-member, which is rather similar to giving a waiter $1 after an exceptionally good meal. The crew was bitterly disappointed, and the usual spirited farewells were somewhat muted with this particular lot.

I was now sensing an opportunity. In November of 1994, the yacht was scheduled to go to the shipyard for a major refit, after which we would cross the Atlantic for the Caribbean charter season. It was during this crossing that I hoped to do all that was required for my Ocean Yachtmaster certification. After a busy season in the Mediterranean that saw us visiting Corsica, Sardinia, Bonifacio, Portovechio, Elba, Girolata, Ajaccio, Cap d'Ail, St Tropez, Menorca, Formentera, Cala San Vincente, San Remo, Portofino, Porto Venere and Viareggio, we finally came to a shuddering halt in Palma Majorca and began our refit.

It would have been nice to paint the entire yacht, but this was beyond our allocated budget of $250,000. We opted instead to get the shipyard to paint the horizontal blue stripe at the main and bridge deck levels in their entirety and the whole hull from cap rail to waterline. This alone accounted for $100,000. The main, bridge and sundecks would have to wait for another year. The sanding machines and plastic tents came out, turning the yacht into a complete shambles. In addition to the topside work, the engineers had an extensive work list including the removal of the port shaft and the replacement of the bearing. In addition, they planned to strip down both generators to the blocks by themselves.

The generator work alone, if subcontracted, was estimated to have cost $35,000. During all this chaos, I set to with a team in the forward, aft and galley bilges to get them cleaned, chipped, primed and painted. This kept us busy for the full six weeks, but in the middle of all this, the engineers, needing some light entertainment and sensing I needed a break from the confines of the bilges, asked for my assistance. Absolutely delighted not to have a chipping hammer in my hand for a while, I leapt at their request. I reported to the engine room, where the two of them looked, rather more than usual, happy to see me.

"Ah," said the chief. "Good to see you. Would you mind getting that on, and then, we can help you with the rest of the kit?"

"Sure," I replied and started pushing first one and then the other foot through the legs of the paper suit, followed by my arms through the sleeves before zipping it up. Once complete, they handed me thick rubber gloves, which I put on before they taped them around the wrists. With all the machinery shut down, there was no way to move the air around, and it was hot in the engine room. I was beginning to sweat. With grins on their faces, they taped the suit around my boots and then got to work around my head. I was given safety goggles and a respirator, both of which I put on, and they then sealed the paper hood around the edges until I was buttoned up good.

"Perfect," declared the chief, apparently much to the amusement of his number two.

"Right. Here's the spray gun. Could you climb in that tank there and give it a good spray so we can get it painted?"

"No problem," I replied, although it came out as a muffled mumble through the respirator. I clambered inside and was passed the spray gun while a waterproof light was hung in the access hatch. With light, the interior scene became apparent. The floors, walls and ceiling were covered in a filthy brown sludge, which was a couple of inches deep where I stood.

"What is this?" I asked, as the disgusting stench began to permeate through even the finest carbon membranes within my respirator.

"I don't know what you're saying," said the chief, "but in case you're wondering, it's the shit tank you're cleaning out!"

It was too late now. I chuckled to myself at having been quite so gullible and set about spraying down the tank. Within a few hours, it looked spic and span, and was ready to be dried before repainting. I stepped out and was surprised, now that I was covered from head to foot in the contents of the tank, that the engineers weren't quite so keen to help me get all my protective kit off. Having cleaned up, I departed back to the confines of the bilges and my chipping hammer, which considering from where I had just come, didn't seem quite so bad.

By now, the topside paintwork had progressed towards the final coats, and the filthy mess on deck had to be cleaned up. The plywood boards that had been placed all over the main and boat deck to preserve them were removed, along with the tangle of compressed air hoses. Finally, the old plastic tents were removed before the entire surfaces to be given a final topcoat were cleaned. Once complete, the areas were masked off, and final preparations were made to apply the final topcoat. Work in the bilges was complete, and the port shaft had been put back and the propeller reattached. The entire cushions for the sundeck area had been given new covers. The sundeck awning was renewed. The final topcoats were applied to the blue and the white of the hull. By the time we slid down the slipway with everything complete, she looked all the better for the work that had been done.

We now had a short period alongside. During this time, we had much to do. First off, we needed to get the decks cleaned and a washdown complete. The decks were almost black from two months' neglect in the shipyard and required some aggressive scrubbing with the two-part cleaner. Once complete, while not yet perfect, they looked much better. Following this, we did a wash down. The combined effect of a deck scrub and washdown transformed the yacht from a filthy shipyard mess to the yacht she had been prior to arriving here. The engineers began the workup of equipment and machinery they had serviced. During this time, I began work on how I would tackle the Ocean Yachtmaster work. I decided that this time it would be extensive. I spoke with the both the chief engineer and head chef to understand all their requirements for a passage from Palma Majorca via Gibraltar to the Caribbean. *Blue Shadow* carried 111,200 liters of fuel. Consumption for the two main engines and one generator ran at 4,240 liters per day. That was enough for twenty-six days. In other words, more than enough for a crossing from Gibraltar to St Croix at our cruising speed of twelve and a half or thirteen knots, with a healthy margin of reserve. The food was now under my jurisdiction as the passage planner, and it was quite the eye opener. Anselmo, our cheerful, bulky Italian chef, sat down with me and ran through what he intended to carry to feed a crew of fourteen for two weeks, with a healthy reserve to carry into the season within the freezers. The list included:

FRUIT	
Kiwi	300
Lemon	50
Pineapple	15
Avocado	20
Apples	150
Pear	70
Oranges	500
Bananas	200

VEGETABLES	
Onions	10 kilos
Potatoes	50 kilos
Carrots	10 kilos
Lettuce	20
Tomatoes	50
Cucumber	20
Zucchini	10 kilos
Celery	10 bunches
Basil	100 grammes
Parsley	400 grammes
Spring onion	2 kilos
Eggplant	5 kilos

FROZEN

Baguettes	100 brown
	100 white
30 loaves	
Salmon	15 kilos
Cod	20 kilos
Prawn	15 kilos
Veg	15 kilos mixed
Chips	15 kilos
Yeast	2 kilos
	(to make bread)

DAIRY

Milk	100 liters
	(long life)
Cream	5 liters
Butter	6 kilos
Eggs	300
Cheese	10 kilos
Yoghurt	100 small pots

MEAT (FROZEN)

Chicken	20 whole
Chicken breast	50 pieces
Turkey breast	50 pieces
Steak	50
Hamburgers	100
Beef (for stew)	10 kilos
Pork Chops	50
Lamb Chops	100

CANS

Tomatoes	100
Mixed Veg	100 Including Mushrooms, Green beans, Sweet corn, Carrots
Mixed fruit	100 including pears, peaches and pineapples

There were, of course, additional dry store items, including forty kilos of flour, ten liters of vinegar, ten kilos of rice, five liters of mayonnaise, thirty boxes of cereal, twenty kilos of pasta, twenty cans of jam and five kilos of fresh bacon. The list was impressive but not half as impressive a finding a place to store everything.

I had decided by now that charter yachts were not for me. Chartering was impersonal and very much a "get them in and get them out" business. I much preferred the unique relationship that develops between a single owner and his crew, and with this in mind, I tendered my resignation, leaving the skipper with plenty of time to find my replacement and for me to do a very respectable "transatlantic handover".

By the time we had slipped our lines in Palma and made our way to Gibraltar for our final refuel, I was able to concentrate on my Ocean Yachtmaster. I pulled together a file containing all the elements of planning, including our planned track; detailed engineering information, including fuel carried against consumption; weather forecasting during our journey, which would come via facsimile; the food carried aboard and extracts of any publications and almanacs consulted or used. I had decided I would provide the sun-run-meridian altitude as my preferred method for daily position finding.

Having departed Gibraltar, we headed further south until we found our way into the trades, where there were endless sunny days and deep blue seas with perfect small white horses breaking over them as far as the eye could see. I loved to stand on the port bridge wing with the sextant in hand, making small adjustments as I battled to keep the sun on the horizon through the eyepiece. I continued with my sun sights and calculations daily. After a few days, I rewrote my own site reduction forms on the computer and printed out the daily sheets showing my full workings, and it dawned on me: I was navigating at a truly extraordinary moment in time. For centuries, mariners had struggled with finding their position at sea. As the techniques needed to use sextants and almanacs developed, the struggle for accurate timekeeping continued. With the advent of the quartz watch and GPS, every problem of position finding and accurate timekeeping had been resolved, but for me, it was even more fun. With a GPS onboard, I was in the unique position of checking my final midday position, which I noted from the GPS, at the same time as my sight for midday latitude. At no other time in the history of open water position-finding have navigators been able check their sextants and calculation work against the immediate, proven accuracy of a complex navigation system like GPS. From Sunday the 13th of November to Wednesday the 23rd of November, 1994, I entered all my sextant workings in the file, producing probably my finest fix on Saturday the 19th of November, when from my sextant sights and subsequent calculation I produced a position of 21°19′.4 N and 39°13′.1 W, while the GPS position was 21°19′.23 N and 39°14′.51 W. This was good enough for me, and I hoped, along with all the other work I produced, good enough for the examiner.

By the 30th of November, 1994, we had passed through St Croix and arrived in Antigua. Since joining the vessel in June, I had logged a further 8,129 nautical miles. It was time to return to the U.K.

Wasting no time, I sent the full file in for final examination. This time, considering the extensive effort that had gone into the preparation, I hoped it would be enough. It was not long before the examiner summoned me. I went down to retrieve the file and hear his verdict. I had made the grade, and I was now an Ocean Yachtmaster. There was no higher certification within the yachting world, or so I thought!

I was about to get my new found Yachtmaster status tested to the full and it was to occur during a rather innocuous short delivery from Milford Haven to Guernsey. This vessel was a full fledged racing machine. A stripped out racer built of exotic carbon and Kevlar where the mearest of ripples against the hull echoed noisily around the interior. Anyway the three of us were all Yachtmaster Oceans with one being an instructor. So a short trip to Guernsey would be a piece of cake! We left bright and early one morning in the middle of February 1995 and headed south across the English Channel with a rising wind which the vessel relished making light work of the Channel chop. By late that evening the wind had risen to gale force 10 as we rounded the bottom of Guernsey. It was a disgusting night and thankfully the skipper for this voyage had brought with him a hand held GPS making accurate position plotting, in this treacherous area, a piece of cake. It was with a certain smugness that we headed north towards the bright lights of St Peter Port looking forward to getting alongside for some well-earned rest. The outer marker was sighted and we steered towards it. Whilst closing in I noticed a rather worn wooden pole, gently swaying back and forth in the current, slide inches down our side and thought little more about it. We got in and secured the yacht before getting some shut-eye. The next morning during our walk about we peered over the harbour wall and were horrified to see, with the low tide, our post and the huge pyramid shaped rock, to which is was attached, fully exposed. Upon return to the yacht we checked the chart and sure enough it was clearly marked. All three of us had been careless the previous night having paid more attention to the bright lights, with the promise of imminent sanctuary, than to the basic task of safe navigation right to the berth. It was only by sheer luck that our arrival, that evening, had coincided with enough height of tide that we motored right over the top of the rock. Sheer good luck was no way to proceed at sea and I knew it. It was a poor start to my new found status as an Ocean Yachtmaster.

THIRTEEN

A Glitch

The glitch was a woman. It was late 1994, and once again, I found myself shore-based, but this time within the "hypnotic embrace" of romance. The woman in question lived in Devon, as indeed I now did. The whole affair was wrong from the start, and I knew it, but the vortex of romance can be most persuasive, and I, having been at sea for far too long, was easily persuaded. Once again, I found myself determined to be a fully-fledged "grown up" with a sensible, shore-based job and budding home life. I resolved to once more enter the field of academics, but this time it was to be in a subject dear to my heart—quite literally. Throughout my adult life, fitness had been an essential activity for me. Even on the yachts, when alongside, I would often slip on a pair of running shoes and get out for a jog, so it was with some interest that I began to search around for a potential job in the field of health and fitness.

Wherever I went and whatever sports facility I visited, I would find freakishly healthy-looking individuals clutching water bottles with ghastly-looking fluids that clearly kept them at their peak of bulging vigor. I began to realize that this was a world I knew nothing about and that I was going to have to get up to speed fast. My rapid research led me to the American College of Sports Medicine, an organization that I think it would be fair to say is the world leader in the technical study of fitness and the body. In my investigation, I began to realize that while there were many other avenues I could explore to become qualified, this was considered the Rolls Royce of fitness instructor qualifications. With the usual dispatch of monies,

I suddenly found myself chained to a desk, trying to get my head around the very technical study of the human body and complex calculations regarding the consumption of calories and oxygen in the activity pursued. The course was detailed and fascinating, and while I resented more time at the desk, there was no doubt I was thoroughly enjoying the intellectual study of a subject that I had always enjoyed on a practical level. The whole study programme was geared towards a two-part exam, which I was not relishing. The academic part of the exam was long and detailed, but the practical was altogether different. It required taking the blood pressure of an individual, at short intervals, whilst he was riding a bike with escalating loads. I tried my utmost to master this skill but found it immensely difficult, and despite my repeated attempts, I really was not of much use.

The exam day arrived, and I felt I did a reasonable job on the academic section, but up next was the dreaded bike test. I sat outside the door along with the rest of the examination candidates, both male and female, most of whom looked disgustingly healthy and chatted incessantly about the field we were studying. I was content to wait nervously in the silence of my own company. I was called in, and there, sitting atop a bicycle, was an extremely fit-looking athlete who was built like a tank. His arms were enormous, and already secured around his left arm was the blood pressure cuff. It was all business as the examiner set up the scenario of an escalating workload. I pumped furiously to inflate the cuff and diligently listened for the heartbeat through the stethoscope on the crook of his arm as I began the slow release of air from the cuff. The general mechanical noise of a person on a bike was about all I could hear as I strained to find any sign that this man was alive. Apparently, on my first attempt, he was dead. I got nothing. There was nothing for it but to try and remain calm and give it another go. I must have been getting the hang of things, for on the second attempt, I was delighted to announce that he was alive, but my joy did not seem to be shared by the examiner, who began to eye me with suspicion. I did my best to get the results required, and with a great sense of relief, I was told I could remove myself from the room and send the next candidate in.

By September of 1995, I received notice that I had met the required standards and was duly qualified as an American College of Sports Medicine Health and Fitness Instructor. Good, now I could get a job. I tracked down a company called Viva Health and Leisure and interviewed for a job as a fitness instructor at their newest operation, currently under construction in Cardiff, Wales. While successful in the interview, they would not need me for some time because the building was not yet complete and a hefty marketing drive was underway to enroll members. The club was situated at the northern end of town in a rather industrial annex of an otherwise residential area. It seemed the perfect spot. Upon entering, there was a large, open-plan foyer with an eating area off to the left hand side. To the right were the offices. At the far end of the foyer area was access to the indoor pool, changing rooms, dance studio, and a very large weight and cardio room with a high pointed ceiling and floor-to-ceiling windows at the far end. At the opposite end to the windows were a couple of small offices where fitness assessments could be conducted on the members as they joined, but as work continued to pull the complex together, we were beginning to sign up a significant number of members who were excited to get started. With this in mind, some bright spark came up with an excellent idea to get the members involved while waiting for the completion of the club. Each of the fitness instructors would offer up an activity to the members who had joined. One started a running club. Another began a cycling club. I decided I needed to see the Brecon Beacons, a beautiful rugged area in the hills to the north of the city, and so I started a hiking club. About fifteen or twenty people signed up. The best time to get everybody together was the weekend, when we would meet at the club car park and head to the hills in convoy.

We started small. I had no idea as to the ability, interest or general health of those who had come along, and I planned to start with short walks and build over a month or so until we finally tackled the Pen y Fan peak, which is the most challenging walk in the area. Over the weeks, we took some beautiful walks and got to know one another. We became quite a strong little group. I was really beginning to enjoy it all, and the scenery in the beacons was second to none. Some of the members had never taken up such challenges, and as our walks progressed in difficulty and duration, they were getting a strong sense of achievement, coupled with the obvious health benefits.

For most, there is either a love of the outdoors or a certain indifference, but this was an area of the world where it was very hard to be indifferent. A typical walk would have us park the cars and start trudging up through a small forest. At first, there would be lots of chatter, but as the slope increased, people settled into a steady rhythm. Most noticeable was the fresh, clean air, and I couldn't get enough of it. Normally, on these walks, the trees would rapidly give way to scrubby grass, and then, before our eyes was the intimidating sight of the day's chosen challenge. I would normally move up and down the line, making sure everybody was all right, but eventually, the steady trudge brought the delighted satisfaction of making it to the summit of the day's climb. The view was always breathtaking, but being the beacons, with its unsettled weather, one had to choose the days to climb with care.

As the group progressed in confidence and experience, the time to have a crack at Pen y Fan drew closer. I needed help, and there was no greater expert than my best mate, Leo. We had met while we were both enrolled in the Yacht Manufacturing and Marine Industry Management course. Our attitudes towards academic "mediocrity" and our preference for life outdoors were evenly matched. A tall chap with darkish ginger hair and blue eyes that gave nothing away, he had a wonderful attitude, always finding humor in everything. He made for very easy company. He also knew the breacon beacons like the back of his hand. I asked if he would be up for helping me assist with the walking group. He said he would be delighted, and so the mixed bag of humanity began its slow and steady progress from where the cars were parked towards the slopes. We made sure to stop plenty, and while the greyhounds at the front stormed off, those at the rear came under the watchful eye of Leo, who with great patience and humor, kept them moving. We had started early, and by lunchtime, all but the slowest were at the top, gratefully munching on their well-earned snacks. Leo continued to do fine work, cajoling those at the rear to never give up. We could watch them as they moved the best they could up the final slope towards where we were waiting until, much to their delight, they too could collapse on the ground. For some, it had been a significant achievement to build to this level, and both Leo and I were impressed with their effort. Now, we had to get those stiffening muscles back into action and down to the bottom. It was a very exhausted team that arrived back at the cars, and with the club opening only days away, I think we could safely say the hill walkers of Cardiff Viva health and fitness club had been a success for all those who took part.

The club opened to great fanfare, and by now, most of the members were familiar faces, but the serious task of getting them on track for their fitness goals began. All the fitness advisors operated under the auspices of our head instructor, Matt. He was extremely well-qualified and ensured that our instruction was given in agreement with a strict protocol. First, we diligently undertook a PAR—Q, or physical activity readiness questionnaire. This was to ensure that we did not get somebody undergoing strenuous activity for which they were medically unfit. As well as asking detailed questions, we also took their blood pressure. If we had any concerns, we would advise them to see their doctors before continuing with us. Personally, I derived the greatest satisfaction from taking individuals who had led a sedentary life to date and getting them comfortable with a fitness workout that became a part of their lives. In the best cases, these individuals would find themselves choosing better food, losing weight and developing an increased appetite for life.

On one particular day, I had finished up my shift when Matt asked if I wanted to go for a run. It was the first and last time I would ever do so with him. As he appeared roadside and stood next to me, I was suddenly aware of how tall he was. I was six foot, and he was a full head taller than me. We began down the road at a nice steady pace, both chatting away, but it was not long before the pace began to quicken until I had to stop talking and start concentrating on moving air in and out of my lungs. Matt, meanwhile, barely paused in conversing. He kept building the pace and the conversation. I was soon making some godawful noises in the battle for air and survival. Sweat began to course down my face, but Matt hadn't even bothered to unzip his tracksuit. My legs were going ten to the dozen, while with enormous strides, he appeared to be barely warming up. Before long, I was at full-bore, and we were easily doing six-minute miles. I was wondering when he might break, but not a hint of concern lay in his features. He looked like a chap enjoying the Sunday afternoon papers. I prided myself on thinking I was fairly fit, but I was not sure I could hang on much longer. Thankfully, we turned the final corner and headed down the long straight towards the club. There, with merciful relief, I collapsed on the ground, wondering if my straining lungs and heart would ever calm down from their hellish fight for normalcy. Meanwhile, Matt stared down at me curiously until I could draw enough breath to say, "Bloody hell, Matt, what the hell have you been doing for training?"

"Yeah, sorry, forgot to mention I used to run the under-twenty-one eight hundred meters for England!" replied Matt, with not the slightest trace of irony.

As I stared up at the sky, I couldn't think of much to say except, "You might have told me that before we started!"

While work was going well, my personal life was not. My relationship with my girlfriend continued to unravel until it was time to call it quits. Having done so, there was no reason to stay on dry land anymore. It was ironic because I was quite enjoying the work, but once more, I felt the tug of the sea and the continuing urge to continue with unfinished business. However, time and age were not on my side, and I was beginning to have concerns that I would not be relevant or able to find a job after having flip-flopped in and out of the industry over the years.

Temporary Status

My first point of contact was a good friend of mine who was working at one the most exclusive yacht brokerages in the south of France. I told him that once again, I was trying to transfer from my "grown up" life ashore back to the world of yachting and asked if he had any ideas. He paused and then said he might have just the thing. He told me to give him a day or two and that he would ring back. True to his word, he did, and he asked me if my bags were packed so that I could be "parachuted" into a new sale that was conditional upon providing a crew ready to go within the week. I had nothing else in the offing, and a job aboard a 41-meter Codecasa seemed like a great opportunity to me. I was to be the first officer. Richard, the captain, was a large bear of a man, Australian and good-natured with a belly to match the cliché of a barbeque and beer "down under" fellow. His wife was blonde, good-looking and the chief stewardess. The deckhand was a young English lad full of energy and keen to help in whatever way was required. The chef, like the deckhand, was a young Englishman relatively new to the yachting industry. Keen to make his mark, he wasted no time in getting the food on the table, but most intriguing of all was the engineer, who we inherited with the sale. He was Italian and thin as a rake, with the look of somebody who took care of himself. He was over fifty, and maintained the engine room immaculately. His patience was extraordinary. No task was too simple or complex to tackle, and he always got the job done with methodical patience. He was a delightful fellow to work with, and I was to find out he had a fascinating past.

However, for now, we had work to do. The boss wanted to get his hands on his new toy and get cruising. Since the previous crew had been dismissed as part of the sale to the new owner, they had taken little care of the yacht once they had received their notice. As a result of a number of weeks of neglect, she was filthy and needed a good sorting out as quickly as possible.

The yacht consisted of four decks. A lower deck containing the crew quarters, engine room and guest accommodation aft. The main deck contained the saloon, galley and owner's accommodation. The bridge deck contained the bridge, the Captain's office and a sitting room at the aft end. Finally, above the bridge deck was the obligatory sundeck. Within the interior, all the cushion covers, curtains, carpets and bed linen had to be cleaned and inventoried. All interior spaces had to be given a thorough spring cleaning. On deck, we had to get all the cushion covers off and cleaned or renewed, the bright work sanded and varnished, the tenders cleaned and scrubbed and all bosun's stores inventoried and restowed. Finally, we did a deck scrub, followed by a hull and topsides washdown. I had a team of ten day-workers helping in the task, as we lay alongside in Antibes, and within four days, we were ready for action.

The boss arrived tucked discreetly among a veritable armada of blacked-out Mercedes motorcars. There also emerged a stunning array of luggage. The action started almost immediately when the chef decided he wanted to impress the boss and his family by preparing a traditional dish from their homeland. For some unapparent reason, this brought forth paroxysms of verbal displeasure from the daughters, who managed to persuade their father that this was an appalling slur and that the chef should be sacked immediately. The poor captain and his wife did their upmost to try to calm the situation, but to no avail, so with great reluctance, the chef and his bags were dumped on the quay. Such is the world of private yachting!

We were now at full throttle, with a new yacht, new crew and new owners, and everybody needed to be fed. A somewhat flustered skipper dashed about, trying to get a new chef as quickly as possible. This is never the best way to get such an important crewmember. It should be done with diligence and time in hand, not under the constraints of urgent immediacy. By the next day, the new fellow was on board, and we knew very little about him. He was rather nondescript in both looks and demeanor. However, he cooked the crew meal and, shortly thereafter, the boss's dinner without an upset, so perhaps, all was not lost. We tried to get settled in after our bumpy start.

The yacht was parked in the outer harbor of Antibes, the very part I had stared at wide-eyed and open-mouthed, having dismounted the train on my first visit to this part of the world all those years ago. We really had no business being in the outer harbor. At just over forty meters, we were dreadfully outsized by our neighbors. We were the "tiddler" on the block, but on the block we were. She could not be described as beautiful; rather, she was "boxy" as yachts are when too much effort has gone into gaining vertical and horizontal accommodation space at the expense of aesthetics. She was all white with respectably-sized windows; although no belle of the ball, she was in good condition now and ready for action.

"Sardinia!" came the cry from the boss, so Sardinia it was. The boss made instant decisions and wanted instant action. We were now full of fuel, food, crew and guests, so we let go all lines and headed southeast. We made the passage overnight, arriving at Porto Cervo the next day. As usual, as we entered the harbor, the fleet of line attendants flying around in their inflatables assisted us as we reversed up to the quay for our stern-to berth. With the lines secured and the gangway ashore, the boss's wife headed ashore, and I could have sworn she had a mischievous gleam in her eye. The boss looked on nervously as she slipped into a car and sped away. We did not see her again for the rest of the day, and the boss began to pace around the interior. When she did return, the look of alarm on the boss's face was very much on display. Out of the car came bag after bag after bag. This shopping expedition was one of the most impressive I had ever seen. It took considerable time for the crew to get it all aboard and into the saloon, where we left an increasingly heated debate taking place between husband and wife. It would seem that not even the extremely wealthy are immune from the "what the hell have you been spending our money on" variety of discussion, in which only a husband and wife can so charmingly engage. Whatever the outcome of the discussion, it certainly brought forth a rapid curtailment of our cruise itinerary. Slip the lines and back to France was the order, and when we arrived in Antibes, the wife was dispatched back home.

This turn of events did little to deter the boss, who immediately sent orders to depart to Ibiza. When we arrived, we slid along to the far end of the port and maneuvered carefully around Coral Sea, which was berthed at the outer end of the finger quay, and dropped port and starboard anchors before backing up slowly to the quay. Richard did a great job, and all lines were secured ashore. As we put out the gangways and finished tidying up at the aft end, a Rolls Royce with an appalling paint color that defied imagination pulled up. The driver of the car started yelling at the boss, who replied in kind. A brief conversation took place, and the car departed. It was to return shortly thereafter with a fleet of humanity, some of whom were preposterously beautiful young ladies. They all came aboard and the boss was immersed in his friends.

All seemed fine. The evening meal for the crew was cooked, and shortly thereafter, the boss and his gang were fed, but no sooner had the plates been cleared away and the galley scrubbed down than the chef reported to the skipper that he would just like to pop ashore for a quick leg stretch. The skipper told him that that was fine but that tomorrow would be another long day and he would do well to get turned in as soon as possible for some shuteye. I was sharing a cabin with this individual. He departed as I was turning in, and I thought little more about it. I awoke early, around 5.30 a.m., and was a little surprised as I clambered out of my bottom bunk to see that there was no sign of the chef. This did not look good. I got scrubbed up and headed topside in the vague hope that there might be some sign of our missing crewmember—no such luck. Once the skipper had come out of his cabin, I reported to him that the chef was not on board. We decided that all we could do was wait. The boss was a very late starter, rising around noon generally, so we had no real emergency. By late morning, we were all getting edgy and wondering what serious situation might have befallen the chef. The skipper's wife started to prepare lunch. Luckily for us, not only was she an excellent stewardess but she could also cook. Lunch was dealt with and, by good fortune, the boss did not wish to go out on the yacht. That bought us more time to figure out what the hell was going on.

I was sent ashore to try to find the chef. I walked the streets and checked the police stations, asking if anybody had been in an accident last night. Richard checked the hospitals, but after a fruitless search, we returned to the yacht, wondering what to do next. While standing on deck late that afternoon, I spotted a familiar-looking figure wandering, with obvious difficulty down the quay towards the yacht. I informed Richard, who, along with the rest of the crew, came topsides to observe the chef coming back. His difficulty in walking was not due to an injury. He was out-of-his-mind drunk! The boss was still oblivious to our plight, and we wanted to keep it that way. Seeing what he did to the last chef, we thought we would all be on the quay if he got wind of this one. We grabbed the chef by the scruff of the neck and, with a certain roughness, guided him across the gangway and got him below. We wanted to grill him, but he was in no condition to answer any questions. He was dispatched to his bunk. The rest of us got through the day by everybody pulling together to help out. The boss was none the wiser. All the crew was happy to turn in that night. It had been a long day. I fell into a deep sleep.

I awoke in a sleepy panic. There was water cascading down my face. I was on the verge of reaching for my lifejacket and running down the corridor yelling we were "going down" when it dawned on me, as I stood there, that the cabin was dry and nothing was dripping from the deck head. Utterly disgusted, I realized what had happened. The chef had pissed in his sleep, and it had flowed down all over me on the lower bunk. I was incensed and about to beat the living daylights out of him when I decided the skipper needed to be informed about this. I went out into the corridor and knocked on the skipper's door. A very sleepy wife answered, and I explained what had just happened and that I wanted it witnessed. Both the skipper and wife came through, and when they saw the mess, neither were amused. The guy was still comatose drunk, and nothing could be done while he was in this state. I scrubbed up and moved cabins to get some shuteye. Dawn bought a furious skipper and wife to the chef's side, who was roused with no ceremony. He was informed that he was fired but would first scrub the entire cabin from top to bottom, including the sheets. He was also to continue with his chef's duties until the replacement was found, at which point he would be dumped on the quay wherever we were. He was not a popular man.

A great effort was made with regards to due diligence for the replacement of the chef. The skipper informed us that the new chef would join us shortly. In due couse, the yacht arrived in Monaco, and on a day much like any other, while working away on the aft deck, I looked up to see a tall stunning blonde approaching the gangway. I immediately stopped what I was doing and paid very close attention to her moving lips.

"Hello, I'm the new chef," she said. "Is the skipper around?"

I was blown away. Nice choice! I couldn't care less if she burnt the corn flakes in the morning. As far as I was concerned, she looked perfect for the job. As calmly as I could, I showed her up to the skipper and left him to show her around. Hmmm! I hoped this one turned out okay.

I need not have worried. Not only did she bring glamour to the job, she also brought professionalism. The crew was once again able to settle down and keep the season moving along professionally.

I wrote earlier about my worst night at sea aboard a yacht in an easterly blizzard around Lands End. Well, this yacht was to give me one of my finest nights. Being a skipper has its privileges, and one of them is that you get to choose your watches. That means as first officer, you normally get the dull middle-of-the-night watches, often midnight till four. This yacht was no different, and while on a passage returning to Antibes and still well out to sea, I arrived on the bridge. It was late as usual, and before I knew it, Richard had darted below and left me to it. There was nothing to report. Having had a cursory glance out of the bridge windows, I settled down to look over the instrumentation, check the chart and scan the log. All seemed well. I checked the radar—not a thing in sight. It was peaceful. I decided to open the bridge door and check outside. As I stepped outside, I realized it was an absolutely stunning night. It was a beautiful, warm evening—just perfect—not too hot, not too cold. There was not a ripple on the water. The only breeze was generated by our forward motion, and it was a gentle caress. As I walked around the bridge surround to the front of the bridge windows, it was to the sky above that I looked, and what a magnificent sky it was. It was crystal clear, without any clouds or light pollution from all the cities lurking far below the horizon. This is unusual, particularly in the Mediterranean. Normally, there is, at the very least, a shimmering heat haze that dulls the heavens, not to mention clouds or a bright moon. I had never in my time at sea seen a sky like it, even in the deep Atlantic. Every star in the sky was on full display, and in the caressing warmth of the night, it was spellbinding. I leaned back against the bridge windows, and with the bow of the yacht piercing the inky black sea, I just gazed at the beautiful scene before me. I kept returning to the bridge to check the instruments and the radar, but I would always return as quickly as possible to my position in front of the bridge windows. For some reason, the chef, having finished the long day, could not sleep, and she joined me on the bridge to enjoy the finest nighttime display of the heavens I had ever seen. I shall never forget that night, and as my watch came to an end, I found myself in the unusual position of being reluctant to head below to my bunk.

We continued on through the summer until Richard announced, as was his right, that a first mate from his previous yacht would be joining him and that I would be released once we hit the shores of Italy. Our Italian engineer was very excited to be heading back to his home country and was going to take some time off. It was his return that was of interest because he brought his photo album from a life gone by. As he flicked slowly through the album, there appeared photo after photo of his time as a cyclist competing at a high level. He told me how he had been cycling on the Italian team in the Giro d'Italia and had been both doing well and getting ready for the Tour de France when, while hurtling downhill from a mountaintop on a closed-off section of the course, a car had reversed out of a driveway and the ensuing devastating crash had ended his cycling career. He had spent almost two years in hospital and rehabilitation before taking on the world again. Cycling was no longer a possibility due to the severity of his injuries, and so he had found his way into the world of engineering and then yachting. On a yacht, you always know when a department runs well because nobody on board, crew or guest, ever talks about it. This was the way it was with him—charming, hard-working, quiet and knowledgeable. It was a pity there were not more like him. After fifty-four days onboard, we had visited San Remo, Golfe Juan, Ibiza, Palma, Antibes, Monaco, Portofino, Portocervo and Viareggio, but in September of 1997, I found myself on the quay and once more looking for work.

FIFTEEN

A Great Beauty

I wasted little time struggling to find work. Surprisingly, it came to me rather quickly. I was summoned to London to meet the boss, an Englishman, for an interview. We met at his understated but cozy apartment in a rather expensive part of town. He described a little of his background in both the business world and yachting. With the constraints of work and raising a family, he had gradually escalated in size to his present commission. In time, he was interested in some serious world cruising, but for now, it was a matter of continuing to get used to the yacht and the task of running it. For the most part, he had kept all his previous yachts in the British Isles, and the young lad who had been the skipper no longer wanted involvement in this new venture. He asked if I would be interested in coming aboard. I leapt at the offer, and once again, found myself with bags packed, heading to the airport. Destination: Florida.

While I considered *Pilar* to be the most impressive and elegant of oceangoing motor yachts, this next yacht was without doubt the most beautiful sailing yacht I was to skipper. *Copihue* was a 75-foot Andre Hoek-designed staysail sloop. I think it would be fair to say that Andre was synonymous with designs of classic elegance. Within his yachts, there is a powerful connection with acres of teak deck and much varnish work that belonged to a bygone era. Beneath this veneer of timeless good looks beat the heart of a modern yacht. With a dark royal blue hull and just a hint of tumblehome at her substantial beam, her proportions were beautiful. On deck, she was even more so. Her deck hatches and deckhouse were constructed with just the right amount of height above deck to provide a perfect balance. Capping it all was a magnificent varnished wheel and, just forward of it, a majestic compass binnacle. The mast rose high above the deck, and both it and the boom had been painted a cream colour that perfectly blended with the overall look of the yacht. She was, in looks, like a mini J-class yacht, and it was a look that I never grew tired of.

The interior was equally impressive with its tasteful, understated theme. Upon stepping through the cockpit hatch, offset to starboard, was a set of steps at the bottom of which there was a door to the left and a short corridor forward. Turning left into the master cabin not only led to this space but also to the master heads on the port side forward. The cabin itself was situated under the doghouse, with the double bed lying aft under the cockpit sole. When standing up, there was an excellent view port and starboard through the small doghouse windows. Throughout the interior, the décor was the same satin varnished wood with a white painted deck head. It was an excellent combination that provided warmth and freshness. The boss's cabin and heads were not excessive in terms of space; in fact, they could be described as restricted, but it was to the forward end of the heads that the uninitiated were drawn because located here was a door. Looking at it, one thought to oneself, *to where*. Opening the door inwards revealed a businesslike watertight bulkhead door. Undogging it and pulling it open gained entry into a very impressive engine room. The boss had made very clear to Andre that he did not want the engineering to be confined in a tight and inaccessible place, as was so often the case on yachts. He, the boss, was well-aware of the importance of access to engineering for the well-being of the yacht and crew alike, and he wanted no compromise in this area. Located next to the bulkhead was the generator in a soundproof box, which when running, was exceedingly quiet. To the right of the generator was a water maker. On a sailing yacht of this size, it was a first for me, and I never did get used to being mid-ocean and able to take a shower if I felt so inclined, without worrying about the repercussions on our drinking supply. It was a neat, compact and well-engineered unit that if maintained and operated correctly, provided excellent service and made for longer cruising periods in comfort. To the right of the water maker was the caterpillar main engine. In the centre of these three pieces of equipment was just enough deck plate to sit upon with a few tools around while performing maintenance. It was an impressive engine space for a yacht of this size.

Retreating out from the engine back into the owner's cabin and then forward along the starboard corridor led to the main saloon and galley. The saloon was very traditional, taking up the entire width of the vessel, with the galley on the port side aft and the nav station on the starboard side aft. This meant that whoever was in either the nav seat or the galley was very much involved in whatever was happening in the saloon. The saloon itself had a large central table with seats around three sides, forward, to port and aft, with the walkway separating the table from the sofa to starboard. Outboard of the saloon seating on each side were the usual bookshelves, while below the seats, there was ample storage. In front of the saloon were two cabins, port and starboard, with bunk beds in each. Guests used the port side, while the deckhand and myself used the starboard side. Past this was a shared heads. Finally, beyond the forward heads was a large foredeck locker, which contained a dive compressor, plus all the other usual bosun's stores associated with the running of a yacht.

By the time I arrived aboard, *Copihue* had done a certain amount of cruising in Europe, as well as a transatlantic delivery to Florida. She was in need of a refit and clean-up. In particular, I was unhappy with the state of the varnish work, which was going to need considerable effort to be upgraded to what I considered an acceptable standard.

We settled on a small local boatyard that could lift her out. During this time, the usual engine and generator services were completed, along with a full antifoul below the waterline and the replacement of the anodes. Much of the worklist had been drawn up by the boss prior to my arrival. With my lack of familiarity with the boat, I could only oversee the completion of this work in the hope that it covered all that needed to be done. The boss also wanted some rather unusual extra work completed, namely installing a secret gun compartment on board. He had purchased a couple of pump-action Remington shotguns due to his concerns regarding piracy and security in general. How we used these I had not the faintest idea, but somehow, we would have to get trained.

There is a saying in the flying world that any landing you can walk away from is a good one. Well, in a similar vein, any boat maneuver you can undertake without damage is also to be encouraged! I had always prided myself on my boat handling, but I was about to almost get it very wrong. We had decided to continue upgrading the yacht at a different facility in Fort Lauderdale, and our time at the yard was complete. The yacht had been lowered into the water and was pointing bow out of the berth while we tested all the main engineering. Satisfied that the yacht was neither leaking nor malfunctioning in any way as a result of our brief refit, I was now about to undertake the move. Directly ahead of us, about a boat's length away, was a covered berth with the height of the shed rather less than the height of our mast. The boss, not knowing me well, was quite concerned at the first move of his beloved yacht and wanted assurance that I was quite happy moving her with just myself and the deckhand. I told him not to worry. As we slipped all lines, I was about to pat myself on the back at a very sedate departure from the berth as I almost immediately applied full port rudder to clear the covered berth and overhanging shed almost directly ahead. To my sudden alarm, I realized that the yacht was not coming around fast enough. In fact, it was hardly coming at all. In an instant, I realized the problem. It was the simply hydrodynamics of the paddlewheel effect. The yacht had a single engine with a very large propeller and no bow thruster. The water pressure at the bottom of the propeller is larger than that at the top. As a result, during rotation, not only does a propeller produce thrust either forward or aft but also the greater paddlewheel sideways bite at the bottom of the propeller overrides the counteracting sideways thrust at the top. As a result, especially at slow speeds and particularly with a single large propeller as measured from top to bottom, the vessel's aft end can move sideways. During maneuvering, this can be very useful when used to full effect, but when ignored or in my case just plain forgotten, you can get into trouble very quickly. Thus, with the very slow forward speed of the yacht, the paddlewheel effect from the occasional nudge astern was counteracting the full port rudder, and we were turning ever so slowly. I was suddenly feeling quite unwell as I stared at the top of the mast and the shed and wondered when we would make contact during our creeping sweep to port. Outwardly, I tried to appear the very epitome of supreme calm and confidence, but inwardly I began to see my shortest posting yet coming to a very quick halt. With agonizing slowness, the yacht reluctantly came ticking round, and all the while, the mast and shed moved towards their inevitable collision. Miraculously, and it must have been by millimeters, a collision was avoided, and I applied a little more throttle to clear the shipyard. Trying my best to emanate an air of calm nonchalance, I was happy to get away from here with a lesson very well-learned. We continued to our next yard, where we were going to completely redo the interior varnish work, repaint some of the mast and finally rebuild the aluminum boom to incorporate some halogen deck lights.

With the mast work underway and the boom in the welding shop, we could strip out the interior and get sanding. It soon descended into semi-disorganized chaos, with filth and mess everywhere, but slowly and surely, we began to apply finishing coats to the interior surfaces until we could stand back and pronounce ourselves satisfied that the work was done. She looked good, but she needed a spring cleaning, which would have to wait until we were back at our berth in the marina. The newly painted mast from deck to about ten feet up was complete. Shortly thereafter, the boom returned looking fabulous and completely repainted. We got the boom reattached and all lines roved, and once more, we were in a position to return to our berth for a thorough clean up. I tackled boat handling very differently now. I already knew where our berth was in the marina and had figured out a battle plan using the paddlewheel to best effect to get us alongside. For our short journey there, I was thinking ahead as we proceeded and made absolutely sure not to get into any sticky situations. To get into our berth required three ninety-degree right hand turns: the first to exit the inland waterway into the marina, the second to enter the lane between the lines of berthed yachts and the third to enter our berth. Fortunately, the right hand turn favored the natural kick to port of the back end when engaging slow astern, but the last turn into the berth had to be conducted, due to the limited space between the rows of berthed yachts, almost within the confines of our own boat's length. For my first time at this, I was a little apprehensive and approached with great caution. Luckily, there was no wind or current, so I only had to choose, while moving ahead at the slowest possible speed, the right moment to apply full starboard rudder and slow astern on the engine control. As I did this, in a majestic fashion, the forward speed of the boat dropped away, and she spun ninety degrees to the right and came to a complete halt. As I put the engine in neutral and gave a tiny nudge ahead, we slid gently forward into our berth. We put the forward spring on and braked the yacht to a complete halt. The rest of the lines were run ashore, and with some relief, I shut down the engine. The small crowd that had gathered in the hope of some seamanship mishap dissipated. Now back in our berth, we could get cracking on cleaning the yacht. We arranged to have the sails returned to the yacht. The task of attaching the headsail and staysail was done first, and then, we got the main aboard. This was a large and heavy sail, and surprisingly, it was a traditional rope reefing system rather than some form of in-boom or in-mast furling. We had a calm day as we attached the halyard to the head of the sail and slowly hoisted away, attaching the mainsail slides to the sail and running the reef lines. Satisfied it was all done correctly, we lowered the sail, flaking it carefully either side of the boom. Finally, we secured the neat flakes with sail ties and put the main cover on. The work of cleaning the interior continued, along with a complete scrub-down of the yacht. She was beginning to look shipshape. One evening, after a long day, I decided to enjoy the fruits of our labor. I put on all the deck lights and new halogen boom lights to enjoy the full effect of the clean yacht while enjoying a quiet evening drink in the cockpit. She really did look magnificent with fresh clean decks and new varnish work. The freshly scrubbed main cover over its flaked contents and the halogen boom lights, along with the spreader lights, added a touch of class that brought out more than a few admirers. Finally, I shut everything down and turned in.

The following morning, I had to remove the mainsail cover to do some work on the main. Peeling the cover back, my heart sank. Where the neat flakes of the main had been pulled tight under the boom by the sail ties, we now had neat round holes where the halogen lamps had burned through while on during the previous evening. I was gutted. Not only had I nearly crashed this beauty while leaving the yard, I had now burnt holes in the mainsail. In hindsight, it was an obvious mistake. I now had to ring the boss and confess to my stupidity. He was remarkably good about it and let me get on with the obvious task of removing it once again and getting it to North Sails for repair. With the sail laid out on the floor, the holes dotting the main looked worse than ever, but North was able to effect excellent patches before once again returning it to the yacht and getting it back where it should be, on the boom. I treated the boom lights with great suspicion from then on and made it a point to have small flakes and a very careful study of the situation before the boom lights were used. I now hoped that I had put my careless mistakes and stupidity behind me, but I was not to be so lucky. I was about to learn another very hard lesson.

We had done a very great deal of repair refit and general upgrades to the yacht, and besides one short hop to the Dry Tortugas, at the end of the Florida Keys, we had been nowhere. It was time to stretch our legs. The boss wanted to move north for the upcoming summer season. On the 10th of April, 1998, with the boss's wife, two sons, the deckhand and me onboard, we slipped our lines and departed from Fort Lauderdale. It was a beautiful day—clear skies, warm and calm. We settled on a track that took us north with just a hint of east to keep us well away from land. The boss's wife was also the chef and made sure we never went hungry. With plentiful cups of tea and coffee, the day drifted by very pleasantly. It was also an excellent opportunity for me to gain familiarity with our E.C.D.I.S (Electronic Chart Display Information System). This was technology that was relatively new and very impressive. It was now possible for the entire admiralty charts to be downloaded to disc, for which you pay as you would if you purchased a paper one. This downloaded disc, once installed, could display the purchased electronic charts on a screen. Although a prudent mariner would carry all the paper admiralty charts, the real beauty of the E.C.D.I.S was in passage planning. With paper, a waypoint had to be manually drawn on and then the latitude and longitude measured off and noted down. On the screen, you could just move the cursor and press the mouse for a chosen waypoint position, and this could be quickly repeated for a complex coast route. What used to take hours of diligent hard work subject to easy errors could be done in minutes.

However, my work at the screen was interrupted by the rising wind. As evening fell, we were reefing the sail until, well into the night, we were reduced to storm canvas beating into a gale from the north. Normally, a gale would not be much to write home about, but these winds over the Gulf Stream, which could move north in this general proximity at between three and four knots, produced a unique sea state. This kind of forward motion of the sea into the teeth of a gale produced some appalling seas, and we were laboring hard into it. The waves had a steepness to them that I had never encountered, and nobody on board was enjoying it. I tried to keep a course as close to land as I dared to keep us on the fringes of the Gulf Stream and out of the worst of the seas. The ceaseless violent pitching motion as we climbed up the face of these waves before crashing down the backside was exhausting and unsettling for all. I kept my foul-weather gear on and rested on the saloon floor for the entire night, leaping between the chart table and topside as needed. We tacked whenever I thought we were quite close enough to dry land for the current conditions. When I felt the violence of the pitching and crashing was becoming too much as we headed further out into the Gulf Stream, we would tack back in. By dawn, we were glad of the company of daylight, which made things seem not quite so bad, but I was in for a rude shock and about to learn my hard lesson. The helmsman yelled down for me at the same time as the yacht came head-to-wind with sails flapping before bearing away in an uncontrolled fashion.

"What's up?" I asked.

In response, he spun the wheel, which continued spinning until he put his hand back on it. Clearly, the steering cable had snapped, and upon further investigation in the aft locker, this was confirmed. The noise of the sails flogging was not helping the situation. I decided to get the headsail furled and lie on the port tack under a heavily reefed main heading slowly away from land while we got things sorted out. I had not planned a stop in this area, but as luck would have it, we were very close to Cape Canaveral. Upon examination of the chart and available literature, I established that there was a small marina there. With the decision made to head in to port we now needed to get the steering sorted out. I extracted the emergency steering tiller and, having removed the cap over the rudderstock, inserted the tiller onto it and set course for Canaveral. As we continued to close land, the seas abated and order returned to the yacht. The main was taken down, flaked and secured with sail ties. The interior was cleared of the general detritus that scatters around during rough weather, and the crew began to sense the relief of making port after some bumpy weather.

We had now passed the outer markers, and as I often did before arriving at a destination, I tested the engine controls to confirm that the engine would go into neutral and astern with no problem; all was fine there. Next, I decided to test the emergency rudder through a full swing all the way to port and then a second swing all the way over to starboard before returning back to amidships. In the process of leaning heavily on the tiller, the square welded cap at the base of the tiller that sat over the top of the rudderstock gave way at one of the welds. I was now a truly worried man. We were proceeding up the channel and were well into the commercial area of the port, and my steering had failed. I immediately brought the engine to neutral. Quickly removing the tiller, I studied the problem. The cap was made from four square pieces welded at each corner to form the box that sat atop the rudderstock. While it had been welded on the outside of the square cap, there was no weld on the inside to back it up. Clearly, it was just not strong enough for the full loads demanded of it. Despite the broken weld, the box was still in place, and it was all I had. I placed it back on the stock and hoped that with the gentlest of motions, I could get five degrees of helm either way of amidships. This could be done, but only just and very very slowly. I was now going to have to dock the single-screwed yacht with almost no steering and a hefty northerly wind blowing.

We were proceeding down the channel heading west. I got the crew to get ready with every available fender, and all lines were prepared. The anchor was lowered to the waterline, ready for immediate deployment if all else failed. After a brief conversation on the VHF with the marina, it was not entirely clear where our berth was, but there would be a man standing ready to help take lines once we arrived. This was not helpful in terms of planning my maneuver. Looking at the chart, I could see that there was a decent patch of water at the most northern and western end of the marina, which would allow me room to spin the yacht around. As we approached the marina from the east, heading almost due west, a man was standing on a dock lying on our port side, with the berth itself lying on a bearing of about 120 degrees. I couldn't control the turn of the yacht to port with the strong northerly wind, so I decided to try and turn the bow through the wind to starboard with a brief aggressive forward thrust on the engine, followed by slow astern to make full use of the paddlewheel kick to port of the back end. This maneuver, coupled with five degrees of starboard rudder, did the trick, with the bow just making it through the wind. Now, I had to apply a little ahead with a few degrees of port rudder to control how quickly the bow paid off to starboard as the wind bore down on the port side of the vessel. We moved slowly forward and our "port side-to" berth, which had been lying just below our starboard bow, was now dead ahead. We crept ever closer, with a few degrees of port rudder and forward speed just holding the bow on course. We continued drifting forward until we could throw the bow line to the arms waiting for it on the dock. With the bow line secured, I nudged the engine control into astern, and the back end drew into the pontoon and came to a halt—perfect. With an enormous sigh of relief, we secured all lines. I was feeling damn pleased with myself and rang the shipyard to berate them for their shoddy work on the emergency tiller. They listened intently to my diatribe, and when I finally drew breath, a heavily accented northern European voice asked, "Why didn't you use the autopilot extension?"

I was dumbfounded by my own stupidity. Of course! The auto-pilot had a long cable, at the end of which, on a box, were buttons to engage or disengage it. In addition, there were buttons to select one degree and ten degree course alterations. It was rarely used and lay in a tidy coil at the bottom of the locker. It would have been the perfect emergency steering, and I had been a fool to forget about it. The execution of the maneuver onto the berth may have been undertaken satisfactorily, but as the shipyard pointed out, it shouldn't have been undertaken in this manner at all. Once again, I had learned a very valuable lesson. I needed to sharpen my act, and it would not be long before I would be tested once again. Our trip to this marina had an unforeseen benefit. One day, as the repair work got underway, I noticed an individual approaching the yacht who did not look like your typical yachtie. He carefully looked the yacht over from every angle, and while he did so, I had the opportunity to study him. He was of medium height with a neat crew cut and glasses. He was wearing a plain short-sleeve button-down shirt and looked like somebody from the set of a television series about the astronauts of the 1960s. He began asking questions about the yacht that were intelligent and technical. Having struck up a conversation, I asked him what he was doing down here. His response got my attention. He informed me that his name was Rick and that he was one of the senior technical engineers responsible for putting the shuttle back together when it returned from space prior to its next launch. I had always had a fascination with the space game, and it became an easy conversation to get lost in. I asked if he would like to look around, and he leapt at the chance. He was particularly interested in the engine room and electronics, more specifically the navigation electronics. After having spent some time aboard and received answers to his questions, he asked if he could return the favor and give a guided tour of some of Cape Canaveral. The deckhand and I leapt at the opportunity.

We got in his car, and he whisked us through security. I naturally assumed we were heading to the working area of the NASA complex, but instead, he took us to the old launch sites of some of the early Gemini and Mercury programs. He also took us to a site that seemed to be full of "space junk". There was everything from old capsules and rocket stages to rocket motors with their bell housings lying around.

Whenever I pointed at something, he would explain what it was and how it functioned. He also had wonderful stories about the problems of developing, testing and maintaining some of these complex machines. It was a magnificent tour and thoroughly enjoyable to be moving around this area with somebody who had security clearance and knowledge. Rick's wife was no less interesting. She was a developmental engineer working on the design of future rocket propulsion systems. These were not dull people to hang around with. I was beginning to regret not paying closer attention in school. Sadly, the day came to an end, and they deposited us back at the yacht and our waiting work list.

We made fast work of the repair to the steering gear cable. With the guests gone, we found ourselves with some time on our hands. The marina had a small clubhouse on the south side, and following work one day, I decided to try it out. The bar/restaurant area within the clubhouse had a few scattered tables and chairs occupying most of the floor and a large window with a view over the top of the Marina to the north. I made my way over to the bar, deciding a pint of beer was in order. It was deserted, and before long, in my hand was a frosted glass full of my ice-cold favorite. I leaned against the bar and stared out over the scene, with nothing in particular going through my mind. As I surveyed the scrub bush scenery stretching away into the distance, suddenly, from what seemed like every direction, military helicopters appeared, darting back and forth at low altitude. This got me standing up straight. I wondered what they were looking for. As I continued staring out the window at this helicopter mayhem, the door swung open and in came a small troop numbering about fifteen or twenty souls. They did not look like your average weekend sailors. No beer guts among this lot! They ordered drinks and came to the window, and I found myself surrounded. I asked if anybody here knew what all these helicopters were about, which bought forth a round of laughter. Putting me out of my misery, one of them told me that these helicopters were security prior to a shuttle launch. I asked how they knew so much, and this brought forth more laughter as I was introduced to each of the astronauts on NASA's current roster, who were obviously not flying today. Apparently, it was tradition for the off-duty roster to come to the bar here on launch day. It is rare that I am rendered speechless, but this was one of those moments. I thought I was enjoying a quiet pint on a dull afternoon in a remote marina bar, and I was suddenly surrounded by America's select few, giving me a blow-by-blow account of what was happening out of the window in front of me. Each time I turned around, another individual would introduce himself or herself as either a shuttle commander or pilot or even mission specialist. All of them seemed extraordinarily experienced and qualified, and they delighted in chatting and telling me all about life in the shuttle program. The countdown continued until we watched a thin contrail disappear vertically into the sky. As the shuttle disappeared down-range, so too did the astronauts, and once again, I was alone in the bar, staring out the window. As I stared down at my empty glass, I couldn't help but wonder about the surreal moment that had just taken place. Another glass of beer was quite unable to compete with meeting the astronauts and watching the shuttle launch, so I decided to call it a day and head back to the yacht.

Cape Canaveral had been a truly memorable visit, but it was time to move on, so with the yacht full of supplies and crewed up once again, we departed with the full advantage of operational steering. The crew spent the usual twenty-four hours settling down. With thoughts of our approach to Cape Hatteras and our turn north building, I did not consider in any great detail the line of white clouds visible in the very far distance. It was a beautiful day as we ghosted along under a bright blue sky and calm seas. There was a generally relaxed atmosphere onboard and everything was functioning perfectly, but as the hours ticked by and the distant line gained some definition, what we were looking at was clear: a line of cumulonimbus clouds stretching as far north and south as the eye could see. By late afternoon, it was clear we would be entering this lot during the night hours. As the sun began to sink towards the horizon, it lit up the billowing clouds with amazing shades of pink and yellow. Everybody was thoroughly enjoying the view of this vertical wall of cloud that sat benevolently before us only a mile or two away. It was flat calm. I got the main reefed as a precaution, not trusting what might lurk within as we continued our approach in the flat, calm sea. Quite suddenly, out popped a warship that I decided to call up on the VHF for some information on what it was like inside the front. He seemed reluctant to respond, despite my repeated calls, until he finally relented. I asked what the weather was like, and he told me it had been blowing a steady thirty knots with gusts to fifty and that he had come through in about thirty minutes. *Well*, I thought, *that all seems manageable*. I made final preparations, reduced sail to the minimum and, with the engine chugging away, we continued to close until, with a final stare straight up at this impressive wall of cloud, we went in. In a heartbeat, things changed. The rain started immediately, and it was torrential. Following close behind the rain was a steady rise in the wind until true to the report, it was steady on thirty knots. The boat began to lurch about in the rapidly rising seas, but with heavily reduced canvas, we were riding comfortably enough. After several hours of banging around in this mess, I was beginning to wonder about the report of going through in thirty minutes. With the reduced visibility we were experiencing, I didn't believe he would have been moving at any greater speed, and then, it dawned on me. He had been heading west, while the front, even though very slow moving, was heading east.

By now, we were beginning to experience heavy lightning that forked around the sky and lit up our rain-soaked world for brief instances of time. Following the lightning were deep rumbles of thunder. As each hour wore on, the flashes became more intense, and the time between them and the thunder became shorter as we approached the centre of the front. The wind was indeed gusting to fifty knots and holding there for considerable periods of time. The motion on board was wild. The seas were steep and confused as the rain lashed down, beating a steady rhythm on deck. Watch-keeping was extremely difficult because each flash of lightning destroyed one's night vision and left one in extreme darkness. By the time the eyes had adjusted, another brilliant flash started the whole process all over again. The lightning appeared all around us until eventually we must have been struck. The VHF turned itself on and screamed static at full volume. This in itself made everybody jumpy, but at the same time, the lightning strike shut down the engine that had been chugging us along at low revs. Everyone turned to me, waiting for my next move, as if I had experience with lightning strikes turning on VHFs and shutting down engines! Trying to look every inch the cool, calm, collected skipper I most definitely was not, I instructed the nearest individual to shut off the breaker to the VHF and then turn it back on to see if it would still function. Next, I told the watch keeper on deck to put the engine control into neutral while I shut the breaker off and reset it. I had no other weapons in my arsenal, and if this did not work, we would have to sail to our destination. With the breaker off, I searched the engine room to check all was well, as I did with the electrical panel. I could find nothing out of order, so with breakers reset, I went through the start-up procedure and got the engine running. All seemed fine. There was no further excitement throughout the night. In fact, from that moment on, the wind steadily decreased, as did the intensity of the rain, until by dawn, some degree of normalcy seemed to return and we were free to continue on a somewhat quieter note up to Annapolis at the top of Chesapeake Bay.

Our stay in Annapolis was brief, and the boss was keen to keep moving towards Maine, our eventual goal for the summer. To this end, we continued to the top of Chesapeake Bay and found ourselves in thick fog, navigating a narrow channel just prior to crossing over into the top of Delaware Bay. This was where the ECDIS and radar really came into their own. The boss was on the wheel, and I was at the nav station. While I could monitor our position on the electronic chart with our updated GPS position continually on display, the radar would confirm this with the next pair of navigation buoys moving slowly down the picture until they were on top of us. The boss would confirm he had them as they appeared out of the soupy gloom. It was not long before the sun burnt off the fog and we proceeded into and back out of Delaware Bay into the Atlantic once more to resume our passage north.

The boss wanted to transit the city of New York into Long Island Sound, and I had to time our arrival precisely to ensure favorable tides through Devil's Cut. As New York City began to fill our horizon and we passed under the Verrazano Bridge, this whole new vista became a very welcome break from the more traditional views of the sea and far off coastlines. It was a unique and magnificent skyline, but my focus had to return to the navigation, which I remained lost in as we continued down the cut and into Long Island sound.

I had no expectations of Maine. I had read no literature on the area, save what little I needed for navigation to arrive, but with our entry into Portland, I was beginning to think that this was an area I could enjoy. The first thing we did was get taken ashore by the boss for a lobster dinner, and while in any other part of the world, this would break the bank, up here, it seem little pricier than ordering burgers and fries. The boss wasted little time. We got the yacht fueled up and loaded with supplies and set off to discover what lay out there. The reading that I now had to do made it quite clear that there was much to concentrate on with tides, currents, tricky inlets and fog. They weren't kidding. When on the move, I spent my life at the chart table or topside, with chart and cruising guide in hand in a continual quest to keep our position updated, correct and safe. However, the rewards were worth it—anchorage after anchorage of beautiful and wild seclusion surrounded by pristine forests. Every so often, a lobster boat would pass, and we would trade a basketful of them for dinner, giving up little more than some beer or a few dollars. Lobster pots were everywhere and a continual threat to the propeller. Having settled at a spot for the night as the sun went down, the dark night sky full of stars was breathtaking framed against the silent dark silhouette of the forest. There was neither sound nor light. It felt wild, pristine and utterly peaceful. Upon waking in the morning, we would be reluctant to leave the anchorage for fear the next might not be as beautiful, but they always were. Time and again, we would gingerly turn the corner and find another magical spot. I was falling in love with cruising here. We continued up the coastline, and the further we went, the more the tides and currents were a factor. We finally arrived at our furthest point east. Due to the amount of incredible cruising further west, there was very little boat traffic here. As we turned the final corner into our chosen anchorage, we were presented with a wide sweeping bay fringed by a long beach and the usual backdrop of unspoilt forests. If possible, it felt even more isolated and wild than our previous stopovers.

The tides were now enormous, and we anchored accordingly. We lay well offshore, far out into the bay. It was a good thing we did because by the next morning, the scene was quite different. Where the water had been lapping at a neat, narrow strip of shoreline just below the forest that we could gaze upon at eye level, we now had to look up vertically from our small puddle in the bay at acres of exposed seabed, at the top of which was the narrow strip that had been last night's shoreline.

Our time in Maine couldn't last. The boss had an office to return to, and we had a major refit to undertake. With enormous reluctance on all our behalves, we turned our back on what may have become my favorite cruise ground and headed south to Newport, Rhode Island.

The boss had really enjoyed the upgrade of the yacht in Florida following a certain period of professional neglect. As such, he wanted to continue the theme. We choose a well-renowned shipyard inland from Newport, and our refit began. The boss wanted to continue upgrading the varnish work, so with the mast removed, we set about sanding the entire upper deck down and getting several more coats on. The shipyard, meanwhile, was engaged in a full repaint of the hull, including the white boot stripe. For the final topcoat of our deep royal blue, the yacht was wheeled into a state-of-the-art paint shed, where the air conditions were carefully controlled so that the lads were able to apply the final coat that gave it an absolutely unbelievable mirror finish from stem to stern. Finally, the undersides were antifouled, and new anodes were put on. This brief surmise within a paragraph encapsulates two full months of intense hard work, by the end of which she looked magnificent. Before the boss arrived, we gave the yacht's teak decks a two-part clean, which gave them a golden sandy color, and finally a full wash-down. Despite her heavy cruising schedule, it would be fair to say she was looking better and better all the time, but I wasn't satisfied and determined that once in the Caribbean, we would get some more varnish on the topsides bright work. For now, we were done.

It was late October of 1998. The Atlantic hurricane season was over, and before the North Atlantic turned foul on us, we needed to get south. We departed on the 28th of October for our next destination, Bermuda. I was glad to leave the chaos of a refit behind and get back to doing what this yacht did best—sailing! Once at sea, it was not long before we got some ideal sailing conditions, a steady force six close on the beam. Both the yacht and crew loved it. It was almost the perfect point of sailing, where she creamed along at a steady ten knots and barely any healing. The wave action was dampened not only by our powerful forward motion but also her substantial beam and the steadying influence of her full hard-working sails. To stand at the back of the yacht and watch as she pounded along, barely acknowledging the seas of the North Atlantic sliding beneath her belly, was pure bliss. We also knew that as each mile slid by, we were getting closer to warmer weather and that the chills of the north would shortly be our concern no longer. With Bermuda looming on the horizon and the guests' phones coming within range, a great deal of phone chatter started up. I paid little attention due to the demands of navigation. Once alongside in St. Georges, dealing with the usual myriad of customs and immigration paperwork, I was fully absorbed in my duties when, quite suddenly, on leapt a delightful blonde, who introduced herself as Philly. She began to eye me up and down as she sought out her friends, who were guests on board. She leaned in and told me that she had someone she wanted me to meet. Once again, I paid little attention and returned to my endless tasks as skipper, trying to keep some semblance of order. The boss, for his part, wasted little time getting organized and suddenly announced we had a berth at the Royal Bermuda Yacht Club in Hamilton. Once more, I got the charts out and prepared for our next leg. We departed St. Georges and proceeded north around the top of the island and entered the sound at the western end. The color of the water was beautiful, a bright blue in the sunshine, and on the sea bed, there was beautiful pink coral sand. We anchored for lunch and a swim before proceeding to our berth, which seemed the best in town, portside to on the finger pontoon, right next to the yacht club. The yacht had done its shakedown cruise and was in perfect working order. We were now secure alongside, and we remained here for a few weeks.

Before we left Newport, I had spoken with the boss and told him that we seemed no further on with getting the crew trained with the firearms. I suggested that my friend Leo might fit the bill for both a firearms work-up and professional training for the crew. The boss agreed and suggested that Leo should arrive a day or so before he, the boss, was due to leave the yacht for London and we were due to head to the Caribbean. I rang Leo and asked if he might be interested in leaving behind the delights of a British winter for the misery of weapons training aboard a private yacht heading to the Caribbean, all food and drink thrown in. Surprisingly, he seemed only too happy to drop everything and dash to the airport!

I now had my weapons training officer organized, but I had two further problems looming. The first I could handle; the second I wasn't so sure about. The first was a late-season hurricane approaching the island. The second was a blind date. The hurricane's track, as always, was a little indeterminate, but it looked to be heading well offshore to the west and then curving a little more north east before dashing off across the Atlantic to entertain Europe. I now had to prepare the yacht for the possibility of hurricane-force winds, severe gales at the minimum. The yacht seemed to be moored in almost the perfect spot for the southwesterly winds that were forecast. Her high bow was tucked in under the lee of the finger pontoon pointing north, while the stern's port quarter would bear the brunt of the forecast wind from the southwest. I put out every line I had available to as many different stanchions on the pontoon as I could. Antichaff was placed at all points of contact of the lines through fairleads or over the lips of the concrete finger dock. Our fenders were large and inflatable, and while, generally, we might only have a couple on deck for use, with the approach of this storm, I got them all out and ready. Full engine checks were completed, and the engine was placed on turnkey stand by for emergency maneuvering. The storm was good enough not to ruin a good night's sleep and began manifesting itself in the early hours of a new day. The winds, true to the forecast, began to build from the southwest, as did the seas, until by the middle of the day, we had waves crashing into the stern and sending up clouds of spray that would tear off downwind. We monitored the situation carefully as the yacht danced on her mooring lines. The hurricane was moving at speed and becoming extra tropical. Her influence on the island began to abate until by the next day, we once again lay quietly at our berth.

A hurricane is one thing, but a blind date is quite another. I arrived at the bar on Front Street and headed upstairs. Having ordered a drink, I stood and surveyed the scene. The usual end-of-day workers clasped their cocktails and chatted animatedly among themselves. It didn't seem particularly busy, and I was beginning to regret coming, conjuring up ghastly images of assignations I would have to spend the rest of the evening trying to wriggle out of. Then, I spotted her. She wore a linen suit, pale green, fitted at the waist, and flared trousers with expensive high-heeled shoes popping out at the bottom. Her jacket was open, revealing a white shirt that hugged her trim figure. She had fine features and short-cropped hair, with two large eyes that were intelligent, beautiful and managed to intimate "mess with me at your own peril." She was way above my pay grade, but I threw caution to the wind and dove right in. The rest of the night was lost in great company, good food and alcohol. I had met Sylvie, my future wife, and I was smitten.

I was not on the island to court beautiful women. I had a yacht to look after and our "weapons officer" was about to arrive. The boss was about to return to the U.K. and wanted to meet Leo for his own piece of mind. I met Leo at the airport and was delighted to see him again. It felt strange that I should be able to have a friend along during the course of my working life, and I was a little apprehensive that things would work out okay. I needn't have worried. Once the boss met him and they opened the bar, I realized there would be no problems, because among Leo's many talents, his ability to consume alcohol and function at a high level was impressive. I left them to it and resumed preparations for our departure to Antigua.

It was early, very early, on the 18th of November, 1998 when Sylvie and I had managed to destroy any chance of sleep with our goodbyes. I stepped aboard, and with little time other than that needed to make final engine checks, I decided we were ready for the off. With the crew roused and first light upon us, we slipped lines and experienced about the easiest departure you can have: exit the channel from St.

Georges and turn right. That was it. Mind you, with no sleep, that was quite enough to concentrate on, and with sails set and our bows pointing south, we could all settle down. With everything set and orderly, a quick nap was in order for me.

Without doubt, by the next day, I was much better. It was time for Leo to work his magic. He pulled both guns from their storage and set about stripping them down and cleaning them before putting them back together, making sure that at every stage, everything was in perfect working order. Having reassembled the weapons, he pronounced himself satisfied and ready to start firing. We had bought along some biodegradable paper bags that we secured and threw over the back. Once about ten meters clear, he proceeded to destroy the bag with the devastating accuracy and skill of a professional. It was now time for the deckhand and me to take our turns. I was feeble, but the deckhand seemed quite relaxed and skilled with a pump action shotgun in his hand. He proceeded with such vigor and enthusiasm that as soon as the paper bag hit the water, he blasted the living daylights out of it, nearly taking the back end of the yacht with it. Leo continued to coach and guide us until, with a depleted inventory of ammunition, we called it a day. Finally, Leo discussed the issue of the use of a weapon. He made the point that to elevate a situation to the moment of using a gun was serious indeed and should never be done lightly. It was an interesting point and gave me another subject to engage my mind during the long night hours when sleep failed me.

We continued south, and the weather continued to warm. There is always something very pleasant about heading towards the sunnier climes of the Caribbean, and this trip was no exception. I was hoping that Leo was enjoying it all, but he seemed utterly content with leaving the troubles of the office thousands of miles away and particularly relished spending a few moments on the night watch just gazing at the stars against the backdrop of the faint glow of the instruments in the warmer air of the approaching Caribbean.

For some reason, I was getting jittery about timing, mainly because Leo had to catch a flight back home, so as Antigua approached, I ran the engine, as well as us sailing at good speeds. I also determined that we should arrive in daylight because this was my first time skippering a yacht in this part of the world and I wanted no exciting challenges during our arrival. As the misty grey outline of Antigua appeared in the distance, I kept upping the engine revs to ensure our daylight arrival until we were doing an excellent impression of a World War II destroyer at full tilt, our stern dug down as we barreled along. Eventually, we shot around the eastern and southern end of Antigua before gingerly entering Falmouth harbor and finding a suitable spot to anchor. With the splash of the anchor, I reversed, laying out the cable on the seabed in a seamanlike fashion before I pronounced myself satisfied and shut down the engine. We had arrived in plenty of time for an excellent dinner ashore in celebration. By the next day, Leo was dispatched to the airport, and the deckhand and myself set about getting things shipshape.

We were to spend Christmas in Antigua, with the boss and his family visiting, and it was on Christmas day that we had one of the finest days of sailing I can remember. The boss had determined that Christmas should be low-key for everyone, but he insisted, quite rightly, on a quick sail before settling down to a relaxed day. We awoke to a stunning day with temperatures rising to between seventy-five and eighty degrees and very few clouds. The wind was perfect, around eighteen to twenty knots from the east, with a touch of south. With the anchor hoisted aboard, we departed Falmouth harbor and set both the main and headsail. We broad-reached out for about an hour and then went back on the other tack. It was her finest point of sailing. With her great beam reluctant to give up more than a hint of heel, she just kept accelerating as the warm gusts leaned against the sails. A sparkling bow wave leapt up from the stem, and she left a boiling wake behind as we powered along in excess of ten knots. It was spectacular, and the yacht and crew relished the conditions. It

222

seemed sad that as promised, within a couple of hours, the boss declared it was time to return to Falmouth harbor. Once more, we lay anchor to enjoy the rest of the day.

My time aboard was coming to an end. I knew that if I was going to continue in the yachting industry, I had to set my sights on larger vessels, but first I had to deliver this one to Florida, so on the 21st of January, 1999, with the boss aboard, we lifted the anchor for the final time in Falmouth harbor and set our course northwest. We were to sail via Virgin Gorda, the Turks and Caicos and the Bahamas before finally entering Fort Lauderdale on the 31st of January, 1999. I spent a further month onboard, upgrading all the varnish work and making sure she was in perfect working order before departing the yacht in February. I had completed a circuit that started in Fort Lauderdale and covered the east coast of the United States as far up as Maine before heading south to Bermuda and the Caribbean and then back up to Fort Lauderdale. In my fifteen months on board as skipper, we had sailed 6,422 nautical miles and completed a major refit.

SIXTEEN
The End. Well—almost!

By this stage, the yachts that were beginning to appear from ship-yards, due to their size, barely fit the description of yachts. They were now ships, some of them of quite considerable size. When I had first arrived in the south of France, a 50-meter yacht was a good size. Now, they were a dime a dozen. With this new demand for larger yachts, a greater burden was being placed upon the humble Ocean Yachtmaster Certification. This qualification had really been designed for the much smaller private yacht that had chosen to wander further afield. It was not designed for the demands of the large private yachts in the 65-meter and upward range that were beginning to appear on the scene with regularity. The qualification I had fought so hard for was no longer relevant. Various professional bodies had come together and decided that those individuals who wished to be captains of large motor or sail yachts would now have to return to "school" and gain the "Certificate of Competency (Deck Officer) Class 4 Limited to Yachts". This, once complete, would allow an individual to sail as Master of Yachts under 3,000 gross tonnes. It would also certify an individual to sail as chief mate or officer in charge of a navigational watch, again on yachts under 3,000 gross tonnes. This was all very well, but how the hell was I going to pass this one? Getting the Ocean Yachtmaster had stretched my limited intellect to the breaking point. I really had no interest in pushing it further. After all, I wasn't sure what might happen! However, upon further investigation, if I didn't wish to be piloting rowing boats around a duck pond, I had no choice.

Having established that I had the appropriate amount of time skippering yachts to date and enough sea miles under my belt, I enrolled in the course. In April of 1999, I arrived at Warsash Maritime Collage near Southampton, where not many years before, I had done my engineering diploma and degree. The course consisted of modules, some of which were completed in a week and some of which took two. At the end of each module, you had to pass an exam, and upon satisfactory completion, a certificate stating as such was issued. In total, nine modules had to be completed, at the end of which there was an oral exam. It was the oral exam that sent the fear of God through most us, but more on this later. First, the mostly self-explanatory modules are listed below:

   i) Professional Yachtmaster Business and Law.
  ii) Certificate of Proficiency in Medical First Aid Aboard Ship.
 iii) Personal Survival Techniques.
 iv) Vessel Construction and Stability.
  v) Certificate of Proficiency for Persons in Charge of Medical Care Aboard Ship.
 vi) Certificate of Completion in GMDSS Radio Communications (GOC).
 vii) Commercial Yachtmaster Navigation & Radar Course.
viii) Training in Advanced Fire Fighting.
 ix) Certificate of Proficiency in Survival Craft and Rescue Boats.

The entire course was comprehensive and designed to equip a captain with the framework of knowledge necessary to deal with all manner of situations. It was also designed to get the captain to think. Particular emphasis was placed on navigation, rule of the road and radar work. The college had been recently equipped with a state-of-the-art bridge simulator, from which they could conduct navigation exercises at all times of the day or night in a variety of conditions. Planning was done in a classroom under the leadership of a team captain, whose responsibility it was to lead a bridge team in the simulator through the exercise. It was realistic and induced considerable sweat on the brow as one navigated up Southampton waters in the dead of night as a squall came through, obliterating visibility as you continued to pilot the vessel under these most trying of situations. The instructors could change things in a heartbeat and never failed to do so. It was hard work. The master mariner who led us through the rules of the road was no less talented and demanding. Whereas to date I had struggled to master what to do when confronted by another vessel either by day or by night, he went one step further and analyzed each sentence of the rules and made us understand the various interpretations. It gave clarity to the rules that I had studied, often in picture form, over so many years. He also took the art of passage planning to a whole new level. The detail of work he required to just head from port around a headland to an anchorage was impressive. Once again, he took our attitudes and experience to date and expanded it, equipping us with a whole new methodology for the business of the safe passage of a vessel. In other words, he got us to think hard about our current situation, as well as our planned future one, and what to do should things go wrong.

All these courses, with their associated exams, were demanding enough, but we had a final hurdle to overcome: the oral exam. This exam was conducted by a highly experienced master mariner. He was quite free to roam across the oceans, anywhere in the world, and come up with all manner of weather and traffic situations, at all hours of the day or night, and see how you coped as master of this fictitious vessel. For candidates wanting assistance in preparing for this final exam, a retired master mariner, who lived within a stone's throw of the college, was available for hire. He would offer up as much time as you wanted to pay for. His time was invaluable. Not only did he instruct me but he also probed my knowledge for gaps and weaknesses, which I would then go back and study before returning again to continue the process until he pronounced he was done. I had passed all the modules, revised all the material and been coached by a master mariner until he seemed satisfied I would pass. I hated exams, particularly oral exams. I was a bag of nerves and knew that my overloaded brain was trying to leak information as fast as it could to make room for the usual nothingness that occupied it. I just hoped I could retain enough to make it through.

I reported to the office in Southampton at the requested time. Having completed the paperwork, I found myself waiting in a narrow corridor on one of the seats next to a rather unobtrusive door. I don't recall how long I waited, probably not much more that half an hour, but it felt like an eternity. My palms were sweaty, and adrenaline coursed through my veins, making me edgy. I sat, trying to recall all I had learned, and found my mind had gone blank, which served to make me even more restless. Suddenly, the door swung open and one of the candidates with whom I had been through the course came out. He was currently skippering a large yacht and had considerably more experience than I. There were tears welling up in his eyes.

"How did it go?" I asked.

"Not well," he replied. "I failed. Your turn."

With that, he was gone. We had been warned about the high failure rate for this course, and I had just witnessed it firsthand. This did nothing to calm my nerves, and with sweaty palms, a now-empty mind and rapid sense of doom enveloping me, I headed towards the door and entered. The square room was empty, save one desk scattered with a plethora of all things nautical, behind which sat a man with neat graying hair and gold half-rimmed spectacles balanced on the end of his nose. His bearing was the very epitome of a respectable master mariner with considerable decades of experience at sea under his belt. He peered at me, taking me in, assessing me, examining me. I realized he had begun. For a brief moment, my concentration was broken by the view out of the window behind him to the buildings beyond, but my attention was quickly drawn back to matters at hand when he began.

"You're the master of a 40-meter, and you have just been called from your bunk in the middle of the night as you approach the Dover Straits shipping lane. You were called due to failing visibility and a report of some lights that have now disappeared into the mess closing in. What are you going to do?"

I began to reply with what I considered a logical response. By the time I was halfway through, he interrupted to add new information and scenarios, never anything that helped the building crisis, and so we went on for a couple of the most intense hours of examination in my life. Under pressure, I was pleased that my brain kept dredging what felt like the right information from the depths, which I then tried with all the calmness of a budding master mariner to deliver verbally to my examiner. His constant interruption halfway through my responses left me wondering whether he was satisfied with my response or beginning to formulate the opinion that I was rather a waste of space. In a couple of hours, he did a very thorough job of covering almost all the topics I had studied in the previous months. Eventually, he pushed back from the table and lifted the glasses from his face before twirling them gently in one hand while he studied me again. I tried to return his gaze with calm nonchalance.

"Right," he said, "we're done. You might be interested in what I am doing here. I need to know that when I lie in my bunk asleep on passage with you in command of the vessel, I can sleep comfortably in the knowledge that you will keep me and the vessel I am on safe at all times in all situations. I am delighted to tell you that you have achieved that today."

I was truly elated. This was the academic pinnacle I had been determined to achieve and, much to my surprise, it was done.

With all my paperwork in order, I now began to hear rumors of a potential job. It was taking time to gel, not least because the yacht in question had to be shipped across the Atlantic from its summer

Mediterranean cruising ground to the East Coast of the United States, more specifically Fort Lauderdale. In the process of transporting the yacht, discussions regarding operational details, to which I was not privy, continued in the background. All I knew was that early in November of 1999, I was on a jet to Fort Lauderdale and told to stand by. The first few days were peaceful and calm as we awaited the arrival the yacht aboard the transport ship. This ship was no ordinary vessel. It had the capacity to sink deep into the water and have yachts of various sizes drive on to the back end before being secured. Once all yachts were aboard and lashed down, the ship would pump out the ballast tanks, rise up and be ready to transport the yachts across the Atlantic. The ship arrived on schedule, and I, along with the other captains and crew, reported to the commercial docks where the transport ship was tied up. As I clambered aboard, I caught sight of my next command. She could best be described as a speedboat on steroids. At almost 110 feet, she was not small, and above her large hull, there was little superstructure apart from the open bridge, which was enveloped by a snug cover that was secured along the top of the bridge windows, aft, to the swept-back radar arch. The large sundeck aft was open, with steps leading down to the swim platform.

I had a far larger problem than admiring the view. With the ship now fully submerged, the crews on the yachts at the aft end had their engines running and were in the process of disengaging various bow and stern lines before slowly departing. I, on the other hand, didn't have the faintest idea of how to even turn the engine on. On top of which, this yacht had a unique propulsion system consisting of two diesel engines coupled to Ka Me Wa water jets. The jets could be rotated port and starboard to act as rudders, and they had a bucket that could drop down, which would redirect the water jet back underneath the yacht to provide astern thrust. I had never operated a system that was anything like this. Now, to add further confusion to the situation, the Captain I was replacing had been ordered to assist me in the handover of the vessel. He was French, as was the deckhand, and quite understandably extremely put out at having been fired. He refused to assist in any way, except to say, "You are the Captain now. You must sort it out!"

The deckhand, who was also the engineer, decided that he liked working on the yacht and that despite his reservations at having this new "English dog" of a Captain aboard, he had better show his willingness to help if he was to stay on. He broke off his French conversation with the old skipper and ran through the start-up procedures for the two diesel engines. When the grand moment came to start them up, we pressed the button, and nothing happened. With much rushing about, the deckhand checked and rechecked everything until we realized the engine start batteries were dead. By now, the crew of the transport ship was getting irate at our lack of progress and threatened to call in the expensive tow vessel that was standing by for such situations. I pleaded for a few more minutes as the old skipper looked on with smugness at the general chaos descending upon me. Truth be told, I wasn't really enjoying my first day on the job! Usually, I got to look the vessel over carefully alongside over a number of days, learning where everything was and how it worked. This, on the other hand, was chaos and confusion at its finest, and I still hadn't the faintest idea how to operate the drive system.

I was at a loss until the deckhand suggested there was a small emergency battery for generator start-up that we might be able to use. I told him to jump on it, and with great satisfaction, I heard the generator tick over and burst into life. We now had the ability to run power directly from the generator through the dead batteries, and soon, after a rather disgusting belch of black smoke, the engines came rumbling to life. This was none too soon because the crew aboard the ship were jumping about all over the place. I was now going to have to drive this beast and was much relieved to know we had a bow thruster, at least relieved right up to the moment the deckhand told me I shouldn't use it because it leaked oil. We had an almost dead-astern 100-foot departure off the back end of the submerged ship between two funnel stacks that stuck out high above the water. The engine controls were two handles that could be pushed forward from neutral to ahead or back upright and aft for astern. The handles were on a rotating bezel that turned the water jet left or right. I opted to not rotate the bezel, but just to use the forward and astern thrust. I had no idea how the vessel would handle within the confines of a submerged ship. With all lines aboard, I pulled both levers gently aft until I felt the gear box engage the water jet, which with the bucket down, directed the water jet back underneath the yacht, and we started moving slowly astern. I held my breath, hoping the bow wouldn't swing in some strange direction and make me look like the brand-new unfamiliar skipper I was. Luckily, nothing exciting happened, and we continued drifting astern until we cleared the ship and her stacks and I could breath a sigh of relief.

We had no marina berth, as currently we were trying to sort out with the boss which shipyard we would go to for a refit. The lines of communication for this process were not simple. I had gotten the job through a broker who also had a representative on the ground in Fort Lauderdale. I was also getting messages via the deckhand from the owner's accountant, who spoke only French; hence, he had to deliver his message via the deckhand. These two "separate parties" often imparted different questions and information, and because I never spoke to the boss in person, it rapidly became extremely boring trying to disseminate the boss's wishes through these often opposing forces. However, we had a small refit to undertake in Miami, and I was determined to get a decent job done. The boat was lifted from the water, and once on the hard, all the antifouling was repainted, and the anodes were replaced. The bar on the fly bridge was removed and repainted, and new cushion covers made. The usual extensive machinery overhaul was done, including oil changes for the main engines and generators.

With the vessel complete, we slid back into the water and tested all systems before pronouncing all was well, at which point the yard informed me we could not leave, due to some problems with getting the bill paid. More communications took place between the various parties, with me stuck in the middle. We needed to conduct sea trials, which the yard allowed us to do, so we slipped our lines and proceeded down the canal to the main port of Miami and headed out to sea. As we exited the channel, I slowly ran the engines up to full speed and enjoyed the power of two 1,500 horsepower diesels digging in. As the turbos wound up, we picked up speed to around seventeen or eighteen knots. It felt good to be at sea as we rode comfortably up and down to the light swells.

Now, the fun began. This yacht was also equipped with a gas turbine aero engine that sat amidships between the two diesel engines. It was coupled to a fixed water jet, i.e., it could not alter its thrust port or starboard, and there was no astern bucket. It was just on! We had tested it running in port, but now we were going to run it properly at sea at full power. I went through the start-up procedure and listened to the metallic aero whine as it picked up speed to its full operational power. Being an aero engine, it needed little warm up, and so I engaged thrust, and instantly, a small jet of water arched out from the back of the yacht as we picked up speed. I continued to push the throttle forward, and the effect was dramatic; 108 feet of Mangusta motor yacht lurched forward, and this was from a respectable speed of over twenty knots. We continued to accelerate past thirty-five knots, then forty. I pushed the throttle all the way forward until I had 7,500 horsepower thrusting us forward. While the diesel engine water jet spewed out directly astern, the central water jet, from the gas turbine, arced up and out as high as our heads while we stood on the open bridge before falling back to sea far astern. It was impressive, as was our forward speed. We continued accelerating until we settled at around forty-eight knots. This was awesome. I had never been on a vessel of this size with such power at my disposal.

We set up a beautiful rhythm, with the bow rising up and over the well-developed swells, which were perfectly spaced for our speed to prevent any slamming. I was really beginning to enjoy this. I turned both water jet bezels, and we went into a long, slow high-speed turn as we headed back to Miami. All machinery seemed to be running fine, and we continued to thunder along at full speed until we hit the outer marker of the channel leading to Miami, by which point I had throttled back the gas turbine to idle and was slowing down the diesels. By the time we had slowed to about fifteen knots, it felt as if we were standing still. I continued throttling down as we entered port, at which point I heard an announcement that no Captain ever wants to hear.

"We have a fire in the engine room," announced the out-of-breath deckhand.

I slowed the engines to a halt, and with no traffic around, I told the engineer to stand watch for a second while I dashed to the engine room. I leapt down below and into the engine room, which was thick with smoke. I could see no flames, but clearly, something was not right. If I stayed any longer, I was going to choke on the noxious fumes. I had no choice. I had to contact the harbor authorities and seek assistance. I got onto channel sixteen, announcing myself and my problem and requested assistance. Eventually, I got the following puzzling response.

"Very good, sir. We will have the fire brigade standing by. Could you come alongside the fuel quay, where they will be able to assist you."

The fuel quay? I thought. *Is this really the best place for a vessel on fire?* I thought I had better ask him. Perhaps they had a special fuel in Miami that put out flames!

"This is the vessel on fire requesting assistance. Is the fuel quay the best place for a vessel that is burning with full tanks of fuel?" I asked.

"Standby, sir," came the response.

By now, my predicament must have reached some of the powers that be in the media empire because a news helicopter arrived and began hovering overhead. You could almost hear him licking his chops at the thought of catching me going skyward at a hundred miles an hour, sitting atop a fireball as my command goes up in smoke! However, I was determined not to fulfill his desire for some outstanding breaking news.

The VHF crackled back to life, informing me the fireboat was on his way. He must have concurred with my desire not to blow up at the fuel quay, taking their fuel supply with me. Sure enough, within moments, the fireboats arrived and unloaded a squad of very large men, who proceeded to destroy much of the beautiful work that had taken place over the previous couple of weeks. Numerous feet surrounded by steel-encapsulated rubber thundered all over the vessel, running hose lines everywhere. I shrank into a corner, wishing I could lose myself in a cup of tea and newspaper. There was little else I could do as semi-disorganized chaos descended around me. The senior fireman reported to me that the fire and/or smoke seemed to be coming from the lagging around the exhaust from the gas turbine. This was odd because it was the one material that was designed not to burst into flames, in theory anyway. I asked them to keep me informed of the water levels in the engine room as they liberally sprayed everything in sight. At the same time, they cut away the lagging and left the sodden lumps lying all over what had been our gleaming engine room floor. By the time they had finished, the mess was impressive. As fast as they had come on board, they began to retreat, taking their hoses and equipment with them until the final one leapt over the guardrail.

"Have a nice day, sir!" he cried.

Hmm! I wasn't quite sure that was possible now. It was right back to the shipyard to start again. All this excitement brought forth a further torrent of messages from various parties until I could stand it no more. Whether I was tired from my time aboard the last yacht and going straight into the Masters Course, whether I was just getting too old to put up with too much nonsense, or whether I just had a feeble sense of humor, who knows. Whatever it was, I decided this operation was not for me. I resolved to get the yacht cleaned up and handed over to the new skipper, much to the disgust of the people who got me the job. True to my word, within a week or so, the yacht was right back up to scratch and the new skipper arrived aboard.

It was the 18th of December, 1999, and I had handed command of the yacht over to the new skipper. My last job was to assist him, in whatever capacity, with the delivery of the yacht to the Bahamas. I had set a deep-water passage to Atlantis Marina in Nassau, but the new fellow would have none of it. He knew these waters like the back of his hand and he would cross the shallower reef areas to save time and distance. I made it quite clear that if we did so, it would be on his shoulders and his command. He plotted his course on his computer, and I felt somewhat liberated of my duties. I had shown him the new printed start-up procedures for the engines and gas turbines, which I had made for new incoming skippers. I left him to it to enjoy the ride.

As we left the harbor, the diesels were bought up to speed, followed by the gas turbine, and once again, we found ourselves blasting over the ocean at forty-seven or forty-eight knots. We were across the straits of Florida in no time. I went to the bow and watched with some discomfort as we crossed at full-throttle from the inky blue depths to a much shallower light blue sandy bottom, with occasional black coral heads flashing past at alarming speed. I sincerely hoped this guy knew what he was doing. I asked him what we were looking for. He responded that there was a mark we needed to leave to starboard before we could alter course to starboard down to Nassau. He assured me, looking at his computer, that all was well, at which point I looked to port and saw, about a half mile away, a post sticking out of the water. I asked him what it was. His faced drained, and he reached for the throttles to slow us down. We were way off course. Why we had not hit a reef was a mystery, but he gently threaded our way back to the marker before resuming our course to our final port.

There were no further incidents and perhaps, like myself, a little shaken, he asked if I could assist with parking her, it being his first time handling the vessel. I was delighted. Entering and exiting port was always the fun and challenging part of the job that I enjoyed, and I was beginning to feel a little more comfortable with this beast, so with some final jostling, we came to rest in Nassau, and the engines were shut down. There was nothing more to do except ask him if he needed anything else in the way of assistance before departing. With that, I was gone to the airport.

Sylvie was living in Bermuda. She was renting a small cottage that belonged on a postcard. White with blue hurricane shutters, it sat at the end of a short driveway tucked back from the main road. Palm trees swayed in the background, and when sitting on the terrace in the warm evening sunshine, you could watch the fiery display of the setting sun while sipping on a drink.

"Why don't you stay a while?" she said. "You could swim on the beach before meeting for dinner in town, wherever appeals on the spur of the moment."

I had to think about this for a moment. Option 1: The endless daily requirements of running a private yacht. Option 2: Get up when I wanted, scooter round the island to the finest beach for swimming and snorkeling before returning to join a rather beautiful lady for dinner in town. I think I was game to give Option 2 a go!

As I lay on the bed in the darkened room, staring out the windows at the swaying palm trees beyond, I knew there was a storm coming, but I had a far bigger concern on my mind. Where the hell were we going to have dinner tomorrow night?